SRI AUROBINDO FOR ALL AGES

SRI AUROBINDO
FOR ALL AGES

A BIOGRAPHY

NIRODBARAN

SRI AUROBINDO ASHRAM
PONDICHERRY

First edition 1990
Seventh impression 2009

Rs 90
ISBN 978-81-7058-202-1

© Sri Aurobindo Ashram Trust 1990
Published by Sri Aurobindo Ashram Publication Department
Pondicherry 605 002
Web   http://www.sabda.in

Printed at Sri Aurobindo Ashram Press, Pondicherry
PRINTED IN INDIA

FOREWORD

There are biographies and biographies: each one has its particular value, its particular viewpoint. This new biography stands apart from all other books on Sri Aurobindo's life, its first distinctive feature being that it is written for the young generation, for whom it was a long-felt need. And its other special value lies in the fact that it is written by a disciple who had the great privilege of serving Sri Aurobindo for twelve years as his literary secretary and, before this, of carrying on a long correspondence with him. During the years 1938–1950 Sri Aurobindo's attendants used to speak with him on various general topics, and many interesting anecdotes and experiences culled from both the talks and the letters give a unique flavour, an intimate feel to this book. It is sprinkled throughout with humour and personal touches which bring to the reader a very living contact.

The author had originally made a draft; he gave it to a close friend of his, Ashit Gupta, who was a professor of English in the Centre of Education, to rewrite it in his practised English style. Ashit Gupta took up the work very gladly even though he was suffering from a debilitating illness. Day after day, for nearly fourteen months, he took infinite trouble, carried out an exhaustive research of all available facts and rewrote the entire book, making it a true piece of art. But unfortunately he passed away before he could give the finishing touch to the last two chapters.

The book is written in a simple yet noble style; it preserves the intention of the author, that of a personal narration which gives it a special charm.

This is why the book claims distinction from the other biographies of Sri Aurobindo, often more scholarly and less intimate.

17.11.1989

CONTENTS

Contents

PART II

PART ONE

PART ONE

Sri Aurobindo, 1918-1920

Chapter I

Family Background and Childhood
1872–1879

ON FEBRUARY 6, 1893, a young man, not yet twenty-one years of age stood on the deck of a ship gazing at the far horizon where he could see faintly the shores of his motherland. He was coming back to India after having spent fourteen years in England. As he was returning home, a darkness which had entered his being when he was a small boy in India and had hung on to him all through his stay in England, fell off him like a cloak. And when the ship touched Apollo Bunder, Bombay, and he stepped at last on Indian soil, he had a strange experience. A vast calm and quiet descended on him and remained with him for months thereafter.

This young man was Aurobindo Ghose and he had this profound spiritual experience the moment he reached India. He told us later that it was the experience of the calm and silent Self, a realisation attained by yogis after years of sadhana. Yet it came to Sri Aurobindo, unbidden and without his seeking it. He was not a yogi at the time; in fact, he knew nothing about yoga then, and was not even interested in it. Nonetheless the experience came. It was as if Mother India was welcoming the return of her son by giving him, unasked, her spiritual treasures for a greater rebirth in him of her ancient glory.

This incident illustrates how the unusual and the unexpected are an inseparable part of Sri Aurobindo's life. Indeed I shall be telling you the story of a life that is immensely strange and wonderful. It is a most fascinating life, rich in its many-sided splendours. Sri Aurobindo is pre-eminent in more ways than one:

poet, philosopher, interpreter of Indian culture and spirituality, patriot and revolutionary; but, above all, a supreme Seer and Yogi. He integrated Life and the Spirit, visualizing the transformation of the vast field of all existence through the power and light of spiritual Truth. 'Our ideal is not that spirituality which withdraws from life, but the conquest of life by the power of the Spirit', he said, and his own withdrawal from politics in search of this transforming power of the Spirit, was but an extension of his love of the motherland to all mankind. His most precious gift to humanity is a knowledge of this Truth-Consciousness and the opening of a path for its attainment and its action upon the world.

*

Let me now take you to the beginning of our story. Sri Aurobindo was born on August 15, 1872, the third son of Krishna Dhan Ghose and Swarnalata. Krishna Dhan, known in his lifetime as Dr. K.D. Ghose, was then posted as Civil Surgeon at Khulna. Sri Aurobindo was born at Calcutta in the house of Mono Mohun Ghose, a well-known barrister and a great friend of Dr. Ghose. Just as they were friends, so were their wives who had the same name, Swarnalata. The name given to the child by the father – 'Aravinda' – was new at the time and hardly borne by anyone else. The word in Sanskrit means lotus and its spiritual significance is that it symbolises divine consciousness – a singularly appropriate and prophetic name for the child.

Dr. K.D. Ghose was a remarkable person, a spirited man who was in many ways in advance of his time. After graduating from the Calcutta Medical College he went, in the year 1869, to Aberdeen in Scotland for further medical studies. He was one of the first Bengalis to do so. To cross the 'black waters' in those days, in defiance of orthodox injunction, was to lose caste and invite social ostracism, but Krishna Dhan had no hesitation in running the risk. Even earlier, as a student of the Medical College, he had broken away from orthodoxy by marrying Swarnalata, the daughter of Rajnarayan Bose, in accordance with Brahmo Samaj rites. Rajnarayan himself was an outstanding product of the new India that was then rising. A contemporary of Bankim Chandra Chatterjee and Ishwar Chandra Vidyasagar, and a close friend of the poet Michael Madhusudan Dutt, Rajnarayan represented in himself the composite culture of his time – Vedantic, Islamic and

European. He was also among the first patriots of the country, the organiser of a National Exhibition of *swadeshi* products, called the Hindu Mela, which roused great enthusiasm. Moreover, because of his piety and consecrated life, he was known as Rishi Rajnarayan.

Swarnalata, Sri Aurobindo's mother, was also unusually gifted. Rajnarayan had seen to it that she was well educated. She used to write poems, was endowed with the social graces and was very beautiful – her husband's Indian and English friends at Rangpur used to call her 'The Rose of Rangpur'. But unfortunately her life was blighted in later years by mental illness, a tragedy that not only cast its shadow on the family but particularly affected Krishna Dhan who was deeply attached to her.

After completing his medical studies in England, Krishna Dhan returned to India in 1871 and joined the civil medical service of the Government, serving with great distinction as a Civil Surgeon at Bhagalpur and then at Rangpur and Khulna. He came back to India a 'pucca sahib', determined to model himself on the British and throw away all Indian ways of life, customs and manners. Krishna Dhan admired the English; at the same time, he had a very strong aversion to the inertia, blind orthodoxy and general degradation which were so prevalent in the Indian society of the time. On his return, he refused to undergo any form of expiation for his 'sins'. He was an iconoclast, not so much a breaker of idols as one who was contemptuous of superstition and foolish beliefs. He had also no regard for conventional religious worship – Sri Aurobindo once said of his father that 'he was a tremendous atheist'. But because he admired the English, you should not think he was servile to them. It was because of his independence of character that he could earn many English friends, and he did not hesitate to criticise the Government for its misdeeds or Englishmen for their arrogance. Moreover, Krishna Dhan had a deep love for the poor of his country and his door was always open to the sick and the needy. With money, medicines and in many other ways, he helped the common people – in fact, he was generous to a fault. Wherever he was posted he was very popular and highly respected. At Rangpur, a drainage canal was laid as a result of his initiative and it was called 'K.D. Canal' by the people. Later at Khulna a school was also named after him. Indeed the poor people at these places almost worshipped him as a demi-god and such popularity was not always to the liking of his British masters. So there were clashes at times and despite his admiration for the British the relationship was not always happy. Bepin Chandra Pal, Sri Aurobindo's contemporary and colleague in the political field, has paid a remarkable tribute to Dr. K.D. Ghose in his book, *Indian Nationalism: Its Principles and Personalities*. He writes: 'Keen of intellect, tender of heart, impulsive and generous almost to recklessness, regardless of his own hurts, but sensitive to the sufferings of others – this was the inventory of the character of Dr. Krishna Dhan Ghose.'

As a child Sri Aurobindo grew up in the Anglicised atmosphere of the house. Bengali was not allowed to be spoken, only English or Hindustani, and in food, dress and manners the English pattern was strictly followed. When he was five years old, the father packed off the three brothers to Loreto, a convent school in Darjeeling. It was a missionary institution where almost all the children were British. The little boy spent two years in this alien corner in his own country. The education he received was nominal but the magnificent natural beauty of Darjeeling, with its view of the valleys and snow-capped mountains, its abundance of trees and flowers, must have left its impress on his growing mind. And it was at Darjeeling that Sri Aurobindo had the experience I have mentioned earlier. Many years later he spoke about it. 'I was lying down one day,' he said, 'when I suddenly saw a great darkness rushing into me and enveloping me and the whole universe. After that I had great *tamas* – darkness – hanging on to me all along my stay in England. It left me only when I was coming back to India.'

Very little is known about Sri Aurobindo during these childhood years but, occasionally in a reminiscent vein, he would mention an incident or two and some of the anecdotes have survived.

One night the children had gone to sleep in the dormitory of their school at Darjeeling. Sri Aurobindo's elder brother, Manmohan, had his cot beside the door. A boy was late in returning and began to knock at the door. There was no response from anyone, and the knocking continued. At last Manmohan, enraged, called out, 'I cannot open the door – I am sleeping!'

Another incident concerns Rajnarayan, Sri Aurobindo's grandfather. The three brothers used to visit his house at Deoghar during their holidays. One evening they had gone for a stroll with him. As they went ahead merrily at their own pace, they forgot all about the old man. Suddenly they looked back and found him nowhere in sight. There was not a soul to be seen in the darkness. Retracing their steps they began to shout and, then suddenly, they found him – sleeping in a standing position! On another occasion, young Auro found his eldest maternal uncle shaving before a mirror. The uncle had a fund of good humour. He called Auro and, putting the mirror in front of him, said, 'Look – there is a little monkey.' Perhaps he wanted to tease the boy because, as usual, he was in European dress. But Auro was not prepared to take defeat so meekly. He took the mirror, and holding it before his uncle's face, said, '*baro mama, baro bandar!* (Look, big uncle, big monkey!)'. Sri Aurobindo always had a happy relationship with his uncle Jogendra Bose, Rajnarayan's eldest son, who was a fine man with a genial temperament.

Krishna Dhan cherished great hopes about the future of his sons, particularly of Auro, and to give shape to these hopes he made a second voyage to England with his family in 1879. Auro was just seven. Benoybhusan, the eldest son, was twelve years old and Manmohan, the second, nine. Soon after arriving in England, Swarnalata gave birth to her youngest son. He was named Barindra.

Dr. Ghose's decision to educate his three sons in England all at the same time was not only unusual but even daring for those days. He could carry out his plans because, during his posting at Rangpur, he had become friendly with the English magistrate there, a Mr. Glazier, and the latter had arranged with his cousin, Rev. Drewett, a minister at Manchester, to take charge of the boys. Accordingly, Dr. Ghose took his boys to Manchester to live with the Drewetts.

Chapter II

Manchester and St. Paul's School, London
1879–1890

At MANCHESTER, the boys were readily given shelter by the Drewett family: Rev. Drewett, his wife and his elderly mother. Before he left, Dr. Ghose gave strict instructions that his sons should not be allowed to make the acquaintance of any Indians or to undergo any Indian influence.

Sri Aurobindo was to stay in England for the next fourteen years, from 1879 to 1893. The first five years were spent at Manchester, the next six in London and the last three mostly at Cambridge. During his entire stay, he was virtually cut off from his motherland, the only contact being through occasional letters, newspapers and a few acquaintances at Cambridge. As he was to write himself, he grew up 'in entire ignorance of India, her people, her religion and culture'. But love of the motherland was ingrained in him and, at the destined hour, it burst into flame.

The two elder brothers joined the Manchester Grammar School, but Auro was coached at home by Rev. Drewett, an accomplished scholar in Latin and English. His wife taught the boy arithmetic, geography and French. It took Mr. Drewett little time to realise that Auro was a boy of exceptional qualities: sharp intelligence and deep concentration, a sweet temper and a quiet reserve in manner and speech. Benoybhushan, the eldest brother, has said: 'Auro was a very quiet and gentle boy, but at times could be terribly obstinate.'

There is very little information available about Sri Aurobindo's stay at Manchester as a boy. It was certainly not the practice in

England for a boy of his age to study exclusively at home but perhaps the Drewetts realised that Auro with his very unusual qualities would not fit into the rough and tumble of school life and so he needed special nurturing. Sri Aurobindo did receive help from the Drewetts but at the same time it would be true to say that he was largely self-taught.

As the young boy grew up, his studies covered a wide field: poetry, literature, history; Shakespeare, Shelley and the Bible were his habitual companions. Shelley's 'Revolt of Islam' pleased him a lot, although as he said later, much of it was then not intelligible to him but the vision of freedom from tyranny and injustice appealed to his juvenile sentiment, leaving its impact on his formative mind. Sri Aurobindo has mentioned that from early childhood he had an abhorrence for all kinds of cruelty and oppression. He said that at this time he also wrote some verses for Fox's family magazine.

Five years passed in absorbed growth. Sri Aurobindo has himself said that even at the early age of eleven he received a strong impression that a period of general upheaval and great revolutionary changes was coming in the world and that he was destined to play a part in it. This is indeed unusual for a boy of that age, an indication of an extraordinary life in the making.

There is a rather amusing story about an attempt to convert him during his stay at Manchester. What happened was this. Rev. Drewett's mother was a zealous Christian. The old lady was very fond of Auro and wanted to save his soul by making him a Christian too. So without disclosing her purpose she took him along when she went to attend a meeting of non-Conformist priests at Cumberland. Recalling the incident many years later, Sri Aurobindo said: 'After the prayers were over nearly all dispersed, but devout people remained a little longer and it was at that time that conversions were made. I was feeling completely bored. Then a minister approached me and asked me some questions. I did not give any reply. Then they all shouted, "He is saved, he is saved", and began to pray for me and offer thanks to God. I did not know what it was all about. Then the minister came to me and asked me to pray. I was not in the habit of praying. But somehow I did it in the manner in which children recite their prayers before going to sleep in order to keep up an appearance. I was about ten at that time.' However, it must not be supposed that Rev. Drewett had any hand in all this. He was a man with liberal views about religion and indeed Sri Aurobindo's father had strictly asked that the boys be kept free from religious instructions.

In 1884 Mr. Drewett decided to migrate to Australia, and left the three brothers in charge of his mother. The old lady also decided to leave Manchester and move to London where she took lodgings at 49, St. Stephen's Avenue, Shepherd's Bush.

When Sri Aurobindo came to London he had just completed his twelfth year. There is a painting by a well-known artist, Promode Chatterjee, from a photograph of Sri Aurobindo taken around this time. The portrait was done at the Ashram in Pondicherry and when the Mother saw it she remarked: 'His nature's spontaneous simplicity and freshness have come out very well; he came to this world with these virtues. His inner beauty is visibly in front. He had no idea of worldly life.' Sri Aurobindo has himself mentioned an unusual experience he had when he was twelve or thirteen. He said: 'I was extremely selfish and then something came upon me and I felt I ought to give up selfishness. I tried in my own way – of course imperfectly – to put it into practice. But that was a sort of turning point in my inner life.' This shows how perceptive and sensitive he was, and endowed with an inner strength rare in a boy of that age.

In September 1884 Manmohan and Sri Aurobindo were admitted to St. Paul's School, London, as day scholars. This was Sri Aurobindo's first experience of school life in England and it must have opened up new vistas for him, after his secluded life at Manchester. Fortunately, St. Paul's was then one of the best schools in England and the Head Master, Mr. Walker, a great educationist of the Victorian period. He could spot at once Auro's exceptional merit: like an astute jeweller he knew the worth of a precious gem at a glance. He gave his personal attention to the boy and finding him to be well up in Latin but a little deficient in Greek, he helped him in this and other subjects, pushing him rapidly into the higher classes. Soon the boy caught the attention of other teachers by his quick intelligence and industry. He took an active part in the school literary society and came to be recognised as a good speaker. His faculties began to flower rapidly. Things were proceeding exceptionally well when, suddenly, Auro appeared to lose all interest in his studies. The teachers were puzzled and disappointed that the boy was wasting his immense talents through laziness. But the fact was otherwise, as Sri Aurobindo told us later. Actually, he was then using his time to read all kinds of books outside of the school curriculum – poetry, novels, history, French literature – and even learning a few other European languages. From time to time he composed a poem or two in Greek or Latin, and then he would be complimented by the teachers, but generally they deplored his lack of attention to school studies. However, Sri Aurobindo did in fact find the class lessons quite easy and secured many prizes. I remember his mentioning to us that one of these prizes was a full set of the *Arabian Nights* which he read with great pleasure. In the final examination, the young scholar did very well, securing prizes in literature and history; he had already shown exceptional proficiency in Latin and Greek. Of his school career, perhaps the last word was said by Mr. Walker. When Sri Aurobindo's name came prominently before the British public in connection with the Alipore Bomb Trials, the old Head Master is reported to have said that of all the boys who passed through his hands at St. Paul's, Aurobindo was by far the most richly endowed in intellectual capacity.

You may think that since Dr. Ghose was very well placed in life and had himself taken his sons to England for their education, they would not have to face financial difficulties during their stay there. In actual fact, the situation was very different. It is true that initially they had a fairly easy time at Manchester, for Dr. Ghose used to send £360 a year for them, a sum sufficient to meet their expenses. But, practically from the time they came to London, conditions turned very difficult because remittances from Dr. Ghose became irregular as well as insufficient and almost stopped at the end. The reason for this I have already indicated: Krishna Dhan was generous to others, to the point of recklessness, and in following the bent of his nature, he sadly neglected his sons. And the situation worsened when they had to leave the old lady's house in London.

The story about this is not without amusement. As you know, Mrs. Drewett was a very orthodox Christian and she used to hold prayers at home with readings from the Bible. At times the eldest brother Benoybhusan, had to perform this duty. One day, before their dinner, the Bible reading had just finished when Manmohan, in a mood of exasperation and mischief, cried out: 'This fellow

Moses was rightly served when his people disobeyed him!' This, you can imagine, set the house on fire, for Moses was for the old lady the greatest of prophets and to speak of him with such irreverence was sacrilege. She said that she would not live another day under the same roof with unbelievers, as the house might fall down on her head and she left in a huff. When he recalled this incident, Sri Aurobindo mentioned, 'We felt relieved and I felt infinitely grateful to Dada [Manmohan].... In those days I was not particular about telling the truth always and I was a bit of a coward. Nobody could imagine that I could face the gallows or carry on a revolutionary movement. In my case it was all human imperfection with which I had to start....'

The three brothers were now virtually stranded: the father silent, no remittances, food scarce. In this crisis they were fortunate in finding a timely benefactor in James Cotton, brother of Sir Henry Cotton, who was a well-known figure in India and a friend of Dr. K.D. Ghose. James Cotton was then Secretary of the South Kensington Liberal Club which had its office at 128, Cromwell Road. The boys went and saw him and, realising their predicament, he engaged Benoybhusan on a small allowance. He also arranged for the brothers to stay in a room on top of the office. The room was unheated and not meant to be used as a living room but the boys were grateful for the shelter it provided. This was the beginning of a period of immense hardship. The three brothers had to live in a city like London on a pittance. During winter they could not afford to have a fire in the room and Sri Aurobindo did not have an overcoat to protect him from the cold. He later mentioned that for a whole year he lived daily on a few slices of bread and butter, an occasional sandwich or two, some cups of tea and a penny worth of sausage. In my letters to him I once asked whether the life of poverty he had to endure in England at such a young age had an adverse effect on his growing faculties or whether it acted as an incentive. He replied: 'Not in the least. You are writing like Samuel Smiles. Poverty has never had any terror for me nor is it an incentive. You seem to forget that I left my very safe and "handsome" Baroda position without any need to do it and that I gave up also the Rs.150 of National College Principalship, leaving myself with nothing to live on. I could not have done that, if money had been an incentive.' This shows how equal-souled he was to hardships and comforts even at that early age and gives an indication of his inner strength. I should add that in spite of all their difficulties the brothers never complained about their father's failure to support them.

Manmohan could not endure for long the strain of living at Cromwell Road and left when he found lodgings on convenient terms. His position also improved when he won a scholarship to go up to Christ Church College, Oxford in 1887. Sri Aurobindo seems to have lived at Cromwell Road from September 1887 to April 1889. Then he had the good fortune to find a landlady who was, in his own words, 'an angel', for she did not ask for her dues for months together. Afterwards he settled all the arrears from his ICS stipend.

Amidst these trials, Sri Aurobindo continued with his extensive studies. Now and then the poet in him would seek expression and he would work on a poem in Greek, Latin or English. Sri Aurobindo's interests were manifold and in course of time he tried and left many things but the Muse was his lifelong companion. Perhaps the original impulse came from his mother and he has himself acknowledged the stimulus he received from his elder brother who had the characteristics of a born poet. Manmohan had already attracted some attention as a poet. He was on friendly terms with his class-mate, Laurence Binyon, later to become a well-known literary figure, and with Stephen Phillips, the notable poet. He was also familiar with the famous Oscar Wilde. Sri Aurobindo when he was seventeen, translated from Greek a poem entitled 'Hecuba' and Binyon who happened to read it went out of his way to encourage him to write more poetry.

It was a spartan life that the brothers led but it was not without its times of carefree joy. When they could afford it during the vacations, they went on walking tours and once they visited the beautiful Lake District. Recalling one such excursion, Sri Aurobindo said: 'Manmohan used to have at times "poetic illness". Once we were walking through Cumberland. We found that he had fallen behind and was walking at a leisurely pace, moaning out poetry in a deep tone. There was a dangerous place there so we shouted to him. But he took no heed, went on muttering the lines and joined us in his own unconcerned way.'

In December 1889 Sri Aurobindo passed the Matriculation examination from St. Paul's. In the same month he also sat for a scholarship examination which enabled the successful candidate to go up to King's College, Cambridge. For this examination, which was open to all eligible students in England, Sri Aurobindo took the papers in the Classical languages i.e. Greek and Latin. He was adjudged the best candidate and won the Senior Classical scholarship which was worth £80 a year. With his own efforts and exceptional abilities, Sri Aurobindo had gained for himself the opportunity of going to Cambridge for further studies.

During 1890, his last year at St. Paul's, Sri Aurobindo prepared to sit for the ICS entrance examination which was held annually in London. After a good deal of pressure, the authorities had agreed to allow Indians of the required age and qualifications to take the examination, but they had to sit in open competition with the British candidates and succeed in a very stiff examination. The ICS career, with its immense prestige, power and rewards, held no attraction for Sri Aurobindo and he sat for the examination only to please his father. Krishna Dhan had high hopes that his son would glorify the country by becoming a brilliant administrator and Sri Aurobindo did not want to disappoint him by refusing to take the examination. When the results came out in 1890, his name was among the successful candidates. He had secured the 11th position, scoring record marks in Latin and Greek. In our talks with Sri Aurobindo in later years one of us made the comment that the ICS examination was regarded as an unusually difficult one to pass, but Sri Aurobindo merely said, 'I did not find it so.'

As a probationer in the ICS Sri Aurobindo was now entitled to a stipend of £150 a year. The period of probation was for two years which he could spend at Cambridge whilst pursuing his other studies. In July 1890 Sri Aurobindo left St. Paul's and in October of the same year he joined King's College, Cambridge. He had completed his eighteenth year, two months earlier.

Chapter III

Cambridge: The Call of the Motherland
1890–1893

As a Senior Classical scholar, Sri Aurobindo studied for the Classical Tripos, the B.A. degree examination in Greek and Latin. He was given rooms in the college and, except for vacations, he stayed at Cambridge for the next two years.

In addition to his work for the Classical Tripos, Sri Aurobindo had to study other subjects for his ICS probationership. These included Law and Jurisprudence, Political Economy, Indian History and some Sanskrit. He had also to show a knowledge of his mother tongue, Bengali (which he did not know at all), and learn a little Hindustani because Dr. K.D. Ghose, delighted at his son's success in the ICS examination, had arranged with the help of Sir Henry Cotton to get a posting for Sri Aurobindo at Arrah in Bihar on completion of his probationership. Sri Aurobindo could have avoided the strain of studying so many subjects by taking lightly his classical studies, for after all his career was now assured, but it was not in his nature to do anything superficially. In fact his reputation as a Classical scholar had preceded him at Cambridge and one of the senior tutors, G.W. Prothero, invited him to meet Oscar Browning, a very well-known scholar and intellectual in the university at that time. There is a very interesting letter from Sri Aurobindo to his father which mentions this meeting: 'Last night I was invited to coffee with one of the Dons and in his rooms I met the great O.B., otherwise Oscar Browning, who is the feature *par excellence* of King's. He was extremely flattering, passing from the subject of cotillions to that of scholarships, he said to me, "I suppose you know you passed an extraordinarily high examination. I have examined papers at thirteen examinations and I have never during that time seen such excellent papers as yours (meaning my Classical papers at the scholarship examination). As for your essay it was wonderful." In this essay (a comparison between Shakespeare and Milton) I indulged in my Oriental tastes to the top of their bent; it overflowed with rich and tropical imagery; it abounded in antitheses and epigrams and it expressed my real feelings without restraint or reservation. I thought myself that it was the best thing I have ever done, but at school it would have been condemned as extraordinarily Asiatic and bombastic.'

During his two years at Cambridge, Sri Aurobindo did not spend all his time on academic studies and except for games, in which he was not interested, he participated fully in the University activities. He continued to be in love with poetry, reading widely as was his habit, but also now writing poems more frequently. Some of these poems were included in his first volume of poetry *Songs to Myrtilla* published in 1895 after his return to India. Sri Aurobindo also experimented with translations of passages from Greek and Latin poetry. Later he told us of a significant incident in this connection. Once a class-mate of his, Norman Ferrers, was reading a line from Homer which he thought was one of the poet's finest lines and, as Sri Aurobindo listened, his ear caught the true rhythm of quantitative metre. As you may appreciate, English is an accented language whereas the sound-structure of Greek and Latin, like Sanskrit is based on quantity i.e. the length of a syllable, so that it is extremely difficult to bring the swing of quantitative metre into English poetry successfully and it had eluded Matthew Arnold and other English poets of the past who had experimented with it. In later years Sri Aurobindo wrote some magnificent poems in quantitative metre. Here are the opening lines of the long poem "Ahana" which I hope you will read one day.

> Vision delightful alone on the hills whom the silences cover,
> Closer yet lean to mortality; human, stoop to thy lover.

Incidentally, this same Norman Ferrers passed through Calcutta on his way to Singapore in 1908. Sri Aurobindo was then imprisoned in the Alipore Jail. When Ferrers heard of this, he tried to see him and even went to the court where the trial was being held. Although anxious to help, he had no means of doing so, but the incident indicates how deeply Sri Aurobindo affected those who came to know him.

Even before he went up to Cambridge, Sri Aurobindo's mind had turned towards his motherland and he had begun to take interest in the political and social conditions in India. Ironically enough, it was Dr. Krishna Dhan who was mainly responsible for first arousing patriotic feelings in young Aurobindo. In the course of his official duties Dr. Ghose came across many instances of injustice and harshness to Indians from their English masters. Such treatment was intolerable to his independent character. In one instance, there was an open clash with the English Magistrate of the district in which the doctor was serving. Sometimes reports of misbehaviour and arrogance were published in local newspapers and Dr. Ghose would send the cuttings to his sons. Sri Aurobindo, in particular, used to pore over them with avidity and growing indignation. So it was that Krishna Dhan, who had asked that his sons were not to be exposed to any Indian influence, himself helped to turn Sri Aurobindo's mind towards his motherland.

Sri Aurobindo's growing interest in politics led him to take part actively in the affairs of the Indian Majlis, an association of Indian students studying at Cambridge which had been formed a few years earlier; and although it was apparently a social club, in fact it was more a union of politically-minded students who resented the British rule in India. Debates and discussions formed part of the Union's activities. Sri Aurobindo was a keen participant of the Majlis. Often fiery speeches would be made at the meetings; Sri Aurobindo once told us an amusing story in this connection. One day an undergraduate was speaking eloquently on the subject of independence. Citing the example of the Egyptians, he repeated two or three times: 'The Egyptians rose up like a man.' When he said this for the third time, someone from the audience exclaimed: 'But how many times did they sit down?' Sri Aurobindo has another delightful story about his Cambridge days. He recounts, 'A Punjabi student at Cambridge once took our breath away by the frankness and comprehensive profundity of his affirmation: "Liars! But we are all liars!" It appeared that he had intended to say "Lawyers", but his pronunciation gave his remark a deep force of philosophic observation and generalisation which he had not intended! But it seems to me the last word in human nature.' A.B.

Purani in his *Life of Sri Aurobindo*, has also given us an enjoyable anecdote which goes back to these days. When Sri Aurobindo started learning Bengali for his ICS probationership, his teacher at Cambridge was a certain Mr. Towers, a retired member of the ICS. He was called 'Pandit Towers' perhaps because his knowledge of Bengali did not go beyond Pandit Ishwar Chandra Vidyasagar. Once Sri Aurobindo took a passage from Bankim Chandra to his teacher. The old man could not understand it at all and said, 'But this is not Bengali!'

In May 1892 Sri Aurobindo passed the first part of the Classical Tripos examination in the first class, a fine achievement which fulfilled his promise as a classical scholar. For distinguishing himself in the examination he won 'books bearing the College arms to the value of £40'. Earlier he had also won prizes for Greek and Latin verses. However, in spite of these distinctions Sri Aurobindo never obtained his B.A. degree. Under the rules it was necessary for a student to put in at least three years' residence at the University in order to earn the degree, and Sri Aurobindo left Cambridge after two years. Indeed he was not interested in a degree as such. Sri Aurobindo told us that it was needed only if one wanted to take up an academic career or for securing a job, and he said, 'If one has true knowledge, a job is always available.'

Later that year, in August 1892, Sri Aurobindo passed the ICS final examination which opened the way to joining the coveted service. There was only one more formality left, that of passing the riding test. Between August and November Sri Aurobindo had four different chances of appearing for this test and, on each occasion, he failed to put in an appearance. Evidently he had made up his mind not to go in for the ICS. Once, in our talks with him, we asked: 'Why did you appear at all for the ICS? Was it on account of some (yogic) intuition that you didn't go for the riding test?' 'Not at all,' he replied, 'I knew nothing of yoga at that time. I appeared for the ICS because my father wanted it and I was too young to understand it. Later I found out what sort of work it was and I had no interest in the administrative life. My interest was in poetry and literature and the study of languages and patriotic action.'

In October 1892 Sri Aurobindo left Cambridge and came to London, taking up lodgings there. The last chance given to him to appear for the riding test was on November 15, but on that day he chose to wander in the streets of London. Late in the evening he came home and told his eldest brother, Benoybhusan, 'I am chucked.' Sometime later Manmohan dropped in and when he heard what had happened, 'he set up a howl as if the heavens had fallen'. Sri Aurobindo himself was quite unperturbed. But it was not only Manmohan who was upset at what Sri Aurobindo had done. Both James Cotton and G.W. Prothero, the senior tutor at Cambridge who knew Sri Aurobindo well, thought that grave injustice had been done and decided to intercede with the Civil Service Commission, the final authority for selecting the candidates. In a letter to Cotton, Prothero wrote: 'I am very sorry to hear what you tell me about Ghose, that he has been rejected in his final ICS examination for failure in riding. His conduct throughout his two years here was most exemplary.... He performed his part of the bargain, as regards the College, most honourably and took a high place in the 1st class of Classical Tripos at the end of the second year of his residence. He also obtained certain college prizes, showing command of English and literary ability. That a man should have been able to do this (which alone is quite enough for most undergraduates), and at the same time keep up his ICS work proves very unusual industry and capacity. Besides his classical scholarship he possessed a knowledge of English Literature far beyond the average of undergraduates, and wrote a much better English style than most young Englishmen. That a man of this calibre should be lost to the Indian Government merely because he failed in sitting on a horse or did not keep an appointment appears to me, I confess, a piece of official short-sightedness which it would be hard to beat.

'If he is finally turned out, it will be, however legally justifiable, a moral injustice to him and a very real loss to the Indian Government....

'Moreover the man has not only ability but character. He has had a very hard and anxious time of it for the last two years. Supplies from home have almost entirely failed, and he has had to keep his two brothers as well as himself, and yet his courage and perseverance have never failed....'

In transmitting this letter to the authorities Mr. Cotton wrote: 'It happens that I have known Mr. A.A. Ghose and his two brothers for the past five years, and that I have been a witness of the pitiable straits to which they have all three been reduced

through the failure of their father, a Civil Surgeon in Bengal and (I believe) a most respectable man, to supply them with adequate resources. In addition, they have lived an isolated life, without any Englishman to take care of them or advise them.
'...Should the Secretary of State feel himself able to give Mr. Ghose one more chance, I undertake to provide the necessary expenses of riding lessons, journeys to Woolwich etc.,...'

I have quoted at length from these letters because of the light they throw on the many difficulties Sri Aurobindo had to pass through in England, and which he overcame in his own undisturbed manner, and also because they are two fine letters which speak of the English character at its best.

These representations on behalf of Sri Aurobindo had their effect and the authorities conceded that another chance should be given to him. But their efforts to communicate with him failed and, finally, he was rejected from the ICS for failing to pass the riding test. But there is another point we should bear in mind. There is hardly any doubt that the authorities were anxious to keep Sri Aurobindo away from the ICS. Had they wished, they could have allowed him to take the riding test in India – there were precedents which permitted this. But it is possible that Sri Aurobindo's patriotic activities at Cambridge, such as the speeches he made in the Indian Majlis, had come to the notice of the authorities and they felt that he would be a thorn in the flesh of the Government were he allowed to join the ICS. Little did they realise that, by his other activities later, he would cause the Government far greater injury.

So you see that the truth behind his rejecting the ICS was his love for the motherland. But let us remember that it was not a small matter to have thrown away a glittering prize like the ICS at his age, for he was not even twenty-one at the time. His was the first example of the kind and it is not unlikely that Subhas Chandra Bose, when he rejected the ICS in 1920, drew his inspiration from Sri Aurobindo's example.

We have another instance at this time of Sri Aurobindo's intense yearning to serve his motherland. In London, he became a member of a secret society with the name 'Lotus and Dagger'. Its members had to take a solemn vow to work for the liberation of India and not to serve the alien Government. The society was short-lived and not all the members kept their vow but Sri Aurobindo remained faithful to it.

Eager as he was to return to India, Sri Aurobindo had first to find a suitable job, and it came to him as if by chance. Recalling the circumstances, Sri Aurobindo told us: 'It is strange how things arrange themselves at times. When I failed in the ICS riding test and was looking for a job, the Gaekwad of Baroda happened to be in London. I don't remember whether he called us or we met him. We consulted an elderly person in authority about the pay we should propose. We had no idea of these things. He said we could propose Rs.200/- per month but should accept even Rs.130/- which was then equivalent to £10 and was quite a good sum. I left the negotiations to my eldest brother and James Cotton. I knew nothing about life at that time.' This is how Sri Aurobindo joined the Baroda State Service. The Gaekwad apparently was very pleased and went about telling people that he had got an ICS man for Rs.200/- per month which was much less than the Civil Service scale. Still Rs.200/- per month was a very good starting pay in those days.

Sri Aurobindo now made preparations to return to India. He applied for and received the final payment of his ICS stipend. This helped him to settle his debts and book his passage to India.

About his debts, there is an amusing story which Sri Aurobindo related to us. 'There was a tailor at Cambridge,' he said, 'who used to tempt me with all sorts of cloth for suits and make me buy them: of course, he gave credit. Then I went to London. He somehow traced me there and found Manmohan and canvassed orders from him. Manmohan went in for velvet suits, not staring red but aesthetic, and used to visit Oscar Wilde in them. Then we came away to India but the tailor was not to be deprived of his dues. He wrote to the Government of Bengal and to the Baroda State for recovering the sum from me and Manmohan. I had paid up all my dues and kept £4 or so. I did not believe that I was bound to pay it, since he always charged me double. But as the Maharajah said I had better pay it, I paid.'

Although Sri Aurobindo lived in England for fourteen years, he had no feelings of regret at leaving. To a disciple he once wrote: 'There was an attachment to English and European thought and literature, but not to England as a country.... If there was attachment to a European land as a second country, it was intellectually and emotionally to one not seen or lived in in this life, not England, but France.'

On January 12, 1893, Sri Aurobindo left England by S.S.

Carthage, but a great tragedy marred his homecoming. You can imagine with what eagerness Dr. Krishna Dhan Ghose was waiting for his son to come back to India after all these years. It seems that Krishna Dhan even went to Bombay to receive Sri Aurobindo but, in the absence of any exact information about the ship by which he was coming, he returned to Khulna. Later his bankers, Grindlay & Co. informed him that Sri Aurobindo had left England by the vessel *Roumania* and that this ship had been wrecked in heavy weather off the coast of Portugal with hardly any survivors. This was a tremendous shock to Dr. Ghose, too severe for his weak heart to bear, and he died with his son's name on his lips.

The S.S. *Carthage*, with Sri Aurobindo on board, duly arrived at Bombay on February 6, 1893, and you will recall the wonderful experience he had as soon as his feet touched the soil of India.

Chapter IV

Baroda

1893–1906

I

Sᴿɪ AUROBINDO reached Baroda on February 8, 1893, i.e. only two days after his arrival at Bombay. What surprises us is that instead of first visiting his relatives in Bengal, he proceeded straight to Baroda. Could he have come to know the sad news of his parents – his father's death and his mother's illness? Difficult to surmise; perhaps there was urgent need to report for duty and thereafter he had to wait until he could get leave.

Sri Aurobindo joined service immediately. He started in the Survey Settlement Department as an attaché for learning the work. Then he was shifted to various departments until towards the end of 1895 he joined the Dewan's office or the Secretariat where he remained for the next few years. It seemed to be the same kind of work as in the ICS – files, office-work, touring etc. – then why Baroda? In explaining this Sri Aurobindo told us: 'True, but with a difference. Baroda was a native State under a native ruler. You did not have to be all attention to the superior English officer ruling your fate. There was much room for freedom and dignity.'

As an officer of the State Service he could hardly avoid administrative work but his real interests were engaged elsewhere. The Gaekwad, however, was fully aware of Sri Aurobindo's exceptional abilities and was keen to utilize them not only for his State but also for his personal work. He used to call Sri Aurobindo for drafting letters which required careful wording, preparing important memoranda or special reports, and also to write some of his speeches. A well-known Marathi historian, G.S. Sardesai, has an interesting account which throws light on Sri Aurobindo's relationship with the Gaekwad: 'Sri Aurobindo and myself were together with Sayaji Rao very often.... Once the Maharaja had to address a social conference. Sri Aurobindo prepared the speech. We three sat together and read it. The Maharaja after hearing it said: "Can you not, Aravind Babu, tone it down? It is too fine to be mine." Sri Aurobindo replied smiling: "Why make a change for nothing? Do you think, Maharaja, that if it is toned down a little, people will believe it to be yours? Good or bad, whatever it be, people will always say that the Maharaja gets his speeches written by others. The main thing is whether the thoughts are yours. That is your chief part." '

You see how Sri Aurobindo maintained his 'freedom and dignity'. I could give you another instance of Sri Aurobindo's independent way of working. On one occasion the Gaekwad passed an order that the officers should attend their office even on Sundays. Sri Aurobindo was not willing to accept the order. The Maharaja fined him Rs.50. When he heard of this Sri Aurobindo said, 'Let him fine as much as he likes. I shall neither pay the fine nor attend the office.' Good sense, however, prevailed on the Gaekwad and he did not press the matter.

For his special work for the Gaekwad Sri Aurobindo would often be invited to breakfast at the palace and would then be asked to stay on; but he was not appointed Private Secretary at any time. However, during a tour of Kashmir in 1903, the Maharaja took along Sri Aurobindo in that capacity, but the experiment was not a success. A disciple once wrote to Sri Aurobindo extolling the beauties of Kashmir and he replied, 'Quite agree with your estimate of Kashmir. The charm of its mountains and rivers and the ideal life dawdling along in the midst of a supreme beauty in the slowly moving leisure of a houseboat – that was a kind of earthly Paradise – also writing poetry on the banks of the Jhelum where it rushes down Kashmir towards the plains. Unfortunately there was the over-industrious Gaekwad to cut short the Paradise! His idea of Paradise was going through administrative papers and making myself and others write speeches for which he got all the credit. But after all, according to the nature, to each one his Eden.'

Despite such differences, however, Sri Aurobindo had a very good relationship with the Gaekwad and his family. He considered the Maharaja to be an able ruler, far in advance of most of his contemporaries; and that the Maharani had a profound regard for Sri Aurobindo is apparent from the fact that in later years she wrote to him at Pondicherry seeking his spiritual help and guidance.

Soon there came an opportunity for more congenial work. How can a poet, litterateur, a man of culture be fitted into the cogwheel of administrative routine? In 1897 there was a suggestion that Sri Aurobindo could work in the Baroda College as a teacher of French. Later his services were lent informally to the College from time to time. Early in 1898 he was appointed Professor of English, and taught at the College in addition to his other official duties. Thus began his long association with the Baroda College which continued until he took extended leave in June 1906 to go to Bengal. In 1899 the Principal of the College, (an Englishman), pressed the Maharaja to make Sri Aurobindo's appointment at the College permanent but the former did not agree as he wanted Sri Aurobindo to write official reports etc. (also to ghost-write his memoirs, but nothing came of this!) and assist him generally in other work. However, by 1904 Sri Aurobindo was made the Vice-Principal of the College and in 1905 he became the acting Principal when the regular incumbent went on leave for a year.

Sri Aurobindo was a wonderful teacher – this is but natural since teaching was his *swadharma*. Fortunately, a few of his students at Baroda have recorded their impressions, and I shall quote from these, but occasionally in his talks with us also Sri Aurobindo spoke of his teaching days. His brother Manmohan had likewise become a Professor of English at the Presidency College, Calcutta. His teaching too was greatly admired but there was a difference between them. Sri Aurobindo told us: 'Manmohan was very painstaking.... I saw that his books used to be inter-leaved, marked and full of notes. I was not so conscientious.' When one of his disciples, Purani, demurred and said that people who had heard him in College spoke very highly of his lectures, Sri Aurobindo continued: 'I never used to look at the notes, and sometimes my explanations did not agree with them at all.... What was surprising to me was that the students used to take down everything *verbatim* and mug it up. Such a thing would never have happened in England.... Once I was giving a lecture on Southey's

Life of Nelson and my lecture was not in agreement with the notes. So the students remarked that it was not at all like what was found in them. I replied that I had not read the notes – in any case, they were all rubbish. I could never go into minute details. I read and left my mind to do what it could. That is why I could never become a scholar.'

Sri Aurobindo was loved and revered by his students, as much for his profound knowledge of literature, his original way of teaching, as for his magnetic personality and gentle, gracious manners. One of his students, R.N. Patkar, writes in his memoirs: 'I had the good fortune to be his student in the Intermediate Class. His method of teaching was a novel one. In the beginning he used to give a series of introductory lectures in order to initiate the student into the subject matter of the text. After that he used to read the text, stopping where necessary to explain the meaning of difficult words and sentences. He ended by giving general lectures bearing on the various aspects of the subject matter of the text.

'But more than his college lectures, it was a treat to hear him on the platform. He used to preside occasionally over the meetings of the College Debating Society. The large central hall of the College used to be full when he was to speak. He was not an orator but a speaker of a very high order, and was listened to with rapt attention. Without any gesture or movements of the limbs he stood, and language flowed like a stream from his lips with natural ease and melody that kept the audience spell-bound.... Though it is more than fifty years since I heard him, I still remember his figure and the ring of his melodious voice.'

Patkar writes further: 'I once asked him how I should improve my English, what authors I should read and study. I had read some portion of Macaulay's *Lives of Great Men* and I was fascinated by his style. I asked him if I should read Macaulay. Then, as was usual with him, he smiled and replied, "Do not be anybody's slave, but be your own master. By reading Macaulay or any other writer you will never be like him. You will not be a Macaulay but a faint echo of Macaulay. You will but be a copy to be derided by the world, but never an original. Therefore you may read any good author carefully, but should think for yourself and form your own judgment. It is likely you may differ from the views of the writer. You should think for yourself and cultivate a habit of writing and in this way you will be the master of your style." '

K.M. Munshi, a leading politician both before and after Independence, was a student at Baroda College for a time and writes: 'My own contact with Sri Aurobindo dates back to 1902 when after passing the Matriculation examination, I joined the Baroda College. Though previously, I had, only on occasions, the privilege of being in personal contact with him, the Aurobindonian legend in the College filled me with reverence, and it was with awe that I hung upon his words whenever he came to College as Professor of English.'

Sri Aurobindo left an impression on all those who came to know him in the College. Dr. C.R. Reddy, a colleague, recalls: 'I had the honour of knowing him.... Dr. Clark, the Principal, remarked to me, "So you met Aurobindo Ghose. Did you notice his eyes? There is mystic fire and light in them. They penetrate into the beyond. If Joan of Arc heard heavenly voices, Aurobindo probably sees heavenly visions."'

Whilst teaching was a welcome diversion from administrative work, Sri Aurobindo has himself said that his real interest at Baroda lay 'in Sanskrit, in literature and in the national movement'. During his stay in England, Sri Aurobindo had acquired a mastery of European literature and culture but of his own country he knew very little indeed. He was now determined to make up for the deficiency for, if he were ignorant of his country's culture, civilization and religion, how would he serve her? So he started learning Sanskrit and studying the Ramayana, the Mahabharata, the Upanishads, Gita, Kalidasa's plays and other Sanskrit works. He learnt the language all by himself – no doubt the start he had made in England for his ICS studies as well as his proficiency in Greek and Latin were a help in acquiring another classical language, but so great a mastery did he gain over Sanskrit that he was later able to make a deep study of the language of the Vedas and, with the help of his yogic vision, present a new interpretation of these ancient scriptures. Sri Aurobindo had a remarkable flair for languages and soon acquired a working knowledge of Gujarati, Marathi and Bengali. His immense powers of concentration and his ability to read with great rapidity, whilst retaining the essentials of what he read, enabled him to cover a very wide field of studies. Moreover, Sri Aurobindo had now the opportunity of giving expression to his creative talents. His official duties were not onerous and he could hardly have had the same scope if he had joined the ICS. He once observed quizzically: 'I wonder what would have happened to me if I had joined the Civil Service. I think they would have chucked me for insubordination and arrears of work.'

The amount of literary work that Sri Aurobindo produced in Baroda was formidable. This falls into several categories – translations, poems and poetic drama, and prose writings on a wide variety of subjects; regrettably not all of it has been preserved. In May 1908, when Sri Aurobindo was arrested in connection with the Alipore Bomb Case, his papers and manuscripts were seized by the police. They were scrutinized to dig up evidence to convict him for revolutionary activities. Afterwards they were stored away in the Record Room of the Court. Under the rules, they should have been destroyed after the lapse of some years. But, thanks to the sensibility and initiative of the record-keeper, the papers – although shown as destroyed – were preserved in a corner. Later they were kept in a steel cupboard in the Judges' Retiring Room. Then, in the changed circumstances after Independence, the papers were found and a good many of the manuscripts belonging to the Baroda period were discovered. But, unfortunately, not all – for some disappeared 'in the whirlpool and turmoil of my political career' as Sri Aurobindo once described it. One such disappearance is a particularly sad loss. As he plunged into Sanskrit studies, Sri Aurobindo was inevitably drawn to the poetic genius of Kalidasa. It was his intention to write a full-scale book on Kalidasa for which he drew up an outline but he did not have the sustained leisure to complete it. He did, however, write extensively on Kalidasa – on the important works, the characters in the plays, the age he lived in and on other aspects of his genius. Moreover, he took in hand some translations of Kalidasa. Of these, a very fine rendering of *Vikramorvasie* was later published under the title *The Hero and the Nymph*, but the manuscript of his translation, in *terza rima*, of Kalidasa's *Meghaduta* could not be discovered. I remember that once when we were talking of the subject there was a tinge of regret in Sri Aurobindo's voice at the mention of this manuscript. 'It is a pity that the translation cannot be found,' he said, 'for it was well done.' This makes the loss all the greater, for he seldom spoke of his own achievements. At about this time Sri Aurobindo was also immersed in the Ramayana and Mahabharata and experimented with translations from these epics. When Ramesh Chandra Dutt, the well-known poet, novelist and historian, saw some of these during a visit to Baroda, he is said to have remarked: 'Had I seen them before, I would never have published mine. It now appears that my translations have been child's play before yours.' Besides translations, Sri Aurobindo wrote some 'Notes' on the Mahabharata as well as comments on the poetic genius of Vyasa and Valmiki. Also, he drew on the Mahabharata for a number of his own narrative poems of which *Love and Death* is the most outstanding. And, of course, for his supreme creation *Savitri*, the story was taken from the Mahabharata. In addition to poems, both short and long, Sri Aurobindo wrote a number of plays in blank verse. One of these, *Perseus the Deliverer*, is based on a Greek myth which Sri Aurobindo adapted. It is an imaginative presentation of the ideas of evolution and progress which were to recur so prominently in Sri Aurobindo's later works.

All in all, the Baroda period was wonderfully productive both in terms of interpretation of ancient Indian culture as well as his own literary creations. But the time for political action and his stupendous spiritual experiences was approaching and during the last years of his stay at Baroda he was to be increasingly absorbed in these.

I would now like to tell you how Sri Aurobindo resumed contact with his family in Bengal. Unfortunately, we have very little information to go on and there are many gaps which cannot now be filled.

About eleven months after his arrival at Baroda, in a letter dated January 11, 1894, to his grandfather, Rajnarayan Bose, Sri Aurobindo writes:

My dear Grandfather,

  I received your telegram and postcard together this afternoon. I am at present in an exceedingly out of the way place, without any post-office within fifteen miles of it; so it would not be easy to telegraph. I shall probably be able to get to Bengal by the end of next week. I had intended to be there by this time, but there is some difficulty about my last month's salary without which I cannot very easily move. However I have written for a month's privileged leave and as soon as it is sanctioned shall make ready to start.... As I do not know Urdu, or indeed any other language of the country, I may find it convenient to bring my clerk with me. I suppose there will be no difficulty about accommodating him.

I got my uncle's letter enclosing Saro's. The letter might have presented some difficulties, for there is no one who knows Bengali at Baroda – no one at least whom I could get at. Fortunately the smattering I acquired in England stood me in good stead, and I was able to make out the sense of the letter, barring a word here and a word there. ...

If all goes well, I shall leave Baroda on the 18th; at any rate it will not be more than a day or two later.

Believe me
Your affectionate grandson
Aravind A. Ghosh

We do not have the exact dates, nor do we know if he took his clerk with him, but he did pay a visit to Bengal that year, the first since his return to India. He stayed for some time at the house of his grandfather at Deoghar. Naturally all the members of the family were jubilant. Sarojini, his sister, gives a pen-picture: 'A very delicate face, long hair cut in the English fashion, Sejda was a very shy person.' When his mother saw him, she exclaimed: 'He is not my Auro. My Auro was so small. Very well, let me see if he has a cut in his finger.' The cut was shown and she was satisfied. Those of us who attended on him after his accident in 1938 also remember that cut in his finger.

How greatly Sri Aurobindo enjoyed this visit to the family can be appreciated from a letter to his sister Sarojini on his return to Baroda. Here are some extracts from the letter.

Baroda Camp
25th August, 1894

My dear Saro,

... It will be, I fear, quite impossible to come to you again so early as the Puja, though if I only could, I should start tomorrow. Neither my affairs, nor my finances will admit of it. Indeed it was a great mistake for me to go at all; for it has made Baroda quite intolerable to me. There is an old story about Judas Iscariot, which suits me down to the ground. Judas, after betraying Christ, hanged himself and went to Hell where he was honoured with the hottest oven in the whole establishment. Here he must burn for ever and ever; but in his life he had done one kind act and for this they permitted him by special mercy of God to cool himself for an hour every Christmas on an iceberg in the North Pole. Now this has always seemed to me not mercy, but a peculiar refinement of cruelty. For how could Hell fail to be ten times more Hell to the poor wretch after the delicious coolness of his iceberg? I do not know for what enormous crime I have been condemned to Baroda, but my case is just parallel. Since my pleasant sojourn with you at Baidyanath, Baroda seems a hundred times more Baroda....

You say in your letter 'all here are quite well'; yet in the very next sentence I read 'Bari has an attack of fever'. Do you mean then that Bari is nobody? Poor Bari! That he should be excluded from the list of human beings is only right and proper, but it is a little hard that he should be denied existence altogether. I hope it is only a slight attack. I am quite well. I have brought a fund of health with me from Bengal, which, I hope it will take me some time to exhaust; but I have just passed my twenty-second milestone, August 15 last, since my birthday and am beginning to get dreadfully old.

I infer from your letter that you are making great progress in English. I hope you will learn very quickly; I can then write to you quite what I want to say and just in the way I want to say it. I feel some difficulty in doing that now and I don't know whether you will understand it.

With love,

Your affectionate brother,

Auro

P.S. If you want to understand the new orthography of my name, ask uncle.

In what a delightful vein have laughter and tears mingled here! Mark too that he draws attention to the orthography or spelling of his name – the old 'Arvind' giving way to 'Aurobindo'.

When this letter was written, 'Bari' or Barindra, the youngest brother was fourteen years of age and Sarojini a couple of years older. The eldest brother Benoybhusan, had returned to India by then to make a career in the Cooch Behar State Service. Manmohan had just completed his studies at Oxford and earned his M.A. degree; he would be returning shortly to India to distinguish himself as an outstanding Professor of English in Government Service. Amongst his family members his maternal uncle, Jogendra, the eldest son of Rajnarayan Bose, was perhaps the closest to Sri Aurobindo. He was a cheerful and kindly man and Sri Aurobindo always enjoyed his company, calling him the 'Prophet of Ishabgul' for he used to prescribe this indigenous laxative to all with any kind of stomach complaint.

After this first visit Sri Aurobindo generally went to Bengal when he could obtain leave or during the College vacations. In Calcutta he often stayed with his maternal uncle, Krishna Kumar Mitra, an ardent patriot, who was later the editor of the Nationalist weekly *Sanjivani*. His daughter, Basanti Devi, has recorded her impressions of her cousin: 'Auro Dada used to arrive with two or three trunks, and we always thought they must contain costly suits and other articles of luxury like scents etc. When he opened them, I used to look and wonder, – what is this? A few ordinary clothes and all the rest books and nothing but books. Does Auro Dada like to read all of them? We all want to chat and enjoy ourselves during our vacations; does he want to spend even this time in reading books? But because he liked reading, it did not mean that he would not join us in our chats and merry-making. His talk used to be full of wit and humour.'

These few authentic accounts we have of Sri Aurobindo's early meetings with his family reveal the affectionate side of his nature. He was by no means aloof and indifferent but interested in life and the people around him. Yet, the overall impression is one of inwardness, quiet poise and easy good humour.

Let me now give you a few glimpses of Sri Aurobindo's personal life at Baroda. In his biography of Sri Aurobindo, A.B. Purani has described the routine as follows: 'After morning tea Sri Aurobindo used to write poetry. He would continue up to ten o'clock. Bath was between ten and eleven o'clock and lunch at eleven o'clock – a cigar would be by his side even while he ate. Sri Aurobindo used to read journals while he ate. He took less of rice and more of bread. Once a day there was meat or fish....'

There exists for us, fortunately, a vivid and detailed pen-picture of Sri Aurobindo at Baroda by a contemporary. This writer was a man of letters, sensitive to atmosphere and personality, and the circumstances under which he wrote were interesting. At Baroda,

Sri Aurobindo soon came to acquire a good grasp of literary Bengali which enabled him, as early as 1894, to write a series of articles of great depth and penetration, on Bankim Chandra. But, for want of practice, he could hardly express himself in spoken Bengali and he must have felt this deficiency during his visits to Bengal. So he arranged with his maternal uncle that Dinendra Kumar Roy, a well-known writer in Bengali, should come and stay with him as a companion at Baroda so that Sri Aurobindo could practise speaking with him in the vernacular. Roy stayed at Baroda for two years, from 1899 to 1900, and later wrote a charming little book of reminiscences in Bengali called *Aurobindo Prasanga*, in which he throws an authentic light on many aspects of Sri Aurobindo's life.

Of his first meeting with Sri Aurobindo, Roy writes:

'Before I met Aurobindo, I had formed an image of him somewhat like this: a stalwart figure, dressed from head to foot in immaculate European style, a stern gaze in his spectacled eyes, an affected accent and a temper exceedingly rough, one who would not tolerate the slightest breach of form. It is needless to add that I was rather disappointed in my estimate when I saw him for the first time. Who could have thought that this darkish young man with soft dreamy eyes and long, thin, wavy hair parted in the middle and reaching to the neck, clad in coarse Ahmedabad dhoti and close-fitting Indian jacket, his feet shod in old-fashioned Indian slippers with upturned toes, a face sparsely dotted with pock-marks – who could have thought that this man could be Mr. Aurobindo Ghose, a living fountain of French, Latin and Greek? I could not have received a bigger shock if someone had pointed to the hillocks about Deoghar and said: ".Look, there stand the Himalayas."...

'He had gone to England as a mere boy, almost on the lap of his mother, and it was much after the first flush of his youth that he had returned to his motherland. But what struck me as amazing was that his noble heart had suffered not the least contamination from the luxury and dissipation, the glitter and glamour, the diverse impressions and influences, and the strange spell of Western society.'

The portrait drawn by Dinendra Kumar is truly astonishing. Fourteen of the most formative years of his life Sri Aurobindo had spent in England and yet within a few years of his return he had become an Indian to the core. This could happen only because of his inner strength which could imbibe and assimilate the best of European culture whilst rejecting its outward trappings to which most others so readily succumb.

In this book Roy also gives us a graphic description of Sri Aurobindo's immense powers of concentration and his deep absorption in books and studies: 'Two well-known booksellers of Bombay were his regular suppliers of books.... They used to supply his selected books on deposit account. He seldom received books by post; they came by railway parcels, packed in huge cases. Sometimes small parcels came twice or thrice in the course of a month. He would finish the books in eight or ten days and place fresh orders. I have never seen such a voracious reader....

'Aurobindo would sit at his table and read in the light of an oil lamp till one in the morning, unmindful of the intolerable bites of the mosquitoes. I used to see him seated there in the same posture for hours on end, his eyes fixed on the book he was reading, like a Yogi plunged in divine contemplation and lost to all sense of what was going on outside. Even if the house had caught fire, it could not have broken his contemplation. Often he would read through the night, poring over books in the different languages of Europe – books of poetry, fiction, history, philosophy, etc.'

Another side still of Sri Aurobindo has been brought out very well by Roy. He writes:

'Aurobindo used to get a handsome pay. He was single, he had no luxuries and did not waste an anna. Still at the end of the month he ran short of funds. He used to remit something regularly to his family. One day seeing him fill up a money-order form I too had the desire to send some money home. So I asked him for the amount. He laughed and, offering me whatever he had, said, "This is all I have – send it." I replied, "That can't be – as you were filling a money-order form, I thought – no, I shall send something later." But he shook his head and added, "Your need is greater than mine."'

R.N. Patkar, from whose memoirs I have quoted earlier, has also dwelt on these very traits. He writes:

'Sri Aurobindo used to be so absorbed while reading that he often forgot to have his dinner. At the servant's request, I had to remind him of it.... Another thing I noticed was his total absence of attachment for money. Whatever monthly salary he received he used to place in an open tray and keep no account. One day I asked him why he didn't keep his money safe somewhere. He answered: "Well, it shows we are living among honest and good people." "But how will you know this unless you keep an account?" He replied quietly, "God keeps my account. Why should I worry when he is taking care of me?"'

Finally, a few more revealing sketches of Sri Aurobindo from the pen of Dinendra Kumar Roy: 'He was not in the habit of dressing up. I never saw him change his ordinary clothes even while going to the Maharaja's court.... Like his dress, his bed was also ordinary and simple. The iron bedstead he used was such that even a petty clerk would have disdained to use it. Baroda being near a desert, both summer and winter were severe there; but even in the cold of January I never saw him use a quilt – a cheap ordinary rug did duty for it. He always appeared to me nothing but a self-denying *brahmachari*, austere in self-discipline and acutely sensitive to the suffering of others. Acquisition of knowledge seemed to be the sole mission of his life. And for the fulfilment of that mission, he practised rigorous self-culture even amidst the din and bustle of an active worldly life. I never saw him lose his temper. No passion was ever seen getting the better of him. It is not possible to have such control without the highest self-discipline.

'Marathi food did not agree with my taste, but Aurobindo was accustomed to it. Sometimes the cooking was so bad that I could hardly take a bite, but he ate quite naturally. I never saw him express any displeasure to the cook. He had a particular liking for Bengali food. The quantity of food he took was very small; and it was because of his abstemious and temperate habits that he kept perfectly fit in spite of heavy mental labour. He took good care of his health. For one hour every evening he would pace up and down the verandah of his house with brisk steps.

'His laughter was simple as a child's, and as liquid and soft. Though an inflexible will showed at the corners of his lips, there was not the slightest trace in his heart of any worldly ambition or of selfishness. There was only the longing, rare even among the gods, of sacrificing himself for the relief of human suffering.

'Aurobindo was always indifferent to pleasure and pain, prosperity and adversity, praise or blame. He bore all hardships with an unruffled mind.'

Yet it should not be thought that at Baroda Sri Aurobindo led the life of a recluse, or of an intellectual immersed in books. On the contrary, it was always Sri Aurobindo's nature to study life in its various manifestations. He was interested in music, dancing and other cultural activities – from time to time, he would attend Court functions, entertainments, etc. Also, he had his circle of friends in whose company he relaxed. Amongst these may be mentioned Khaserao Jadav, who was a magistrate and a colleague in the Baroda State Service, his younger brother Lt. Madhavrao Jadav of the Baroda State Army, and Phadke, a young Maratha Brahmin of genial temperament and a man of letters. In fact, for some years Sri Aurobindo lived in Khaserao's house at Baroda, a beautiful two-storeyed building situated on the main road of the town; Madhavrao too was close to Sri Aurobindo and helped him in his political work. But Sri Aurobindo's life was never lived on the surface and behind the apparently placid external routine, he had started secret revolutionary work. And, within, burnt a blazing fire.

II

Sri Aurobindo was not a politician in the ordinary sense of the word: he was not interested in position, fame or money and, characteristically, he preferred to work silently from behind the scenes. His outward participation in Indian politics lasted only a few years but his vision of India was his own and by his own genius he projected it into the political sphere. In this way he planted a seed which has taken root and continues to grow. To help you understand this, I shall sketch briefly the background of the political scene of those days.

You must remember that when India entered the last decades of the nineteenth century, Indians had very little say in the administration of their country. After the Revolt of 1857, the East India Company was dissolved. Instead, the British Government directly assumed power over the Indian territories. A new political office was created in London, that of the Secretary of State for India, who became an important minister of the British Government and was put in overall charge of Indian affairs; but he seldom interfered in the internal administration of India. Here the Governor-General, now given the additional title of Viceroy to signify that he was the representative of the British monarch, was supreme. There were two small Councils, with legislative and executive functions, to assist the Viceroy but these bodies had only a handful of nominated members and Indians were not admitted to these Councils. This was the structure at the top. The vast territories over which the British ruled in India were divided into provinces which in turn were divided into smaller districts. Each province was under a Governor who was directly responsible to the Viceroy for the administration of his area. The Governor also had small Councils, again without any Indian members, to assist him; and a powerful secretariat of British officials to oversee the administration. The actual civil administration of the country was carried on through the Indian Civil Service. This was an exclusive cadre of service with immense prestige and authority. Recruitment was made through an open examination held once a year in London. In theory, Indians could become members of this service but the rules were so framed that until 1870 only sixteen Indians had ever attempted the examination and only one had been able to get into the ICS. So you can easily see that Indians had hardly any voice in the government of their own country. There can be no doubt that it was the painful recognition of this fact that prompted Dr. Krishna Dhan Ghose to send all his three sons at such a tender age to England so that they could be equipped to compete with Englishmen in every way.

During the nineteenth century there were two parallel movements in India. On the one hand, there was an almost continuous growth of British power and domination in the political sphere. On the other, in the social, religious and cultural spheres there were far-reaching changes and reforms. Many a factor contributed to these changes but the most important was the impact of the new ideas and forces from the West as a result of the growth of education and the spread of the English language. At first there was a good deal of blind acceptance and servile imitation of western life but soon a number of powerful thinkers started examining their own ancient heritage in the light of the western impact. Raja Rammohan Roy is generally recognised to be the first of these pioneers and he was followed by many other great men such as Dwarkanath Tagore, his son Debendranath, Ishwar

Chandra Vidyasagar, Dayanand Saraswati, Sri Ramakrishna, Keshav Chandra Sen, Bankim Chandra Chatterji, Swami Vivekananda, Balgangadhar Tilak, Rabindranath Tagore, and others. The list is by no means exhaustive and I have given the names of only those who were Sri Aurobindo's precursors or contemporaries. They are outstanding figures and you are surely aware of their great contribution to national life. It will be sufficient here to say that not only did they represent the spirit of resurgent India but each, in his own way, was a link between India's past and her present. What is equally important is that by their integrity and example these great men inspired many others to follow and emulate them with the result that there was a great awakening in the religious, cultural and social life of the country.

It was inevitable that these changes should have repercussions in the political sphere also. The formation of the Indian National Congress in 1885 was an expression of this new political awareness. But the political awakening, when it came, was slow and uncertain in its beginnings. The first generation of Congress leaders, among them M.G. Ranade, Surendranath Banerjee, Pherozeshah Mehta, Gopal Krishna Gokhale, were sincere patriots but they were men of prudence and moderation, who sought to cooperate with the British, not to confront them. Their group came to be known as the Moderates. They had faith in the justice and good intentions of the British and believed that if Indians could prove that their demands were reasonable and just, the British would grant them. So they advocated various economic reforms, sought representation of Indians on the Viceroy's and the Provincial Councils, pressed for increased admission of Indians to Government services, and asked for other similar concessions. At their meetings, the Congress would debate these issues at length and pass eloquent resolutions. The British attitude to all this was simple. So long as British authority and their right to rule over India were not questioned, the Congress could be allowed to act as a harmless safety-valve to keep Indians away from greater mischief. Occasionally some concessions would be announced with much fanfare but nothing much would really be conceded. The overriding consideration for the British was to retain their hold over India and the plea to justify their imperial rule was that the Indians were not yet ready for self-government; only the British could resolve their quarrels and differences.

This, in brief, was the background when Sri Aurobindo returned to India in 1893. Soon after he had settled down at Baroda, Sri Aurobindo was approached by his Cambridge friend, K.G. Deshpande to contribute articles to the *Indu Prakash*, an English-Marathi weekly, which he was then editing from Bombay. Deshpande was aware of Sri Aurobindo's uncompromising views but he was willing to take the risk of publishing them. Accordingly, Sri Aurobindo wrote a series of nine articles over the period August 1893 to March 1894, under the title 'New Lamps for Old', to imply that these were new thoughts he was presenting to replace the old ideas and views of the Congress. He did not sign the articles because, as a member of the Baroda State Service, he did not wish his own views to cause embarrassment to the Gaekwad.

Sri Aurobindo started on a striking note. He wrote: 'If the blind lead the blind, shall they not both fall into the ditch? So or nearly so runs an apophthegm of the Galilean prophet, whose name has run over the four quarters of the globe.... I myself two years ago would not have admitted that it can truthfully be applied to the National Congress. Yet that it can be so applied... is the first thing I must prove.' He then pointed out that the Congress had failed to fulfil the expectations of the people and went on to comment on the attitude with which it had started: 'There was a little too much talk, about the blessings of British rule, and the inscrutable Providence which has laid us in the maternal, or more properly the step-maternal bosom of just and benevolent England. Yet more appalling was the general timidity of the Congress, its glossing over of hard names, its disinclination to tell the direct truth, its fear of too deeply displeasing our masters.' He conceded however, that this initial posture could perhaps have been the sign of 'amiable weaknesses which would wear off with time'. But then he added with telling effect: 'Those amiable weaknesses we were then disposed to pass over very lightly, have not all worn off with time, but have rather grown into an ingrained habit; and the tendency to grosser errors has grown not only into a habit, but into a policy.'

In his subsequent articles Sri Aurobindo criticised the organisation, policy and aims of the Congress from many angles. He pointed out that the Congress 'was not national... it did not represent the mass of the population'. He wrote that the Congress had not heard 'the distant rumbling of the volcano of the ailing and tortured Indian proletariat', and warned that the volcano might erupt one day. He added: 'The proletariat is... the real key of the situation. Torpid he is and immobile; he is nothing of an actual force, but he is a very great potential force and whoever succeeds in understanding and eliciting his strength, becomes by the very fact master of the future.' Sri Aurobindo was particularly critical of the way in which the Congress relied on legalistic arguments to win its case, as if it was conducting an appeal in a court of justice. He wrote: 'Our appeal, the appeal of every high-souled and self-respecting nation, ought not to be to the opinion of the Anglo-Indians, no, nor yet to the British sense of justice, but to our own reviving sense of manhood, to our own sincere fellow-feeling – so far as it can be called sincere – with the silent and suffering people of India.' But if it was useless relying on the British sense of justice it was equally pointless blaming the individual Englishmen who ruled over India. Sri Aurobindo wrote: 'I cannot really see why we should rage so furiously against the Anglo-Indians and call them by all manner of opprobrious epithets. I grant that they are rude and arrogant, that they govern badly, that they are devoid of any great or generous emotion, that their conduct is that of a small coterie of masters surrounded by a nation of Helots. But to say all this is simply to say that they are very commonplace men put into a quite unique position... they are really very ordinary men, – not only ordinary men, but ordinary Englishmen – types of the middle class or Philistines, in the graphic English phrase, with the narrow hearts and commercial habit of mind peculiar to that sort of people. It is something very like folly to quarrel with them for not transgressing the law of their own nature.' Then, with unerring insight, Sri Aurobindo went to the root of the problem: 'Our actual enemy is not any force exterior to ourselves, but our own crying weaknesses, our cowardice, our selfishness, our hypocrisy, our purblind sentimentalism.'

And his final indictment of the Congress was devastating: 'I say, of the Congress, then, this – that its aims are mistaken, that the spirit in which it proceeds towards their accomplishment is not a spirit of sincerity and wholeheartedness, and that the methods it has chosen are not the right methods and the leaders in whom it trusts, not the right sort of men to be leaders; – in brief, that we are at present the blind led, if not by the blind, at any rate by the one-eyed.'

We have to remember that Sri Aurobindo was only twenty-one

when he wrote this. I do not know of a comparable instance of another political writer of any country who had at that age such rare qualities of the intellect, heart and pen. These articles created a turmoil in political circles. But as to the outcome, I shall give you Sri Aurobindo's own words as he recalled the events to us many years later: 'When I came to Baroda from England I found out what the Congress was like at that time and I formed a strong contempt for it. Then I came into touch with Deshpande, Tilak, Madhavrao and others. Deshpande requested me to write something in the *Indu Prakash*. There I strongly criticised the Congress for its moderate policy. The articles were so fiery that M.G. Ranade, the great Maratha leader, asked the proprietor of the paper not to allow such seditious writings to appear in his columns; otherwise he might be arrested and imprisoned. Deshpande approached me with the news and re-quested me to write something less violent. I then began to write about the philosophy of politics, leaving aside its practical aspect. But I soon got disgusted with it.'

Sri Aurobindo's first entry into Indian politics was marked by an immediate clash with moderate opinion and, although he then withdrew from politics for a time, the fight was renewed in later years. But even at that time those with foresight must have divined that one day he would give the lead to India. There was an interesting sequel to these articles. Justice Ranade was so dis-turbed at what had appeared in the *Indu Prakash* that he wanted to meet the author and a meeting did take place at Bombay. This is what Sri Aurobindo wrote about it in his reminiscences of prison life, *Karakahini* written in Bengali, from which I give a translation. 'I remembered that fifteen years earlier after returning home from England, I had written some bitterly critical articles in the *Indu Prakash*. Realising that these articles were influencing the mind of the young, the late Mahadev Govind Ranade had told me, when I met him, that I should give up writing these articles and take up some other Congress work. He wanted me to take up the work of prison reform. I was astonished and unhappy at the unexpected suggestion and refused to undertake that work. I did not know then that this was a prelude to the distant future and that one day God himself would keep me in prison for a year and make me see the cruelty and futility of the system and the need for reform.'

There was another remarkable series of articles that Sri

Aurobindo wrote for the *Indu Prakash*. These were occasioned by the death of Bankim Chandra Chatterji and appeared between July 16 and August 27, 1894. Each of the seven articles on Bankim Chandra is brilliantly written and worth quoting in detail, but I will have to content myself by giving you only a few examples. Commenting on the versatility of Bankim's genius, Sri Aurobindo summed up: 'Scholar, poet, essayist, novelist, philosopher, lawyer, critic, official, philologian and religious innovator – the whole world seemed to be shut up in his single brain.' Of the student Bankim Chandra, Sri Aurobindo wrote: 'He ascended the school by leaps and bounds; so abnormal indeed was his swiftness that he put his masters in fear of him... and indeed his ease and quickness in study were hardly human. Prizes and distinctions cost him no effort in the attaining. He won his honours with a magical carelessness and as if by accident while others toiled and failed.... [At the Hubli College] he left behind him a striking reputation, to which, except Dwarkanath Mitra, no student has ever come near. Yet he had done positively nothing in the way of application or hard work. As with most geniuses his intellectual habits were irregular. His spirit needed larger bounds than a school routine could give it, and refused, as every free mind does, to cripple itself and lose its natural suppleness.... At the eleventh hour and with an examination impending, he would catch up his prescribed books, hurry through them at a canter, win a few prizes, and go back to his lotus-eating.'

These words are of particular interest because, perhaps unconsciously, they reflect Sri Aurobindo's own genius as a student and, in fact, there is a remarkable temperamental affinity between them in other spheres too of their activities. And here is Sri Aurobindo's concluding assessment of Bankim Chandra: 'When Posterity comes to crown with her praises the Makers of India, she will place her most splendid laurel not on the sweating temples of a noisy social reformer but on the serene brow of that gracious Bengali who never clamoured for place or for power but did his work in silence for love of his work even as nature does, and just because he had no aim but to give out the best that was in him, was able to create a language, a literature and a nation.' Again, we have to marvel at the depth of perception and the mastery of language which found expression in one who was barely twenty-two years of age.

After his initial experience with the *Indu Prakash*, Sri Aurobindo

kept away from any public connection with politics for a number of years, but he continued to study conditions closely so that
he could judge and decide on the lines of action he would take
at the appropriate time. He also plunged into studies, as you
know, so as to understand better the culture and civilization of his
country.

Sri Aurobindo's study of history led him to the conclusion that
without a revolution no country could win its freedom. He has
himself said that his politics ran on three lines. First, revolution: to
build up a secret revolutionary organisation and to propagate
revolutionary thoughts and ideas. Secondly, a public movement to
make people accept the idea of complete independence, for most
Indians then believed that to think or speak of independence was a
madman's delirium – the British Raj was too powerful. Thirdly, to
prepare the common people's mind for non-cooperation and
passive resistance by which the government machinery could be
paralysed. This anticipated Mahatma Gandhi's movement on
similar lines in later years.

When we asked him once how he could even conceive of an
armed insurrection against the vast well-equipped British garri-
sons, he answered: 'At that time, warfare and weapons had not
become so lethal in their effect. Rifles were the main weapons,
machine guns were not so effective. India was disarmed, but with
foreign help and proper organisation, the difficulty could be
overcome; and in view of the vastness of the country and the
smallness of the regular British armies, even guerilla warfare
might be effective, provided that the people gave their support. In
the Indian Army, a general revolt was also a possibility.'

Around 1900 Sri Aurobindo made his first move when he sent a
young Bengali soldier of the Baroda Army, Jatin Banerji, as his
lieutenant to Bengal with a programme for preparation and action
which he thought might need thirty years for fruition.

Dinen Roy has given us a vivid picture of how this step was
taken. He writes: 'A tall, well-built Bengali youth came to our
house one day with a *lota* and a long staff in his hand. The visitor
told me, "Bengalis are not admitted to the British Army, so I am
knocking about from place to place to see if by any good fortune I
could enlist myself in the army of a native Prince." Aravinda was
much impressed by the young man's courage, ardour and
ambition.'

Sri Aurobindo got this young man into the Baroda Army,

concealing his identity and passing him off as a Brahmin from the north. After a year's training, he sent Jatin to Bengal to prepare the necessary revolutionary climate and provided him with a programme of action: he should recruit members for the revolution, collect money and equipment, organise the young men into groups and units and give them intensive physical training so that in a future warfare they could play their role as efficient soldiers. Centres were to be established in every town and eventually in every village.

Since his initial visit in 1893, Sri Aurobindo went to Bengal whenever he could and especially during the college vacations. During his visit to Calcutta in 1901 he took an important step in his life. In April, he married Mrinalini, daughter of Bhupal Chandra Bose, a senior official in Government service. Sri Aurobindo was then 28; the bride Mrinalini, 14. She was beautiful, educated and belonged to an aristocratic family. It was an arranged marriage resulting from an advertisement inserted by Sri Aurobindo, which caught the notice of Principal Girish Chandra Bose of Bangabasi College, a close friend of Bhupal Chandra, and it was Girish Babu who negotiated the marriage. The wedding was attended by many distinguished persons of Calcutta, like Jagdish Chandra Bose, Lord Sinha and others. Sri Aurobindo had insisted on the marriage ceremony being performed according to the Hindu rites. And this raised a problem. He was told that he would have to go through *prayaschitta*, a purificatory ceremony, for having crossed the 'black waters'. Like his father, he refused and also turned down other alternatives which were suggested. Eventually, some money passed into the hands of an obliging Brahmin priest and saved the face of society and *shastra*! After the marriage Sri Aurobindo reached Baroda along with his wife and sister Sarojini, via Deoghar and Nainital where the Gaekwad was holidaying at the time.

About this time Sri Aurobindo's youngest brother, Barin, also joined him at Baroda. Because of his mother's illness and the untimely death of Dr. K.D. Ghose, Barin's education had suffered, but he had managed to pass the entrance examination, then tried various occupations, including running a tea-shop (then a most novel undertaking) at Patna; eventually he decided to try his lot with 'Sejda' at Baroda. He was a young man of valour and exceptional ability but of a volatile, somewhat unstable, temperament. He had already been initiated into a revolutionary coterie at Deoghar and proved to be an eager disciple at Baroda. He soon became friendly with Lt. Madhavrao, Khaserao Jadav's brother, who was in the Baroda Army, and took lessons from him in the use of fire-arms etc. Later, Madhavrao was sent to Europe for further military training. Sri Aurobindo helped Madhavrao meet the expenses from his own resources.

Among Barin's varied interests was spiritualism – experiments with planchette, table-tapping, etc. Sri Aurobindo would join him on some evenings and came across some startling results. Once a spirit assuming their father's name came and said: 'I gave a gold watch to Barin when he was a child.' This was confirmed by Barin who had forgotten all about it. When Dr. Krishna Dhan's spirit was asked what kind of a man Tilak was, the answer came: 'When all your work will be ruined and many men bow down their heads, this man will keep his head erect' – a remarkable prediction about Tilak's political greatness. On another occasion Sri Ramakrishna's spirit was invoked. He said, '*Mandir gado*' (make a temple) which was construed to mean that a temple for political sannyasins was to be built like the Bhavani Mandir of Bankim Chandra's *Ananda Math*.

After training Barin, Sri Aurobindo sent him to Bengal to help Jatin Banerji in the organisation of revolutionary work and himself followed up with a visit in 1902 during the college vacation. He went to Midnapur for the first time accompanied by Jatin and Barin. There he met Hemchandra Das, the revolutionary leader. On his return to Calcutta Jatin arranged a meeting between Sri Aurobindo and Barrister P. Mitter who had started an organisation of young men for revolutionary work under the guise of youth clubs for physical exercises etc. Mitter readily joined hands with Sri Aurobindo who administered the revolutionary oath to him and Hemchandra: holding a sword and the Gita in their hands, they vowed to strive to secure at any cost the freedom of Mother India. It was also resolved to form six centres of revolutionary work in Bengal and to give training in rifle-shooting.

Earlier Sri Aurobindo had learnt of a secret revolutionary society in Maharashtra under the leadership of Thakur Ram Singh, a Rajput prince from the State of Udaipur. Sri Aurobindo joined its Bombay branch and took the oath of the party. The Thakur was actively engaged in winning over regiments of the

Indian Army to the revolutionary movement. Sri Aurobindo paid a visit to Central India and met some regimental officers. He thus forged a link between eastern and western India, with Tilak working from behind in Maharashtra. Here I should also mention that Sri Aurobindo had a long meeting with this great Maharashtrian leader in December 1902 when both were present at the Ahmedabad session of the Indian National Congress. Sri Aurobindo had an exceptional regard for Tilak and their collaboration in the political field was both close and of immense significance for the national movement.

In 1903 Sri Aurobindo paid another visit to Calcutta to patch up differences which had cropped up between Jatin and Barin. Jatin, it appeared, had become too rigid a disciplinarian and was losing his hold on the youth. Sri Aurobindo formed a committee of five consisting of P. Mitter, Sister Nivedita, C.R. Das, Surendranath Tagore and Jatin to be in overall charge of the revolutionary work in Bengal. Although some differences continued, the work under P. Mitter's leadership increased enormously. Hundreds of young people joined the movement and even some government servants lent their secret sympathy and help. And by 1905 the movement received a tremendous fillip as a result of the Government's ill-conceived decision to partition Bengal.

From this time a relationship of firm friendship and cooperation grew up between Sri Aurobindo and Sister Nivedita. It had started when Nivedita visited Baroda in 1902 to give some lectures. Sri Aurobindo went to the station to receive her. She had heard of him as a worshipper of Kali and Sri Aurobindo had appreciated her book *Kali, the Mother*. Nivedita had an interview with the Maharaja at which Sri Aurobindo was present. She tried to persuade the Maharaja to support the revolutionary movement but he merely said he would send his reply through Mr. Ghose. Of course he had no intention of joining the movement; but he seemed a little surprised that Sri Aurobindo was taking such a keen interest in it.

Sri Aurobindo had great admiration and respect for Nivedita and spoke about her with much warmth. 'She was a true revolutionary leader,' he told us once, 'she was open, frank and talked freely of revolutionary ideas. There was no concealment about her. It was her very soul that spoke. Whenever we met we spoke about politics and revolution. But her eyes showed a power of concentration and revealed a capacity for going into trance. Her book *Kali, the Mother* is revolutionary and not at all non-violent.' 'What about Barin,' we interposed, 'he was also fiery?' 'But not like Nivedita. She was fire, if you like. She did India a tremendous service.'

With the revolutionary movement gathering strength, Barin hit upon the idea of giving a concrete shape to Sri Ramakrishna's words heard at the spirit sessions, *Mandir gado*. So he stalked far and wide in the Vindhya hills looking for a suitable place where a temple, along the lines of the Mandir in *Ananda Math*, could be built. In the course of these wanderings he contracted a 'hill fever', a violent and almost incurable disease, and had to return to his Sejda at Baroda. Now it happened, one day, that a *naga* sannyasi arrived at the house and, seeing Barin laid up in his emaciated condition, asked, 'Who is that lying there?' When he was given the story, he said, 'Fetch a glass of water.' Then muttering some mantra he cut the water crosswise with a knife and asked Barin to drink it. 'Tomorrow the fever will leave you,' he predicted and truly it did. A fever, which had persisted for days, disappeared as if by magic!

About this striking incident Sri Aurobindo wrote: 'This was a first-hand proof of yoga-power. I thought – if yoga has such powers, why not use them for the country's sake? This was the immediate cause of my turning to yoga. Ramakrishna's message gave the necessary push. That is why I have said that I entered yoga by the back door.'

This brings me to the subject which will assume increasing importance as we go on, *viz.*, Sri Aurobindo's turning to yoga. Actually, Sri Aurobindo was a born yogi. I have already told you of the rare spiritual experience which came to him when he first stepped on the shores of India. Let me give you another instance of an experience he had in the first year of his stay in Baroda, again in a most unexpected manner. Sri Aurobindo had then a very old-fashioned horse-carriage, known as a 'Victoria' carriage. Dinen Roy wrote that the horse was a huge creature but in movement it was the cousin-brother of a donkey and whipping had no effect on it! Anyway, Sri Aurobindo was going through the city streets in this carriage when, suddenly it went out of control. A serious accident was imminent. Sri Aurobindo willed that that must not happen and immediately a Being of Light emerged out of him and took control of the situation. Later in a splendid sonnet, 'The Godhead', Sri Aurobindo recalled this experience and if you read the poem aloud, you will feel its power, extraordinary rhythm and vividness. This was probably Sri Aurobindo's first experience of the Divinity within himself. Nearly ten years later, in 1903, he had another remarkable experience. This was in Kashmir where he had gone with the Maharaja. While walking on the ridge of the Takht-i-Suleman or Hill of Shankaracharya, Sri Aurobindo had an experience which too he expressed in a sonnet, 'Adwaita':

> An unborn Reality world-nude,
> Topless and fathomless, forever still...

Probably in the same year Sri Aurobindo visited a temple of Kali on the banks of the Narmada. This he did on the persuasion of his friends, as he himself had at the time no faith in idols or image-worship. 'With my European mind,' he wrote, 'I had no faith in them and I hardly believed in the presence of God.' But when he looked at the image of the goddess, he found 'a living Presence deathless and divine, / A form that harbours all infinity...' and he writes: 'For the first time I believed in the presence of God.' In an indirect reference to this experience, he wrote afterwards: '...You stand before a temple of Kali beside a sacred river and see what? – a sculpture, a gracious piece of architecture, but in a moment, mysteriously, unexpectedly, there is instead a Presence, a Power, a Face that looks into yours, an inner sight in you has regarded the World-Mother.' We can but wonder at such experiences, rare even amongst those who have dedicated their entire lives to the practice of yoga. I should also remind you of the vivid description given by Dinen Roy of Sri Aurobindo in 1899/1900 – his self-control, detachment, equanimity, compassion for the poor – which are all signs associated with a yogi who is far advanced on the path.

   Before he turned to the practice of yoga, Sri Aurobindo had started on certain practices of *pranayam* having learnt some rules from an engineer friend, Devadhar. Sri Aurobindo said that he practised it 'on my own for five or six hours a day for nearly four years. As a result, the brain became full of light, *prakashamaya*. The mind worked with great illumination and power. My power of writing poetry as well as prose increased tremendously. Usually I wrote about 200 lines of poetry a month. After the *pranayam* I wrote pages and pages in a single day and that flow I never lost. I used to feel that an electric energy was all round the brain because of which the mosquitoes did not bite me during the *pranayam*. My health too improved, even the skin became fair and there was a peculiar substance in the saliva which probably produced these changes. I adopted a vegetarian diet. That gave lightness and some purification. But that was all and there was no farther advance. Besides, politics kept me too busy and owing to irregularity in the practice of *pranayam* I fell seriously ill. It nearly carried me off.'

However wonderful as these earlier experiences were, 1904 is usually taken to be the year in which Sri Aurobindo actually commenced the practice of yoga. He himself has said that he had no pull towards yoga to begin with. When asked to explain how the conversion took place, he replied, 'God knows how. At Baroda my friends asked me to practise yoga. I didn't care for it; my idea about yoga was that it was a life-denying affair. One has to retire to the hills and become a sannyasi, while my heart's call was to seek for the freedom of the country. But the cure of Barin's fever opened my eyes and I realised my error about yoga. Slowly my mind turned towards it and when I decided to take up yoga I made this prayer: "If You do exist, You know my mind. You know I don't care for liberation; what others want has no attraction for me. I want power so that I may raise this country and serve my dear countrymen."'

In another revealing letter he explained: 'I didn't know what God was. Deshpande was doing Hatha Yoga *asanas* and other *kriyas* at that time and as he had a great proselytising tendency he wanted to convert me to his view. But I thought that a yoga which required me to give up the world was not for me. I had to liberate my country. I took to it seriously when I learnt that the same Tapasya which one does to get away from the world can be turned to action. I learnt that Yoga gives power and I thought why the devil should I not get the power and use it to liberate my country.... It was the time of "country first, humanity afterwards and the rest nowhere". It was something from behind which got the idea accepted by the mind; mine was a side-door entry to the spiritual life.' It is evident, then, that there was no conflict in Sri Aurobindo between the practice of yoga and politics and one became a part of the other.

At this time, that is around 1905, Sri Aurobindo visited the Ashram of Swami Brahmananda of Karnali on the banks of the river Narmada, had the *darshan* of the *maha yogi* and was greatly impressed. Usually when receiving pranams Swami Brahmananda sat with closed eyes but for Sri Aurobindo he made an exception and gazed at him with his eyes fully open as if some extraordinary person or kindred soul had come. 'He had very beautiful eyes,' Sri Aurobindo said, 'and his penetrating look saw everything inside me.'

In later years Sri Aurobindo made some observations about Swami Brahmananda which were very interesting. There was much speculation about the age of the Swami, some claiming that he was more than 400 years old. Sri Aurobindo wrote: '400 years is an exaggeration. It is known however that he lived on the banks of the Narmada for 80 years and when he arrived there, he was already in appearance at the age when maturity turns towards overripeness. He was when I met him just before his death a man of magnificent physique showing no signs of old age except white beard and hair, extremely tall, robust, able to walk any number of miles a day and tiring out his younger disciples, walking too so swiftly that they tended to fall behind, a great head and magnificent face that seemed to belong to men of more ancient times. He never spoke of his age or of his past either except for an occasional almost accidental utterance. One of these was spoken to a disciple of his well known to me, a Baroda Sardar, Mazumdar .... [who] learned that he was suffering from a bad tooth and brought him a bottle of Floriline, a toothwash then much in vogue. The Yogi refused, saying, "I never use medicines. My one medicine is Narmada water. As for the tooth I have suffered from it since the days of Bhao Girdi." Bhao Girdi was the Maratha general Sadashiva Rao Bhao who disappeared in the Battle of Panipat [14.1.1761] and his body was never found. Many formed the conclusion that Brahmananda was himself Bhao Girdi, but this was an imagination. Nobody who knew Brahmananda would doubt any statement of his – he was a man of perfect simplicity and did not seek fame or to impose himself. When he died he was still in full strength and his death came not by decay but by the accident of blood-poisoning through a rusty nail that entered into his foot as he walked on the sands of the Narmada.' All this shows that the ordinary norms of age or indeed the usual consideration of everyday life can scarcely be applied to great yogis.

Let me now tell you of the booklet *Bhawani Mandir* which Sri

Aurobindo wrote at this time. It was Barin who conceived the idea
that a temple consecrated to the Divine Mother, invoking Mother
India as Bharat Shakti, Bhawani Bharati, would be extremely
effective for the propagation of the new revolutionary gospel, and
at his request Sri Aurobindo wrote the booklet. It begins: 'A
temple is to be erected and consecrated to Bhawani, the Mother,
among the hills.' Bhawani is the Mother, the Infinite Energy that
'looms up in the vision of man in various aspects and infinite
forms. Each aspect creates and marks an age.' In our age, the
Mother's characteristic aspect is Shakti or masterful strength; in
this aspect her name is Bhawani. 'Everywhere the Mother is at
work...remoulding, creating. She is pouring Her spirit into the
old; She is whirling into life the new.'

But in India *tamas* has taken possession of the people. 'We have
abandoned Shakti and are therefore abandoned by Shakti. The
Mother is not in our hearts, in our brains, in our arms.' So Sri
Aurobindo gives the call: India must shake off her lethargy and
rise to her full stature. And what *is* India, our mother-country? Sri
Aurobindo's answer is crystal clear: 'It is not a piece of earth, nor a
figure of speech, nor a fiction of the mind. It is a mighty Shakti,
composed of the Shaktis of all the millions of units that make up
the nation, just as Bhawani Mahisha Mardini sprang into being
from the Shaktis of all the millions of gods assembled in one mass
of force and welded into unity. The Shakti we call India, Bhawani
Bharati, is the living unity of the Shaktis of three hundred million
people; but she is inactive, imprisoned in the magic circle of
Tamas, the self-indulgent inertia and ignorance of her sons.'

Three things are necessary: first, a temple for the Mother;
secondly, a new Order of Karma Yogis, 'Men in whom the Shakti
is developed to the uttermost extent'; and, thirdly, the message of
so-ham, 'the mighty formula of the Vedanta...the knowledge
which when vivified by Karma and Bhakti, delivers men out of all
fear and all weakness.' And India must be reborn because her
rebirth is demanded for the future of the world. Then comes Sri
Aurobindo's final call: 'Come then, hearken to the call of the
Mother. She is already in our hearts waiting to manifest Herself,
waiting to be worshipped, – inactive because the God.in us is
concealed by *tamas*, troubled by Her inactivity, sorrowful because
Her children will not call on Her to help them. You who feel Her
stirring within you, fling off the black veil of self, break down the

imprisoning walls of indolence, help Her each as you feel impelled, with your bodies or with your intellect or with your speech or with your wealth or with your prayers and worship, each man according to his capacity. Draw not back, for against those who were called and heard Her not She may well be wroth in the day of Her coming; but to those who help Her advent even a little, how radiant with beauty and kindness will be the face of their Mother."

Neither the Mandir nor the new Order of Karma Yogins materialized, although later Barin sought to give some shape to these ideas on a small scale amongst the community of revolutionaries who gathered at Maniktolla garden. However, the booklet was a source of inspiration and courage to hundreds of revolutionaries, causing much alarm among official circles. And Sri Aurobindo's call still rings for us to respond to in our hearts, for that is where the Mandir has to be built.

We have now come to the closing period of Sri Aurobindo's stay at Baroda. In March 1905 Sri Aurobindo took over as acting Principal at Baroda College and he held that position until February 1906 when he took privilege leave to go to Béngal. Meanwhile much was happening in that province. On October 16, 1905, the Partition of Bengal had become an 'accomplished fact', the decision of an alien Government in complete disregard of the wishes of the people. This was to have far-reaching consequences. Sri Aurobindo remained in close touch with the situation. In December 1905 he attended the Benares Session of the Indian National Congress to feel the pulse of the nation. Mark how many things he had simultaneously taken up by this time: yoga, revolutionary work, politics, teaching, besides his own literary activity. But we can get a glimpse of his main preoccupation from the letters he wrote in Bengali to his wife Mrinalini at this time. These letters were not meant for publication but expressed only his private thoughts and feelings and were written in order to answer some of her anxious queries. They were seized by the Police when Sri Aurobindo was arrested in May 1908 and were produced before the Court as part of the evidence against him. I shall quote only a few extracts to show how his intense aspiration for the Divine had merged with his ardent love for the motherland without any contradiction between these two urges of his being, and how deeply concerned he was that Mrinalini should understand him and follow him in his path.

In the letter of August 1905, Sri Aurobindo writes: 'I have three madnesses. The first is this. I firmly believe that the accomplishments, talent, education and means that God has given me, are all His. Whatever is essential and needed for the maintenance of the family has alone a claim upon me; the rest must be returned to God. If I spend everything for comfort or luxury, then I am a thief.... The second madness which has recently seized hold of me is: I must somehow see God.... If He exists, there must be ways to perceive His presence, to meet Him. However arduous the way, I am determined to follow that path. In one month I have felt that the Hindu religion has not told lies – the signs and hints it has given have become a part of my experience. Now I want to take you along with me.... My third madness is that other people look upon the country as an inert piece of matter, a stretch of fields and meadows, forests and rivers. To me She is the Mother. I adore Her, worship Her. What will the son do when he sees a *rakshasa* sitting on the breast of his mother and sucking her blood? Will he quietly have his meal or will he rush to deliver his mother from that grasp? I know I have the strength to redeem this fallen race. It is not physical strength, it is the strength of knowledge. The power of the *Kshatriya* is not the only power. There is also the power of the *Brahmin*, the power founded upon knowledge. This feeling is not new, I was born with it and it is in my very marrow. God has sent me to this world to accomplish this great mission. When I was fourteen, the seed began to sprout; at eighteen the foundation became firm and unshakable.'

In another letter he wrote: 'In these dark days, the entire country is seeking refuge at my door. Among the thirty crores of my brothers and sisters many are dying from hunger and starvation.... They must be helped. This was the secret I wanted to tell you.'

This is but a bare gist of the letters. You have to go through them in full to realise Sri Aurobindo's greatness even in those early days. The letters were perhaps an enigma to Mrinalini – we must remember that she was only 18 at the time, and even for one more mature it would have been difficult indeed to follow the steep and narrow path of austerity and sacrifice that her husband had chosen for himself. But, to her great credit, she faced her ordeals bravely during the years of her husband's incarceration and remained steadfast in her devotion to him.

On completion of his privilege leave in June 1906 Sri Aurobindo returned to Baroda but only to stay for a few days. On June 19 he took one year's leave without pay to go back to Bengal. This marked practically the end of his long association with Baroda. Bengal was in ferment and the agitation had spread to other parts of the country. Sri Aurobindo was to play a crucial role in the momentous hour which was now on the nation.

Chapter V

The Nationalist Movement: Bande Mataram
1906–1907

YOU have seen that there were three sides to Sri Aurobindo's politics: planning and spreading secret revolutionary action; establishing the idea of complete independence, and creating a movement for non-cooperation and passive resistance so as to paralyse the Government.

Sri Aurobindo was waiting for an opportunity to leave Baroda for good. During his visits to Bengal in 1905 and 1906 he saw that the situation there had undergone a radical transformation and he knew that the time had come for concerted action on the lines he had in mind.

What had happened in Bengal was this. The province of Bengal or the presidency of Bengal as it was called, was at the time a very large area. It consisted not only of West Bengal and what is now Bangladesh but also included Bihar and Orissa. Because of its size there were difficulties in administering it properly and in 1903 the Government announced a plan whereby the presidency would be partitioned or divided into two provinces. There would be one province consisting of West Bengal, Bihar and Orissa; another new province would be created to include East Bengal and Assam.

The plan created an uproar. In the undivided presidency the Bengali Hindus were the leading community. They had been the first to be exposed to the new ideas and forces from the West and the first to take to English education; as a result, they were more conscious, politically, than the rest. So they could realise that the partition was really aimed at them, for in consequence of the division, they would become a minority community in both the new provinces and their strength and influence would be greatly reduced. So they held hundreds of protest meetings, and gathering in thousands, successfully enlisted the support of the other communities in a united opposition to the Government's plan. There was a tremendous upheaval of popular feeling, an unprecedented surge of shock and resentment. And, suddenly, a cry was heard – '*Bande Mataram*', a mantra invoking the Mother for strength and fearlessness, a rallying call as well as a battle cry. This is how Sri Aurobindo describes its significance: 'It was thirty-two years ago that Bankim wrote his great song and few listened; but in a sudden moment of awakening from long delusions the people of Bengal looked round for the truth and in a fated moment somebody sang '*Bande Mataram*'. The mantra had been given and in a single day a whole people had been converted to the religion of patriotism. The Mother had revealed herself. Once that vision has come to a people, there can be no rest, no peace, no further slumber till the temple has been made ready, the image installed and the sacrifice offered. A great nation which has had that vision can never again bend its neck in subjection to the yoke of a conqueror.'

And the people showed their intense feelings not merely through mass meetings, speeches etc., but the demonstrations took the practical form of urging people to boycott British cloth and other goods and to use Indian products instead. This was how the Boycott and Swadeshi movement was born. Like a tidal wave it gained ground in Bengal and soon it spread outside the province. Bepin Chandra Pal was at the forefront of the movement in Bengal and Balgangadhar Tilak and Lala Lajpat Rai gave the lead to it in Maharashtra and the Punjab, forming the well-known trinity Lal-Bal-Pal. Indeed a country-wide campaign was launched with the result that the demand for British goods fell off seriously. Even the Indian National Congress at its annual session at Benares in December 1905, which Sri Aurobindo attended as an observer, could not ignore the intensity of popular feelings and gave support to the movement.

Yet the Government was adamant and the man most responsible for its hardline policy was the Viceroy, Lord Curzon. A very able man and a brilliant administrator, he was a diehard imperialist who believed in Britain's divine right to rule over India. For him, the Partition was a 'settled fact' and the plan was pushed through to take effect from October 16, 1905, a day observed in Bengal and elsewhere as one of mourning. No cooking was done that day and all the shops and market-places were closed. Thousands walked barefoot in silent processions and the ceremony of *rakshabandhan* became a symbolic ritual of unity and brotherhood.

Through his lieutenants, Jatin Banerji, Barindra, Abinash Bhattacharjee and others, Sri Aurobindo had kept himself closely informed of the developments in Bengal, and he sent his directives saying, 'Take advantage of this intense discontent and spread the seeds of revolt amongst the youth. Enlist them in the revolutionary camp.... This is a very fine opportunity. Carry on the anti-partition agitation powerfully. We will get many workers for the movement.' The 'settled fact' of Partition had to be 'unsettled'.

To help you get a feel of the atmosphere of those wonderful days, let me give you a quotation from Nolini Kanta ˙Gupta's *Reminiscences.* He was a very young man then, still in his teens, and yet see how deeply he responded. He writes: 'Almost overnight, how very different we became from what we had been as individuals! We used to be just humdrum creatures, most ignorant and inert; now we became conscious and alert, our lives acquired a meaning, an aim, a purpose. We used to move in the traditional ruts, dull and desperate. Instead of that our lives now got a cohesion, an orientation. Borne along the current and driven with the crowd, the most one could hope for in the past was to become a Deputy Magistrate or Professor, a Doctor or Advocate, worldly men of sufficient means. In a moment, all this got topsy-turvy, our lives were rent in twain as if by an earthquake. There lay across the chasm the deathlike life of the dead past, and here loomed a life of the present that faced the future with new duties.

'Calcutta was at the time in the throes of a great turmoil. The press and the platform were loud with cries of "Freedom" and "Boycott"; the British must be driven out, India must be rid of the Britisher. In the parks and wherever there was open space, crowds would gather to listen to lectures and orations, crowds mostly of boys from the schools and colleges – the girls had not yet come out and joined. Swadeshi, boycott, national education, rural uplift – these were the slogans dwelt upon everywhere. And with it all there went on, in secret, underground preparations for revolution and revolt and armed attack.'

However the Government was not to be caught napping. They resolved to crush the movement and came down with ruthless force on the people. Meetings and processions were banned and the cry of '*Bande Mataram*' was considered seditious. The British were determined to uphold their power and authority.

In March 1906 Sri Aurobindo went to Calcutta on a privilege leave. He attended Barisal Conference. On 14th April the delegates went in a procession to the pavilion, crying '*Bande Mataram*' in defiance of the government's order. The police allowed the leaders to pass and then attacked the volunteers with iron-shod *lathis*. Among the many injured was a young boy whose head bled profusely, but nothing could prevent him from shouting '*Bande Mataram*'.

As a result of the Boycott movement many patriotic students and teachers refused to attend Government schools and colleges. Anxious to help them, the leaders of the Swadeshi movement realised that it was now necessary to set up alternative avenues of education on national lines and free from the control of Government. So a National Council of Education was formed and, during his visit to Calcutta, Sri Aurobindo attended some of its meetings presiding over several of them. A munificent donation of one lakh of rupees was promised by Subodh Chandra Mullick, an affluent and ardent patriot, to found a National College. Through his brother-in-law C.C. Dutt, Subodh Mullick had earlier met Sri Aurobindo, soon becoming one of his closest friends and staunchest supporters in the political field. In making the donation, Subodh Mullick stipulated that Sri Aurobindo should become the Principal of the proposed National College. So the way was now open for Sri Aurobindo to leave Baroda. As Principal of the National College Sri Aurobindo would draw a nominal pay of Rs.150 per month; when he left Baroda, his salary was more than Rs.700 per month, a handsome figure in those days. Characteristically, he accepted this considerable sacrifice without thought for himself or his family, but it was greatly appreciated by his countrymen when they came to hear of it.

There was another notable development during Sri Aurobindo's visit to Calcutta. In March 1906 Barindra and others started a Bengali weekly, *Yugantar*, a revolutionary journal which became immensely popular and influential, particularly amongst the youth. Sri Aurobindo wrote articles for some of the earlier issues of the paper and exercised a general control over it. The Government, alarmed at the popularity of the paper, eventually arrested Bhupendranath Dutt, Swami Vivekananda's brother, who came forward as the editor, and sentenced him to jail on a charge of sedition. *Yugantar* finally had to cease publication in June 1908, but during its short career it attacked the Government fearlessly.

Around this time a book in Bengali entitled *Desher Katha* was also causing a sensation. Its author was Sakharam Ganesh Deuskar, a Maharashtrian revolutionary who was an able writer in Bengali. At Sri Aurobindo's request, Deuskar wrote the book in which he exposed, in vivid detail, how the British had ruthlessly exploited India, commercially and industrially, in the course of their rule. Sri Aurobindo included this kind of activity within the scope of his revolutionary work. The book had an enormous influence, shaking even the Moderates, and provided a powerful impetus to the Swadeshi movement. In fact its influence became so pronounced that the Government had to ban it.

When Sri Aurobindo came over to Calcutta in June, for a while he stayed at Subodh Mullick's palatial house at 12 Wellington Square. There all his requirements were well looked after, but not wishing to inconvenience his host Sri Aurobindo moved to a house in Chukku Khansama Lane, where Mrinalini, Sarojini, Barin and Abinash came to stay with him. Later when they shifted to 23, Scott's Lane, Barin went over to stay at the Murari Pukur Gardens.

At first Sri Aurobindo was absorbed in work connected with the new National College but soon he was drawn into a venture which had a profound influence on the course of events. I have already told you that Bepin Pal was then one of the foremost political leaders in the country. He was a remarkable man – a great orator, perhaps the finest of his day, a powerful writer, a scholar and sadhak. Along with Monoranjan Guha-Thakurta, Brahmaban-dhab Upadhyaya and others, he stood for a new party, the Nationalist, which was opposed to the moderate policy of the Congress. Upadhyaya was successfully conducting the Bengali evening daily *Sandhya*. But the need for an all-India organ was keenly felt. Bepin Chandra, with great courage but hardly any financial support, decided to launch the paper. The first issue of this new journal, *Bande Mataram*, was to be brought out on

August 7, 1906, the first anniversary of the boycott of British goods as a protest against the Partition. However, Bepin Pal had to leave Calcutta urgently and the first issue of the *Bande Mataram* actually appeared on August 5, 1906. Indeed Bepin Pal was able to leave only because he had obtained Sri Aurobindo's assurance that he would contribute an article every day during Pal's absence. In this way Sri Aurobindo was associated with the paper from its very inception and he has himself given a very interesting account of its early career: 'Bepin Pal started the *Bande Mataram* with Rs.500 in his pocket donated by Haridas Haldar. He called in my help as assistant editor and I gave it. I called a private meeting of the young Nationalist leaders in Calcutta and they agreed to take up the *Bande Mataram* as their party paper with Subodh and Nirod Mullick as the principal financial supporters. A company was projected and formed, but the paper was financed and kept up meanwhile by Subodh. Bepin Pal who was strongly supported by C.R. Das and others remained as editor. Hemendra Prasad Ghose and Shyam Sundar joined the editorial staff but they could not get on with Bepin Babu and were supported by the Mullicks. Finally, Bepin Pal had to retire, I don't remember whether in November or December, probably the latter. I was myself very ill, almost to death, in my father-in-law's house in Serpentine Lane and I did not know what was going on. They put my name as editor on the paper without my consent, but I spoke to the secretary pretty harshly and had the insertion discontinued. I also wrote a strong letter on the subject to Subodh. From that time Bepin Pal had no connection with the *Bande Mataram*.' In spite of Bepin Pal's brief association with the paper he lives in our memory for having started a journal which became synonymous with the new spirit of Indian nationalism and patriotism.

The *Bande Mataram* was an instantaneous success but throughout its career it had to contend with many difficulties. From the beginning it evoked the hostility of the Government who were ready to pounce on it with charges of sedition etc. The Anglo-Indian press was alarmed at the appearance of a rival which started stealing all their thunder. Although the *Bande Mataram* became very popular and a public limited company was formed to strengthen the financial position, it was almost always short of funds and Sri Aurobindo had to give time and attention to this problem also. The *Bande Mataram* had no declared editor. As we have seen, Sri Aurobindo's name was given as the editor in one issue but as a result of his strong protest, it did not appear again. Sri Aurobindo did not wish attention to be drawn to himself as he had still not resigned from his Baroda service; moreover, as the Principal of the National College, he wanted to avoid involving that institution in political controversies.

In the day to day running of the *Bande Mataram* Sri Aurobindo had able assistants to help him: Shyam Sundar Chakravarty, Bejoy Krishna Chatterjee and Hemendra Prasad Ghose were writers of exceptional ability but, as the historian J.L. Banerji wrote at the time: 'Whoever the actual contributor to the *Bande Mataram* might be – the soul, the genius of the paper was Arabinda. The pen might be that of Shyam Sundar or whoever else, but the voice was the voice of Arabinda Ghose.' And later, Bepin Pal was to write a moving tribute which catches the tone and temper of the *Bande Mataram*'s intellectual and literary powers: 'The hand of the master was in it from the very beginning. Its bold attitude, its vigorous thinking, its clear ideas, its chaste and powerful diction, its scorching sarcasm and refined witticism were unsurpassed by any journal in the country either Indian or Anglo-Indian...morning after morning not only Calcutta but the educated community, almost in every part of the country, eagerly awaited its vigorous pronouncements on the stirring questions of the day.... Long extracts from it began to be reproduced in the exclusive columns of the *Times* of London. It was a force in the country which none dared to ignore, however much they might fear or hate it; and Aravinda was the leading spirit, the central figure in the new journal.'

Indeed hardly had he settled down in Calcutta when Sri Aurobindo plunged into intense activity which imposed a very heavy strain on him. At Baroda he had practised *pranayam* regularly but he had no time for it now and this, according to Sri Aurobindo himself, brought on a serious illness. He was removed to his father-in-law's house where he was nursed with great devotion by Mrinalini. Later he went to Deoghar to recuperate but returned to Calcutta in time to attend the Congress session which began on December 26. From this time onwards he assumed control not only of the policy of the *Bande Mataram* but also of the Nationalist Party.

The Congress session at Calcutta was held under the presidentship of Dadabhoy Naoroji, the venerable and aged politician who lived mostly in England and who was the choice of the Moderates. The Nationalists had earlier wanted Tilak to be president. However, a split on the issue was avoided. Tilak was present as the leader of the Nationalists, along with Lajpat Rai, G.S. Khaparde and others. Sri Aurobindo avoided the limelight but worked constantly behind the scenes, taking a prominent part in the private discussions. Largely as a result of his influence, it was decided that the Nationalists would press for a resolution adopting independence as the goal of the Congress, along with other objectives such as Swadeshi, Boycott and National Education. However, when the resolution came up for discussion at the open session, the Moderates fought shy of the word 'independence' and their stalwarts like Pherozeshah Mehta, Gokhale and Suren Banerjee opposed the resolution. Heated discussions ensued and at one stage it seemed that the Nationalists, or the Extremists as their opponents called them, would stage a walk-out. Eventually, the President, realising the strength of the Nationalists, proposed Swaraj as a compromise substitute for 'independence' and the resolution was then passed, although no doubt each party interpreted the word in its own way. The other resolutions, on Swadeshi, Boycott and National Education, were all passed and the Nationalists emerged from the session with greatly increased strength. On December 31, 1906, commenting on 'The results of the Congress', Sri Aurobindo wrote in the *Bande Mataram*: 'No strongly worded resolutions have been pressed and we are glad that none has been passed, for we believe in strong action and not in strong words. But our hopes have been realised, our contentions recognised, if not precisely in the form we desired or with as much clearness and precision as we ourselves would have used, yet definitely enough for all practical purposes.... All that the forward party has fought for, has in substance been conceded....' Sri Aurobindo's strategy had succeeded. He had remained in the background, but his diplomacy and political acumen had won the day. However, the Moderates were not ready to give up the leadership, as we shall see later.

Sri Aurobindo's policy in the *Bande Mataram* was based on three clear objectives. First, he kept the ideal of independence constantly before the people. As early as September 1906 he wrote: 'The withdrawal of the Partition by itself will not improve the position of our race with regard to its rulers nor leave it one whit better than before Lord Curzon's regime. Even if the present Government were overflowing with liberal kindness, it cannot last forever, and there is nothing to prevent another Imperialist Viceroy backed up by an Imperialist Government from perpetrating measures as injurious to the interests and sentiments of the nation. The only genuine guarantee against this contingency is the control by the nation of its own destinies.' Here let me emphasise that Sri Aurobindo was the first among political leaders to proclaim the ideal of complete independence in unequivocal terms. When Dadabhoy Naoroji introduced the word Swaraj at the Calcutta session of the Congress as its political objective, the Moderates interpreted Swaraj to mean a form of self-government as it existed in the British Colonies; to many of them even this ideal was too remote and impractical. But Sri Aurobindo was not prepared to gloss over the issue. To make the position perfectly clear he wrote: 'The latest and most venerable of the older politicians who have sat in the Presidential Chair of the Congress, pronounced from that seat of authority Swaraj as the one object of our political endeavour, – Swaraj as the only remedy for all our ills, – Swaraj as the one demand nothing short of which will satisfy the people of India. Complete self-government as it exists in the United Kingdom or the Colonies, – such was his definition of Swaraj. The Congress has contented itself with demanding self-government as it exists in the Colonies. We of the new school would not pitch our ideal one inch lower than absolute Swaraj, – self-government as it exists in the United Kingdom.' India must be free, even as England is free, and if the word Swaraj is ambiguous, let the goal be defined as 'absolute Swaraj' – nothing could be clearer! This theme was to find repeated utterance in the pages of the *Bande Mataram* and in Sri Aurobindo's speeches so that it could be established in the mind of the people, for the very concept of complete independence was revolutionary and unfamiliar at the time.

Sri Aurobindo's second objective was to make the *Bande Mataram* the mouthpiece of the Nationalist party. Through it he explained the ideals and programmes of the new movement represented by the Nationalists and exposed the weaknesses of the other parties, so that the Nationalist party could enlist popular support and then gain control over the Congress. I will give you just one quotation to show how he defined the position with unequalled force and clarity. On April 26, 1907, he wrote: 'The new movement is not primarily a protest against bad Government – it is a protest against the continuance of British control; whether that control is used well or ill, justly or unjustly is a minor and unessential consideration. It is not born of a disappointed expectation of admission to British citizenship, – it is born of a conviction that the time has come when India can, should and will become a great, free and united nation. It is not a negative current of destruction, but a positive, constructive impulse towards the making of modern India. It is not a cry of revolt and despair, but a gospel of national faith and hope. Its true description is not Extremism, but Democratic Nationalism.

'These are the real issues. There are at present not two parties in India but three, – the Loyalists, the Moderates and the Nationalists. The Loyalists would be satisfied with good Government by British rulers and a limited share in the administration; the Moderates desire self-government within the British Empire, but are willing to wait for it indefinitely, the Nationalists would be satisfied with nothing less than independence whether within the Empire, if that be possible, or outside it; they believe that the nation cannot and ought not to wait, but must bestir itself immediately, if it is not to perish as a nation.'

Thirdly, and with the object of involving the people in the struggle for freedom, Sri Aurobindo wrote a series of articles on passive resistance, a strategy developed by him which combined all the elements of the struggle such as Boycott, Swadeshi, National Education, etc. He wrote: '...our policy is self-development and defensive resistance. But we would extend the policy to every department of national life; not only swadeshi and national education, but national defence, national arbitration courts... whatever our hands find to do or urgently needs doing, we must attempt to do ourselves and no longer look to the alien to do it for us.... Our defensive resistance must be mainly passive in the beginning, although with a perpetual readiness to supplement it with active resistance whenever compelled...passive resistance may be the final method of salvation in our case or it may be only the preparation for the final sadhana.' Many of these ideas and programmes were later incorporated in Mahatma Gandhi's non-cooperation movement. However, Sri Aurobindo did not place reliance exclusively on non-violence nor did he preach a gospel of *Ahimsa*. He wrote: 'Under certain circumstances a civil struggle becomes in reality a battle and the morality of war is different from the morality of peace.... To shrink from bloodshed and violence in such circumstances is a weakness deserving as severe a rebuke as Sri Krishna addressed to Arjuna when he shrank from the colossal slaughter on the field of Kurukshetra.' I have given you only a bare outline of Sri Aurobindo's ideas and you will need to read the original writings so as to understand the comprehensiveness of his perceptions.

But what gave the *Bande Mataram* its uniqueness was not so much its brilliant exposition of political ideas and programmes but its tone of high idealism, its spiritual elevation, which distinguished it from other newspapers and political journals of its day as also of the past. Early in 1908 Sri Aurobindo delivered a speech in Bombay which was later reproduced in the *Bande Mataram*. In it he said: 'Nationalism cannot die; because it is no human thing, it is God who is working in Bengal. God cannot be killed, God cannot be sent to gaol.... It is not by any mere political programme, not by National Education alone, not by Swadeshi alone, not by Boycott alone, that this country can be saved. Swadeshi by itself may merely lead to a little more material prosperity, and when it does, you might lose sight of the real thing you sought to do in the glamour of wealth, in the attraction of wealth and, in the desire to keep it safe. In other subject countries also, there was material developement.... When the hour of trial came, it was found that these nations which had been developing industrially, which had been developing materially, were not alive...the forces of the country are other than outside forces.... God is doing everything.... When he throws us away, he does so because we are no longer required.... He is immortal in the hearts of his people.' I could give you quotation after quotation from the *Bande Mataram* breathing this spirit but there is just one point that I would like to stress here. Sri Aurobindo did not want India to be free for her own advancement alone, but always emphasised that free India had a great contribution to make to the world. In an editorial under the heading 'Indian Resurgence and Europe', he wrote: 'If India becomes an intellectual province of Europe, she will never attain to her natural greatness or fulfil the possibilities within her.... Wherever a nation has given up the purpose of its existence, it has been at the cost of its growth. India must remain India if she is to fulfil her destiny. Nor will Europe profit by grafting her civilization on India, for if India, who is the distinct physician of Europe's maladies, herself falls into the clutches of the disease, the disease will remain uncured.... The success of the National movement, both as a political and a spiritual movement, is necessary for India and still more necessary for Europe. The whole world is interested in seeing that India becomes free so that India may become herself.'

There was another side of the *Bande Mataram* that we should remember. It was a daily newspaper (from June 1907 a weekly edition also started) and it reported on all important political developments: acts of commission or omission by the Government, activities of the political parties and personalities, criticisms of the Anglo-Indian press and similar topics. Its comments on these were of a rare brilliance. Sometimes bitingly caustic or sarcastic, sometimes grave or portentous, they set a new standard for Indian journalism. I shall give you just one example. The *Times* of London complained in its columns that 'these nationalists were spreading racial hatred and disaffection against the ruling race'. Sri Aurobindo retorted: 'Our motives and our objects are at least as lofty and noble as those of Mazzini or those of Garibaldi whose centenary the *Times* was hymning with such fervour a few days ago. The restoration of our country to her separate existence as a nation among the nations, her exaltation to a greatness, splendour, strength, magnificence equalling and surpassing ancient glories is the goal of our endeavours: and we have undertaken this arduous task in which we as individuals risk everything, ease, wealth, liberty, life itself maybe, not out of hatred and hostility to other nations but in the firm conviction that we are working as much in the interest of all humanity, including England herself as in those of our own posterity and nation.... If England chooses to feel aggrieved by our nation-building, and obstruct it by unjust, violent or despotic means, it is she who is the aggressor and guilty of exciting our hatred and ill-feeling.'

What a profound impression these articles created! The leading daily English newspaper of that period in India was *The Statesman* and its editor, S.K. Ratcliffe, later wrote about the *Bande Mataram* in these terms: 'It had a full-size sheet, was clearly printed on green paper, was full of leading and special articles written in English with brilliance and pungency not hitherto attained in the Indian press. It was the most effective voice of what we then called Nationalist extremism.' But the person who really appreciated the worth of the *Bande Mataram* and realised that it was creating both political history and literature was a kindred spirit, Sister Nivedita. She wanted the writings in the *Bande Mataram* to be preserved for posterity and, fortunately it was possible to make a selection from the old files of the paper and bring out a book which forms the first volume of the Sri Aurobindo Birth Centenary Library.

One last word about Sri Aurobindo and the *Bande Mataram.* I have already told you that the paper had to contend with financial difficulties and it goes without saying that it did not have any of the facilities of modern newspapers, either by way of staff or equipment. The articles by Sri Aurobindo were often written under severe pressure, sometimes at the last minute and on the nearest available piece of paper. Yet the copy was always practically word-perfect, with the need for hardly any change, even of a comma. Truly inspired writing!

At this time Sri Aurobindo was carrying a tremendous load. Apart from the *Bande Mataram* work, he had his responsibilities at the National College, including teaching; he was now at the centre of the Nationalist party, directing its policy and keeping in touch with its leaders outside Bengal. And all along he maintained his links with the underground revolutionary movement while keeping an eye on the *Yugantar,* the powerful organ of the revolutionaries. This aspect of his secret activities was of course not known to the public at all, indeed none but his closest followers were aware of his actual role in the movement, and they kept the secret. Even later, when Sri Aurobindo had withdrawn from active politics, very few people knew that he was the brain behind the revolutionary movement and its real leader. I remember that in 1935, after I had joined the Ashram and had the privilege of corresponding with him daily, there was a reference in a letter from him to the days when he had 'to live dangerously'. In my ignorance (and also, let me add, in order to draw him out) I wrote to him: 'You wrote that you had lived dangerously. All that we know is that you did not have enough money in England, – also in Pondicherry in the beginning. In Baroda you had a handsome pay, and in Calcutta you were quite well off.' Back came a magnificent reply: 'I was so astonished by this succinct, complete and impeccably accurate biography of myself that I let myself go in answer! But I afterwards thought that it was no use living more dangerously than I am obliged to, so I rubbed it all out. My only answer now is !!!! I thank you for the safe, rich, comfortable and unadventurous career you have given me. I note also that the only danger man can run in this world is that of lack of money. Karl Marx himself could not have made a more economic world of it! But I wonder whether that was what Nietzsche meant by living dangerously?' I submitted my apologies but persisted in my foolish inquiries in order to draw him out further. So I wrote back: 'Kindly let us know by your examples, what you mean by living dangerously that we poor people may gather some courage and knowledge.' And then he wrote: 'I won't. It is altogether unnecessary besides. If you don't realise that the starting and carrying on for ten years and more a revolutionary movement for independence without means and in a country wholly unprepared for it meant living dangerously, no amount of puncturing your skull with words will give you that simple perception.'

Now, let me return to the more outward side of Sri Aurobindo's political activities. In Bengal he had emerged as the undisputed leader of the Nationalists though always he preferred to remain in the background. In June, 1907, he went to Khulna to found a National School; there he was given a warm welcome. 'I received here a royal reception,' he says, 'not for being a leader of the nation, but because I happened to be the son of Dr. K.D. Ghose.' The heart of Khulna was still bound in gratitude to the good doctor who had ministered to the needy and the poor without thought or care for himself.

Late in April, 1907, news reached the *Bande Mataram* that the Government had decided to deport Lajpat Rai. In taking recourse to deportation, they had invoked an old Ordinance, seldom brought into use, whereby due processes of law could be ignored and any person considered politically dangerous by the Government could be sent to a remote location for long years of detention without any charge brought against him or proved in a court of law. The *Bande Mataram* responded immediately, and in an editorial under the heading 'The Crisis' Sri Aurobindo wrote: 'In this grave crisis of our destinies let not our people lose their fortitude or suffer stupefaction and depression to seize upon and unnerve their souls.... Lala Lajpat Rai has gone from us, but doubt not that men stronger and greater than he will take his place. For when a living and rising cause is persecuted, this is the sure result that in the place of those whom persecution strikes down, there arise, like the giants from the blood of Raktabij, men who to their own strength add the strength, doubled and quadrupled by death or persecution, of the martyrs for the cause.' In its comments the *Bande Mataram* added with biting sarcasm: 'We cannot sufficiently admire the vigorous and unselfish efforts of the British Government to turn all India into a nation of Extremists. We had thought that it would take us long and weary years to convert all our countrymen to the Nationalist creed. Nothing of the kind. The Government of India is determined that our efforts shall not fail or take too long a time to reach fruition.... By the deportation of Lala Lajpat Rai, they have destroyed the belief in British justice.'

Naturally the Government was alarmed not only at the growing popularity of the *Bande Mataram* but at the effectiveness of its attacks. The Anglo-Indian press was also complaining that its writings 'reeked with sedition' but had to admit also that they were so cleverly worded that they remained within the limits of the law. So the Government decided to act. They issued a warning both to the *Yugantar* (on June 7, 1907) and the *Bande Mataram* (on June 8, 1907) for using inflammatory language and cautioned them that if they did not desist, police action and prosecution would ensue. The Government followed this up with police search of the *Yugantar* office on July 3 and arrested Bhupendra Nath Dutt, as you know. On July 30 it pounced on the *Bande Mataram*, searched the office and confiscated many books and papers. Nothing daunted, the *Bande Mataram* wrote the next day: 'The wolf has come at last.' In fact a warrant for the arrest of Sri Aurobindo had also been issued on July 30, but it was not served at the time of the raid. The police waited for a few days to examine the papers they had taken away and finally on August 14, the day before his 35th birthday, Sri Aurobindo was arrested. He made no attempt to evade the arrest. At the police court he was interrogated and asked whether he was the editor of the *Bande Mataram* or its printer. Sri Aurobindo answered 'no' to both questions and correctly so, leaving the onus on the Government to prove him the editor – he had no intention of unnecessarily becoming a martyr.

He was released on bail on August 29. The *Bande Mataram* Sedition Trial came up for hearing before the Chief Presidency Magistrate of Calcutta, D.H. Kingsford. Altogether three persons were accused and charged: Sri Aurobindo as the alleged editor, and Hemendra Nath Bagchi and Apurba Krishta Bose as the manager and printer respectively.

The Government fought with great determination to win the case. In order to prove that Sri Aurobindo was the editor a summons was served on Bepin Chandra Pal to give evidence as a witness. The Prosecution had thought that since Bepin Pal had severed connections with the *Bande Mataram* he would be willing to appear and testify that Sri Aurobindo was the editor. But their calculations went wrong. Bepin Pal declined to obey the summons and appear as a witness. For this breach of law he was sentenced to imprisonment for six months. And the next day a moving tribute appeared in the *Bande Mataram*: 'The country will not suffer by the incarceration of this great orator and writer, this spokesman and prophet of Nationalism, nor will Bepin Chandra himself suffer by it. He has risen ten times as high as he was before in the estimation of his countrymen.... He will come out of prison with his power and influence doubled, and Nationalism has already become the stronger for his self-immolation. Posterity will judge between him and the petty tribunal which has treated his honourable scruples as a crime.'

The Sedition Trial created intense excitement in Calcutta and all over the country, but Sri Aurobindo himself was 'wonderfully composed' as Hemendra Prasad Ghosh has recorded in his diary. It was at this time, on September 8, 1907, whilst the trial was going on in Kingsford's Court, that a Bengali poem by Rabindranath Tagore entitled "Namaskar" (Salutation) appeared in the *Bande Mataram*. This is a famous poem in the Bengali language; here are the opening lines from an English translation by Khitish Chandra Sen:

> Rabindranth, O Aurobindo, bows to thee!
> O friend, my country's friend, O voice incarnate, free,
> Of India's soul! No soft renown doth crown thy lot,
> Nor pelf or careless comfort is for thee; thou'st sought
> No petty bounty, petty dole; the beggar's bowl
> Thou ne'er hast held aloft. In watchfulness thy soul
> Hast thou e'er held for bondless full perfection's birth

For which, all night and day, the god in man on earth
Doth strive and strain austerely....

At last on September 23 Kingsford delivered his judgement. He found the *Bande Mataram* guilty of publishing seditious writings, particularly certain articles it had reprinted from the *Yugantar* in translation. However, he added: 'There is no evidence before me that the *Bande Mataram* habitually publishes seditious matter.' He went on to acquit Sri Aurobindo for want of evidence that he was the editor. Hemendra Bagchi was also acquitted but, as the provisions of the law had to be met, he sentenced the printer, Apurba Bose, to imprisonment for three months. The judgement was a severe blow to the Government and greatly lowered its prestige as it had failed either to imprison Sri Aurobindo or to gag the *Bande Mataram*. The printer's imprisonment was unfortunate but unavoidable under the existing provisions of the Press Act.

An immediate result of the Sedition Trial and Sri Aurobindo's acquittal was that it brought him to the forefront in the public eye. Overnight his name was on everyone's lips and, paradoxically, although he was acquitted, everyone now recognised him to be the author of the *Bande Mataram* articles and a great Nationalist leader. Had not the Prosecution thundered in vain during the trial: 'I do not care whether Aurobindo Ghose is the editor or not, I say he is the paper itself!' This sudden fame and attention were not at all welcome to Sri Aurobindo. To a disciple he once wrote: 'I was never ardent about fame even in my political days; I preferred to remain behind the curtain, push people without their knowing it and get things done. It was the confounded British Government that spoiled my game by prosecuting me and forcing me to be publicly known and a "leader".'

Around this time Henry Nevinson, author and journalist, who had come out to India as a special correspondent of the *Manchester Guardian* of London, met Sri Aurobindo for an interview. In his book *The New Spirit of India*, he records his impressions of Sri Aurobindo: 'Intent dark eyes looked from his thin, clear-cut face with a gravity that seemed immovable.... Grave with intensity, careless of fate or opinion, and one of the most silent men I have known, he was of the stuff that dreamers are made of, but dreamers who will act their dream, indifferent to the means.'

After his arrest, Sri Aurobindo resigned from the Principalship of the National College as he did not wish to embarrass the

College authorities, going back however, after his acquittal, but only as a professor. Because of his many preoccupations, he could not give much time and attention to the College and his period of association with it was too short for him to develop it on the lines of a new system of nationalist education that he had in mind. He considered National Education an integral and most important part of the new National movement. His experience at Baroda had convinced him that the system which the British· had introduced was causing immense harm by laying stress on examination results and on the mechanical study of text-books and notes which the students 'mugged up'. As he wrote later, this system 'tended to dull and impoverish and tie up the naturally quick and brilliant and supple Indian intelligence'. During 1909-10 Sri Aurobindo wrote a series of articles on 'A System of National Education' which appeared in the *Karmayogin* and this seems a suitable opportunity for me to tell you briefly what his views on education were – they were indeed far in advance of the conventional ideas on the subject.

According to Sri Aurobindo, the central principle of education is: 'Every one has in him something divine, something his own, a chance of perfection and strength in however small a sphere which God offers him to take or refuse. The task is to find it, develop it and use it. The chief aim of education should be to help the growing soul to draw out that in itself which is best and make it perfect for a noble use.... The teacher is not an instructor or taskmaster, he is a helper and a guide. His business is to suggest and not to impose.... The idea of hammering the child into shape by the parent or teacher is a barbarous and ignorant superstition. It is he himself who must be induced to expand according to his own nature.' These ideas are at the core of the Free Progress System of education followed in the Sri Aurobindo International Centre of Education at the Pondicherry Ashram.

As at Baroda, Sri Aurobindo was held in great respect and admiration by his students at the National College. After his arrest and resignation as the Principal, the students organised a meeting to record their regret and to express their sympathy in his 'present troubles'. At their request, Sri Aurobindo addressed them briefly and the words he used remain as inspiring today as they were on that day in August 1907: 'There are times in a nation's history when Providence places before it one work, one aim, to which everything else, however high and noble in itself, has to be sacrificed. Such a time has now arrived for our Motherland when nothing is dearer than her service, when everything else is to be directed to that end. If you will study, study for her sake; train yourself body and mind and soul for her service. You will earn your living that you may live for her sake. You will go abroad to foreign lands that you may bring back knowledge with which you may do service to her. Work that she may prosper. Suffer that she may rejoice. All is contained in that one single advice.'

Chapter VI

Surat Congress and the Aftermath
1907–1908

AT THE Calcutta Congress session in December 1906, the Nationalists had succeeded, largely as a result of Sri Aurobindo's influence and his effort behind the scenes, in prevailing on the Congress to pass resolutions adopting Swaraj as its goal and Swadeshi, Boycott and National Education as the effective means of realising it. This was a serious setback for the Moderates, who had strongly opposed the resolutions, and they were waiting for an opportunity to get back their hold over the organisation. Moreover, their Bombay group led by Sir Pherozeshah Mehta and Gokhale, could not stomach the resolution on Swaraj. There was talk at this time of political reforms being introduced in India. Lord Minto had replaced Lord Curzon as the Viceroy and in England also there was a new Secretary of State, John Morley, said to be a statesman of liberal views. There were repeated warnings by Sri Aurobindo in the *Bande Mataram* not to be hoodwinked by proposals of political reforms which were paper concessions only, and which in practice would merely strengthen the British position in India. The Moderates, however, were determined to offer their cooperation to the British and not to offend them by cries of Swaraj.

Meanwhile there were developments in Bengal which also clearly indicated the growing cleavage between the Moderates and the Nationalists. Sri Aurobindo was now the recognised leader of the Nationalists and he led the party at the session of the Bengal Provincial Conference at Midnapur from December 7 to 9, 1907.

The Moderates were led by Surendranath Banerjee. At the conference, there was a 'vehement clash' as Sri Aurobindo put it, the first open rupture between the two parties, with the result that the police had to be called in to restore order. Eventually, the Nationalists held a separate conference under Sri Aurobindo's leadership.

Traditionally the annual session of the Congress took place during the last week of December. At first it was proposed that the 1907 session should be held in Nagpur but the Moderates manoeuvred to get the location shifted to Surat which was a Moderate stronghold whereas at Nagpur the Maharashtrian Nationalists were powerfully represented. From the beginning, therefore, it was apparent that this session of the Congress would be a decisive trial of strength and indeed the proceedings at Surat turned out to be both dramatic and fateful.

The Surat Congress was scheduled to begin on December 26, 1907. Delegates came in strength from many parts of India. Sri Aurobindo led a large contingent of Nationalists from Bengal. Tilak was present along with other stalwarts from Maharashtra like Dr. Munje and G.S. Khaparde. The Nationalists also welcomed back Lala Lajpat Rai and Sardar Ajit Singh who came from the Punjab and had both been recently released from detention. The Moderates were equally well represented. The rival parties were accommodated in separate camps; apparently all was peaceful but in reality suspense and hostility were in the air. The Nationalist delegates included some young revolutionaries (Barin was one of them) and they kept a vigilant eye to make sure that their leaders were not subject to unprovoked attacks in a city which was known to be a Moderate stronghold. The Moderates were not above encouraging rowdyism when it suited their purpose!

The Nationalists did not come to Surat to wreck the Congress or divide it. Some Nationalist leaders indeed wanted to avoid Surat and hold a separate Congress at Nagpur. But Tilak sent a wire: 'For God's sake, no split.' Sri Aurobindo acquiesced. The Nationalists were willing to make any reasonable compromise with the Moderates provided it did not mean sacrificing the four resolutions which had been accepted after so much debate at Calcutta. And it was precisely on this issue that the clash took place.

On the eve of the Congress, i.e. on December 25, the Nationalists held their party meeting. G.S. Khaparde has recorded in his diary: 'There is great discipline in our party. In the afternoon we had our Nationalist Conference. Aurobindo Babu presided and Tilak made another masterly statement, clear and concise and yet full, such as he alone can make. Everybody praises it.' There is also a vivid description of this meeting in Nevinson's *The New Spirit of India*. He writes: 'Grave and silent – I think without saying a single word – Mr. Aravinda Ghose took the chair, and sat unmoved, with far-off eyes, as one who gazes at futurity. In clear, short sentences, without eloquence or passion Mr. Tilak spoke till the stars shone out and someone kindled a lantern at his side.'

The Nationalists had come to know by this time that the Moderates were getting ready to scuttle the resolutions on Swaraj, Swadeshi, Boycott, and National Education, but unable to go back openly on them, they had decided on a roundabout method. They had prepared the draft of a new constitution for the Congress, which they proposed to get passed at the Surat session. In this draft, among other changes, the goal of the Congress was defined as 'the attainment by India of self-government similar to that enjoyed by the other members of the British Empire.' Moreover, this was conceived as an ultimate goal, not an immediate objective. This was a far cry indeed from the Calcutta resolution. The Moderates also proposed that, under the new constitution of the Congress, only those who accepted its new creed could henceforward become members of the Provincial Committees. It was at once clear to the Nationalist leaders that if these changes in the constitution of the Congress were adopted, not only would the work done at Calcutta be destroyed, but also the Congress would be dominated by the Moderates for years to come. And, at Surat, the Moderates were very strongly placed to carry through these resolutions. They had been busy enlisting their supporters as delegates for the open session and whilst the Nationalists did their best to follow suit, it was Sri Aurobindo's estimate that the strength of the Moderate delegates (not all of them genuine supporters) was 1300 as against 1100 on the Nationalist side.

This was the background against which the Congress open session began on December 26, 1907, before an audience of over ten thousand strong. And immediately the two parties clashed. The Moderates had selected Dr. Rash Behari Ghosh to be the

President. He was an eminent lawyer but politically he was only a figurehead. When his name was proposed and Surendranath Banerjee, considered the greatest orator of his day, stood up to second the proposal, his voice was drowned in a prolonged clamour of protest and counter protest. This demonstration was not pre-arranged but reflected the tension and antagonism which had been building up between the rival parties. In vain did the Chairman of the Reception Committee, who was then presiding over the meeting, try to control the situation and restore order. The demonstrations continued without a break and eventually the Chairman declared the sitting suspended, although at that stage Dr. Ghosh had still not been officially elected President.

That evening attempts were made to arrive at a negotiated settlement between the parties, but these efforts failed. The Nationalists were prepared to withdraw their opposition to Dr. Ghosh's election as President, provided the Moderates did not try to overrule the Calcutta resolution on Swaraj, but no understanding could be reached.

The Congress session was resumed on December 27. Dr. Ghosh arrived at the meeting in a big procession arranged by the Moderates. He came and occupied the Presidential Chair but hardly had he begun reading his address when Tilak stood up. He had earlier given notice that he would move an amendment and he now ascended the dais to face the delegates. Dr. Ghosh refused to give him permission to speak. Tilak retorted that Dr. Ghosh had not been properly elected as President and that he, Tilak, had every right to address the delegates. With folded arms he faced the audience and began to speak. The rest may be described in Sri Aurobindo's own words: 'There was a tremendous uproar, the young Gujarati volunteers lifted up chairs over the head of Tilak to beat him. At that the Mahrattas became furious, a Mahratta shoe came hurtling across the pavilion aimed at the President, Dr. Rash Behari Ghosh, and hit Surendranath Banerjee on the shoulder. The young Mahrattas in a body charged up to the platform, the Moderate leaders fled; after a short fight on the platform with chairs the session broke up not to be resumed. The Moderate leaders decided to suspend the Congress....'

Thus the Surat Congress ended in a total breakdown. The next day the Moderate leaders gave notice of a meeting, calling it a convention of delegates who were agreed on the changes which they wanted to introduce in the constitution of the Congress. The Nationalists refused to attend this convention, and so split the Congress irrevocably. Both parties issued separate statements on the proceedings of the Congress session. The Nationalist statement was signed by Tilak, Sri Aurobindo and others. That of the Moderates was described as the 'official statement of the Congress'. Students of political history will find these documents of absorbing interest, for they reflect very clearly the conflicting attitudes and objectives of the respective parties.

This is the outward story of the Surat Congress. But, long afterwards, in reply to a disciple's question, Sri Aurobindo stated: 'History very seldom records the things that were decisive but took place behind the veil; it records the shown front of the curtain. Very few people knew that it was I (without consulting Tilak) who gave the orders that led to the breaking up of the Congress and was responsible for the refusal to join the new-fangled Moderate convention which were the two decisive happenings at Surat.'

Why did Sri Aurobindo decide to break up the Congress? We do not have a direct answer from Sri Aurobindo himself but it can be easily surmised that he did not want the Nationalists to be part of a Congress with the anaemic ideals it was proposing to adopt and which the Moderates could get accepted because of their numerical superiority. Besides, he was never in favour of a 'dead or lifeless unity' between the parties. Though he knew that once the Nationalists broke off with the Congress, they would be ruthlessly persecuted. And, in fact, by July 1908 Tilak was charged with 'exciting disloyalty and bringing feelings of enmity towards the Government'. He was sentenced to six years of imprisonment and sent to Mandalay jail in Burma. And then the Government focussed their entire attention on Sri Aurobindo. But Sri Aurobindo also knew that repression would not extinguish the flame of independence which had now been lit and that it would be held aloft by brave patriots until the nation itself became ready to accept the ideal of complete independence, as eventually it did at the historic Congress session at Lahore in 1929. Meanwhile the Surat Congress sounded the political death-knell of the Moderates. Though some individual Moderate leaders were later to occupy eminent positions in the Government, as a political party the Moderates became a waning force and were soon supplanted by other nationalist forces which came to the fore.

The year 1908 was dawning as Sri Aurobindo left Surat for Baroda. This was his first visit to Baroda since his departure for Calcutta in June 1906, and what momentous changes had taken place during these eighteen months! When he left Baroda, Sri Aurobindo was hardly known outside his circle of close associates and followers. Now he was in the forefront of Indian politics, having inspired in a whole nation the ideal of freedom, giving to this a spiritual content and significance not known before. The Principal of the Baroda College had directed the students not to leave their classes and meet Sri Aurobindo, but they simply ignored the ban. When Sri Aurobindo was being taken in a procession, they ran out, unyoked the horses of his carriage and then proceeded to draw it themselves. Many political workers came and met Sri Aurobindo and he also addressed a number of political meetings.

Amongst those who met him were Chhotalal Purani and his younger brother Ambalal. They were initiated by Sri Aurobindo into revolutionary work and played a prominent part in the movement in Gujarat. Ambalal Purani afterwards became a disciple of Sri Aurobindo, joining the Ashram in the early 1920s; he also served Sri Aurobindo as a personal attendant. In the course of this visit to Baroda, Sri Aurobindo also met the Maharaja. We do not know what transpired during the talks but the Gaekwad desired another meeting, which, however, did not take place.

At Baroda, Sri Aurobindo first stayed at Khaserao Jadhav's house. Those who met him were struck by the utter simplicity of his way of life. You may recall that when he was in service at Baroda, Sri Aurobindo was indifferent to comfort but now his needs were reduced to the bare minimum. Although the winter was severe, he wore only a cotton dhoti and shirt and did not even have a wrapper. His friend Sardar Mazumdar presented him with a Pashmina shawl to keep away the cold. Sri Aurobindo carried no bedding on his railway journeys, and slept on the bare, wooden bunks of third-class compartments, using his arm for a pillow. Incidentally, when he went from Calcutta to Surat to attend the Congress session, he travelled in a third-class compartment along with other nationalist delegates – there were no special arrangements for him. A Mr. J. Ghoshal was also travelling by the same train. He was one of the secretaries of the Congress and belonged to the Moderate group. Ghoshal was travelling in a first-class compartment in perfect European clothes and style. The train stopped at various stations en route to enable the large crowds which had assembled to have their *darshan* of the leaders, particularly of Sri Aurobindo. Many flocked to the first-class compartment expecting to find him there and Barin, who was also travelling with Sri Aurobindo, has recounted in his autobiography how the highly embarrassed Mr. Ghoshal, to save his face, repeatedly requested Sri Aurobindo to join him in his compartment. Needless to say, Sri Aurobindo felt no obligation to meet the request!

Sri Aurobindo stayed at Baroda for a fortnight and this stay took on a special significance and importance not so much for political activities, although he was involved in these, but because of a tremendous spiritual experience which, in his own words, was the first of the four great realisations on which his Yoga and spiritual philosophy are founded. I shall now try and give you an account of this, relying largely on his own words.

You know that from the year 1904 Sri Aurobindo was deeply engaged in the practice of yoga but because of the increasing pressure of political work he did not have time for the regular practice of *pranayam* and other concomitant *kriyas*. He himself felt that his progress in sadhana had come to a halt and, being at a loss, he asked Barin if he knew of someone who could pull him out of the impasse and help him to pursue yoga more systematically than he had hitherto done. In the course of his extensive wanderings, Barin had met a Maharashtrian yogi, Vishnu Bhaskar Lele by name, and had been impressed by him. It had been a brief meeting but Barin remembered the occasion and now, with Sri Aurobindo's consent, he sent a telegram to Lele at Gwalior to come to Baroda. It is said that when Lele received the telegram he felt that a great soul needed his help in yoga and so he left at once for Baroda.

It was at Khaserao Jadhav's house that Lele came and met Sri Aurobindo. Lele was ready to help but asked that he should suspend all political activities, at least for a few days, and devote himself completely to yoga. So Sri Aurobindo left Khaserao's house and, keeping only his close associates informed of his whereabouts, went with Lele to the house of another old friend, Sardar Mazumdar. Here in a small room on the top floor he was

closeted with Lele and what happened then is something un-
imaginable, incalculable and, at least to my knowledge, with no
parallel in spiritual history. Let me quote Sri Aurobindo himself:
'"Sit in meditation", he [Lele] said, "but do not think, look only at
your mind; you will see thoughts *coming into it*; before they can
enter throw these away from your mind till your mind is capable of
entire silence." I had never heard before of thoughts coming
visibly into the mind from outside, but I did not think either of
questioning the truth or the possibility, I simply sat down and did
it. In a moment my mind became silent as a windless air on a high
mountain summit and then I saw one thought and another coming
in a concrete way from outside; I flung them away before they
could enter and take hold of the brain and in three days I was free.
From that moment, in principle, the mental being in me became a
free intelligence, a universal Mind, not limited to the narrow circle
of personal thought as a labourer in a thought-factory, but a
receiver of knowledge from all the hundred realms of being and
free to choose what it willed in this vast sight-empire and thought-
empire.'

Much later, when we were serving as his attendants at the
Ashram, he once spoke to us of this experience: 'Lele asked me to
silence the mind and throw away the thoughts if they came. I did it
in three days – and the result was that the whole being became
quiet and in seven days I got the Nirvanic experience which
remained with me for a long time. I could not have got out of it
even if I had wanted to. Even afterwards this experience remained
in the background in the midst of all activities.'

There is much scope for thought here, indeed for amazement
and wonder at this tremendous experience Sri Aurobindo gained
in three days. When I asked him once how he had achieved this, he
answered: 'It was simply through the Divine Grace – because it has
been done by thousands before me throughout the centuries and
millenniums and the Divine did not want me to waste time over
that.' Yet we can but marvel that he should have had this
realisation, which comes as the culmination of a life-long sadhana,
in only a few days. And there are other exceptional features about
Sri Aurobindo's experience. Mark, for instance, how obedient he
was to Lele's instructions and how he followed them to the letter
without questioning. Seldom do we meet an intellectual, particularly one of Sri Aurobindo's attainments, with such unquestion-

ing faith. He speaks of this in a letter to a disciple: '...we sat together and I followed with absolute fidelity what he instructed me to do, not myself in the least understanding where he was leading me or where I was going.' Mark, also, that Sri Aurobindo had this realisation even while he was in the midst of intense political activity. It is true that, for the purpose of concentration, he had withdrawn for a while from outside contacts but he did not have this experience somewhere remote from the world's turmoil, all alone, in Himalayan solitudes. This bears a far-reaching significance, for it shows that *karma* or action is no bar or bondage to spiritual life.

In his sonnet "Nirvana" Sri Aurobindo has given a description of this experience, bringing its reality nearer and more clearly to our vision, understanding and feeling. Here is the poem:

All is abolished but the mute Alone.
  The mind from thought released, the heart from grief
  Grow inexistent now beyond belief;
There is no I, no Nature, known-unknown.
The city, a shadow picture without tone,
  Floats, quivers unreal; forms without relief
  Flow, a cinema's vacant shapes; like a reef
Foundering in shoreless gulfs the world is done.

Only the illimitable Permanent
  Is here. A Peace stupendous, featureless, still,
  Replaces all, – what once was I, in It
A silent unnamed emptiness content
  Either to fade in the Unknowable
  Or thrill with the luminous seas of the Infinite.

One word more. Sri Aurobindo's experience – in fact it was, to quote him, 'a series of tremendously powerful experiences and radical changes of consciousness' – came as a surprise to Lele, for he had not intended it. Indeed to Sri Aurobindo himself the experience came as a surprise, for they were contrary to his own ideas – 'they made me see with a stupendous intensity the world as a cinematographic play of vacant forms in the impersonal universality of the Absolute Brahman.' However, the overwhelming impact of this realisation did not at all mean that henceforward he would give up politics. All along invitations had been pouring in for Sri Aurobindo to address meetings and to meet political workers at Poona, Bombay and other places. The uncompromising stand he had taken at Surat had enhanced his reputation in the eyes of the true patriots who now looked to him for guidance in the critical situation which had arisen.

So from Baroda Sri Aurobindo went to Poona. At his request, Lele accompanied him. Sri Aurobindo's mind had become calm, silent, devoid of all thoughts and as he was not sure how he could give a speech or address meetings in that condition, he asked Lele what he should do. Lele told him 'to make *namaskar* to the audience and wait and speech would come to him from some other source than the mind'. And so, in fact, the speeches came.

From Poona Sri Aurobindo proceeded to Bombay where also he was called upon to address large meetings. The silent condition of his mind continued and the outside world seemed to be bathed in unreality. Sri Aurobindo has described how, at Bombay, when he was standing on the balcony of a friend's house, he saw 'the whole busy movement of Bombay as a picture in a cinema show, all unreal and shadowy'. And yet he continued with his political activities. The most important speech he had to deliver in Bombay was at a meeting of the National Union at Mahajanwadi on January 19. Again he had this problem – how was he to give a speech in that condition. This is what happened, in Sri Aurobindo's own words: 'I asked Lele what I should do. He asked me to pray but I was so absorbed in the silent Brahman consciousness that I could not pray. Then he replied that it did not matter. He and some others would pray and I had simply to go to the meeting, make *namaskar* to the audience as Narayan and then some voice would speak. I did exactly as I was told...when I rose to speak the impression of a [newspaper] headline flashed across my mind and all of a sudden something spoke out.'

Later, during his talks with us, he once explained: 'One result of this silencing was that while I was writing for the *Bande Mataram* the thoughts didn't pass through the mind; they came direct to the pen and I didn't know beforehand what I was writing – sometimes they passed through the mind which was quite passive.'

Let me return for a moment to the famous speech he delivered at the National Union meeting in Bombay. This was later reproduced in the *Bande Mataram* and I have already given you an extract from it while telling you about Sri Aurobindo's writings in that paper. The subject of the speech was 'The Present Situation' and he spoke not as a politician but as an inspired prophet of Nationalism. It made a deep impression on the mind of the audience, for it carried a new note from his new perspective. Here is another fragment from it. Sri Aurobindo says: 'Look for the Shakti within yourselves, bring it forward. Then you will realise that whatever you do is being done by that Shakti, not by yourselves.... There, within you, is that Immortal, Unborn and Eternal whom swords cannot sunder, fire cannot burn and to whom all the power in the world is a trifle.'

Before leaving Bombay Sri Aurobindo asked Lele for instructions, and Sri Aurobindo's words in this connection are most revealing: 'He was giving me detailed instructions. In the meantime I told him of a Mantra that had arisen in my heart. Suddenly while giving instructions he stopped and asked me if I could rely absolutely on Him who gave me the Mantra. I replied that I could always do that. Then Lele said that there was no need of further instructions.'

As Sri Aurobindo explained later: 'The final upshot was that [Lele] was made by a Voice within him to hand me over to the Divine within me enjoining absolute surrender to its will – a principle or rather a seed force to which I kept unswervingly and increasingly till it led me through all the mazes of an incalculable yogic development bound by no single rule or style or dogma or Shastra to where and what I am now and towards what shall be hereafter.'

From Bombay Sri Aurobindo went to several places – Nasik, Dhulia, Amravati, Nagpur – centres of Maharashtrian culture and Nationalist strongholds which he visited at Tilak's request. Political workers came to meet him and he was called upon to give many speeches; everywhere his presence inspired those who met and heard him. The same theme ran through all his speeches — Nationalism as a religion, as an imperative force from God. At Amravati, on January 29, the meeting commenced with the singing of '*Bande Mataram*' and in the course of his speech Sri Aurobindo spoke on the history and significance of the song.

Sri Aurobindo was back in Calcutta by the first week of February 1908. At once he resumed his *Bande Mataram* work and now that he had emerged as an all-India leader, he was also much in demand as a speaker, which meant an even greater increase in his public activities. These activities on the surface seemed to go on as before but as a result of the profound inner change, speech and action acquired a power of spontaneity, free from disturbance and in manner flawless, as if some great and higher Power was working through him and was the source of his thoughts, words and action. And we must remember that not only the speeches he then gave or his writings in the *Bande Mataram* but his later writings in the *Karmayogin*, and the *Arya*, his correspondence etc. as well as *Savitri* and the poems he wrote in Pondicherry all arose out of this mental silence. He told us once: 'You just become an instrument, you have no responsibility of your own. It is a state of great ease and peace.'

Shortly after his return, Sri Aurobindo wrote another letter to his wife Mrinalini who was not then in Calcutta. This, perhaps his last letter to her, is a moving document in which he begins by expressing his regret for not having written to her for a long time. 'This is my eternal failing,' he pleads, 'if you do not pardon me out of your own goodness, what shall I do? What is ingrained in one does not go out in a day. Perhaps it will take me the whole of this life to correct this fault.' And then towards the end of the letter he writes: 'You may think that in my work I am neglecting you, but do not do so. Already, I have done you many wrongs and it is but natural that this should have displeased you. But I am no longer free. From now on you will have to understand that all I do depends not on my will but is done at the *adeśa* [command] of God. When you come here, you will understand the meaning of my words. I hope that God will show you the Light He has shown me in His infinite Grace. But that depends upon His Will. If you wish to share my life and ideal you must strive to your utmost so that, on the strength of your ardent desire, He may in his Grace reveal the path to you also.' Note how totally he has now surrendered to the Divine Will but note, also, how concerned he is that Mrinalini should understand and follow him – Sri Aurobindo was never indifferent to her thoughts and feelings.

Sri Aurobindo's preoccupation with spiritual realities and the new tone his words had acquired can be further felt in a passage he wrote in the *Bande Mataram* on February 18, 1908: 'Swaraj is the direct revelation of God to this people, – not mere political freedom but a freedom vast and entire, freedom of the individual, freedom of the community, freedom of the nation, spiritual

freedom, social freedom, political freedom. Spiritual freedom the
ancient Rishis had already declared to us; social freedom was part
of the message of Buddha, Chaitanya, Nanak and Kabir and the
saints of Maharashtra; political freedom is the last work of the
triune gospel.... God has set apart India as the eternal fountain-
head of holy spirituality, and He will never suffer that fountain to
run dry. Therefore Swaraj has been revealed to us. By our political
freedom we shall once more recover our spiritual freedom. Once
more in the land of the saints and sages will burn the fire of the
ancient Yoga and the hearts of her people will be lifted up into the
neighbourhood of the Eternal.'

About this time a young patriot, Amarendra Nath Chatterjee,
who had contributed generously to the Swadeshi cause, met Sri
Aurobindo and was initiated by him into the revolutionary
movement. Many years later Amarendra wrote about this fateful
meeting and recalled Sri Aurobindo's words to him: 'If we want
India's independence, we have to offer everything... we should be
ready to give up even our life for it and conquer the fear of
death.... Surrender yourself to God and take the plunge in the
name of the Mother. This is my *diksha* to you.' Amarendra says
that these words changed the entire course of his life, removing
fear and attachment in him. This is how Sri Aurobindo effected
miraculous changes in young minds through his presence and the
power of his words which acted as *mantra*.

Meanwhile, at Barin's request, Lele visited Calcutta. He called
on Sri Aurobindo at his residence at 23 Scott's Lane and when he
inquired about Sri Aurobindo's yoga he was astonished to hear
that Sri Aurobindo had given up meditation and other yogic
practices. Lele said that the devil had caught hold of Sri
Aurobindo. When Sri Aurobindo heard this he said to himself, 'If
it is the devil, I will then follow him.' He told us afterwards that
since he was in a constant state of meditation in works, repose,
sleep, there was no need for regular, fixed hours of meditation. So
too Sri Ramakrishna says, 'One who is uttering the name of Kali at
all the three *sandhyas*, where is his need for fixed hours of
worship?' Indeed, in the course of only a few months, Sri
Aurobindo had gone far beyond the depth of an experienced yogi
like Lele.

Barin had another purpose in inviting Lele to Calcutta. Some
time before this Barin had left Sri Aurobindo's residence at Scott's

Lane and moved to Maniktolla Gardens in Muraripukur, North Calcutta. This was a piece of ancestral property, about two and half acres in extent, which was more of a jungle than a garden and had a small building almost in ruins. But it suited his plans admirably. For here he gathered round him a dozen or so of young ardent revolutionaries, recruited by him and made to take an irrevocable pledge to give their lives for the Motherland. He gave them special training which included physical austerities, target practice with weapons and the manufacture of bombs. Along with these, they also practised meditation, reading the Gita etc. Sri Aurobindo was aware of these activities but was not directly involved in them. Nolini Kanta has recorded in his reminiscences how he was once sent by Barin to fetch Sri Aurobindo to visit the Gardens. He writes: 'I went by tram and it was about four in the afternoon when I reached there [Sri Aurobindo's residence].... As I sat waiting in one of the rooms downstairs, Sri Aurobindo came down, stood near me and gave me an inquiring look. I said, in Bengali, "Barin has sent me. Would it be possible for you to come to the Gardens with me now?" He answered very slowly, pausing on each syllable separately – it seemed he had not yet got used to speaking in Bengali – and said "Go and tell Barin, I have not yet had my lunch. It will not be possible to go today." So that was that. I did not say a word, did my *namaskar*. This was my first happy meeting with him, my first Darshan and interview.'

Now, to return to Lele. Barin wanted him to visit Maniktolla Gardens to help the inmates in their yoga practices. But once he was there it did not take Lele long to realise the true nature of their activities and he at once warned Barin to give up these dangerous pursuits, 'otherwise he would fall into a ditch'. Barin, however, was in no mood to listen and, as Sri Aurobindo commented later, 'he did fall into a ditch', soon facing the gravest crisis of his life.

Dark clouds were now gathering on the horizon. On April 30 a bomb was thrown at a carriage supposedly carrying Kingsford, District Magistrate of Muzzafarpur. He was a notorious official who was hated by the people because he had ordered the public flogging of a fourteen-year old boy for a political offence. It so happened that Kingsford was not in that carriage. Two English ladies, who were travelling in it, were unfortunately killed instead. This led to a tremendous hue and cry and the Government immediately ordered a round of arrests. Sri Aurobindo, who was watching developments closely, sent a warning to Barin to remove all arms and other incriminating evidence from the Maniktolla Gardens but before Barin could act upon the message, the police raided the place on May 2, 1908, arrested the occupants and seized the tell-tale materials.

Meanwhile, Sri Aurobindo had shifted residence. On April 28, he had moved from 23 Scott's Lane to 48 Grey Street which also housed the office of the Bengali paper *Navashakti*. Here, in the early hours of May 2, 1908, Sri Aurobindo was sleeping peacefully, when the police entered in force and arrested him.

Chapter VII

The Alipore Bomb Case: One Year in Jail
1908–1909

'ON FRIDAY night I was sleeping without a worry. At about five the next morning [May 2, 1908] my sister rushed to my room in great agitation and called me out by name. I got up. The next moment the small room was filled with armed policemen! Superintendent Cregan, Mr. Clark of 24-Paraganas, the charming and delightful visage of familiar Sriman Benod Gupta, a few inspectors, red-turbaned policemen, spies and search witnesses. They all came running like heroes, pistols in hand, as though they were besieging, with guns and cannons, a well-armed fort. I heard that a white hero had aimed a pistol at my sister's breast, but I myself did not see it.' This is how Sri Aurobindo begins the account of his arrest in *Karakahini* (*Tales of Prison Life*), his book in Bengali which was first serialised in the magazine *Suprabhat* during 1909-10. Those of you who know Bengali will be well rewarded to turn to the original, for it has a special flavour of its own. Written with rare detachment, it is an inspiring record of his intense sadhana in the most unpropitious surrounding imaginable, and of the crowning spiritual experiences he had in jail. Besides, his use of irony, sarcasm, invective and humour in exposing the prison system under the British rule is both devastatingly effective and richly entertaining. And there are brilliant sketches of some of the inmates and officials of the jail as well as of those who were participants in the Trial. I shall quote some excerpts for you from the book and wish there was scope for giving you more.

To resume Sri Aurobindo's description of the arrest: 'I was

sitting up, still half-asleep when Cregan inquired, "Who is Aurobindo Ghose, is that you?" I answered, "Yes. I am Aurobindo Ghose." Immediately he ordered a policeman to put me under arrest.... I asked for the search warrant, read it and then signed it. Finding a mention of bombs in the warrant I realized that the presence of these soldiers and policemen was connected with the Muzzafarpur killing. What I could not understand, however, was why, even before any bombs and explosives had been discovered in my house, and in the absence of a body warrant, I was arrested. But I did not raise any useless objections. Afterwards, under instructions from Cregan my arms were handcuffed, and a rope tied round my waist. An upcountry constable stood behind me holding the rope end. Just then the police brought in Shrijut Abinash Bhattacharjee and Shrijut Sailen Bose, handcuffed and roped round the midriff. Nearly half an hour later, I do not know at whose bidding, they removed the rope and the handcuffs. From Cregan's words it seemed as if he had entered into the lair of some ferocious animal, as if we were a lot of uneducated, wild, law-breakers, and it was unnecessary to behave courteously towards us. But after a sharp exchange of words the sahib grew a little milder. Benodbabu tried to tell him something about me, after which Cregan asked me: "It seems you are a B. A. Is it not a matter of shame for an educated person like you to be sleeping on the floor of an unfurnished room and a house like this?" "I am a poor man, and I live like one," I said. "Then, have you worked up all this mischief with the idea of becoming a rich man?" Cregan shouted in reply. Knowing how impossible it would be to explain the love of motherland, or the sublimity of a vow of poverty to this thick-skulled Briton I did not make the attempt.'

Meanwhile the house was being searched from top to bottom. Sri Aurobindo writes: 'The search began at five-thirty, and was over at about eleven-thirty. All the boxes were turned inside out: exercise books, letters, papers, scraps, poems, plays, prose, essays, translations, nothing escaped the clutches of the all-consuming search but nothing remarkable transpired in the course of it. However, I recollect Mr. Clark looking long and suspiciously at the sacred earth from Dakshineshwar that had been kept in a small cardboard box: he thought it might be some new and terribly powerful explosive. In a sense his suspicions were not unfounded.'

The search over, the three arrested persons were taken first to the local police station and then to the Police Headquarters at Lal Bazar. To quote Sri Aurobindo further: 'After being made to wait there for a couple of hours we were removed to Royd Street [premises of the Intelligence Branch], in which auspicious locality we stayed all evening. It was there that I first came to know the wily detective Maulvi Sams-ul-Alam and had the pleasure of entering into a cordial relation with him.... The Maulvi made me listen to a most entertaining sermon on religion: "To be truthful is part of the religious life. The Sahibs say Aurobindo Ghose is the leader of the terrorist party; this is a matter of shame and sorrow for India. But by keeping to the path of rectitude the situation can yet be saved." The Maulvi was fully convinced that distinguished persons, men of high character, like Bepin Pal and Aurobindo Ghose, whatever they might have done, they would openly confess their deeds.... I was charmed and delighted with his knowledge, intelligence and religious fervour. It would have been impertinent to talk too much, so I listened politely to his priceless sermon and cherished it in my heart. But in spite of his religious enthusiasm the Maulvi did not forget his profession as a detective. Once he said: "You made a great mistake in handing over the garden to your younger brother to manufacture bombs. That was not very intelligent on your part." I saw the implication of his words and said with a smile: "Sir, the garden is as much mine as my brother's. Where did you learn that I had given it over to him, or given it to him for the purpose of making bombs?" A little abashed the Maulvi answered: "No, no, I was mentioning this in case you had given it." '

From Royd Street Sri Aurobindo was taken back to Lal Bazar. To continue his narrative: 'At Lal Bazar Sailen and I were kept together in a large room on the ground floor. Some food was given to us. After a while two Englishmen entered the room; later I was told that one of them was the Police Commissioner, Mr. Halliday himself. Finding the two of us together Halliday lost his temper with the sergeant, and pointing towards me he said, "Take care that nobody stays or speaks with this man." Sailen was at once removed and locked up in another room. When I was alone with Halliday he asked me: "Aren't you ashamed of being involved in this cowardly, dastardly activity?" "What right have you to assume that I was involved?" To this Halliday replied: "I am not assuming, I know everything." At this I said: "What you know or do not know is your concern. I wholly deny having any connection with these murderous acts."'

From these exchanges which took place you can see how careful and controlled Sri Aurobindo was in replying to questions and to the provocations to which he was subjected. He knew enough about law, which he had studied for his ICS examinations, not to be trapped. Despite pressure, he refused to make any statements and stood on his rights. From the beginning the Government were bent on harassing Sri Aurobindo as much as they could. The food he was given was not fit to be eaten. His lawyer sought permission to have food sent from home but this was refused by the Police Commissioner. And three nights were spent in Lal Bazar in this fashion.

On Monday May 5, the prisoners were produced at the court of the Chief Presidency Magistrate, Calcutta. By that time the Government had decided that, in view of the very large number of arrests which had been made (as many as eight different locations were raided and searched by the Police and more than twenty-five persons arrested on the morning of May 2 itself, and further arrests followed), all the individual cases would be joined and sent up for trial by the District Magistrate, Alipore, as the proper jurisdictional authority. So Sri Aurobindo and all the other prisoners were sent to Alipore Jail to await trial which came to be known as the Alipore Bomb Trial.

'My prison life in Alipore began on May 5. Next year, on May 6, I was released,' wrote Sri Aurobindo and he observed philosophically: 'Friday, May 1, 1908... I did not know that it would mean the end of a chapter in my life and that there stretched before me a year's imprisonment during which all my human relations would cease, that for a whole year I would have to live, beyond the pale of society, live like an animal in a cage. And when I would re-enter the world of activity, it would not be the old familiar Aurobindo Ghose.... I have spoken of a year's imprisonment. It would have been more appropriate to speak of a year's living in an ashram or a hermitage.... The only result of the wrath of the British Government was that I found God.'

Meanwhile the news of Sri Aurobindo's arrest and of the large-scale rounding up of the revolutionaries had spread all over the country. People were stunned. The Muzzafarpur bomb outrage had itself created a sensation. Of the two young men who were caught, Prafulla Chaki shot himself as he was being arrested and the other, Khudiram, was awaiting his trial. (Later he was hanged and his very name became a synonym of martyrdom.) Few could believe that Sri Aurobindo was involved in the terrorist plots and yet he had been caught by the Government who were making out that he was the kingpin, the root of all this evil! People were bewildered as much as they were shocked and grieved.

The Alipore Bomb Trial commenced before Mr. Birley, District Magistrate of Alipore, on May 17, 1908. This was the preliminary trial. Altogether forty-two persons had been arrested of whom three were released for want of sufficiently incriminating evidence against them. The Magistrate now proceeded to hear the Prosecution draw up individual charges against the remaining thirty-nine accused, including Sri Aurobindo, on the basis of the evidence gathered.

While the preliminary trial was going on in the District Magistrate's Court, a dramatic event took place. One of the accused, Narendranath Gossain, had become an approver, i.e. in return for a promise by the Government that he would be given full pardon, he agreed to make a confession, provide statements of all that he knew and appear as a witness for the Prosecution. As soon as he had taken this step, Gossain was removed to the European section of the jail, away from his former companions. However, this did not save him. Two of the revolutionaries, Kanai Lal Dutt and Satyendranath Bose had already decided that for this act of betrayal Gossain must pay with his life. They arranged to send word to him that they too would like to turn approvers, and a meeting was accordingly arranged in front of the jail dispensary on the morning of August 31. Here, whilst they were engaged in conversation, suddenly shots rang out. Gossain was seen running away chased by Kanai and Satyen who were themselves being pursued by the warders. More shots were fired and Gossain was seen to fall into a drain by the side of the pathway along which they were running. He was dead. By this time Kanai and Satyen were overpowered and in the midst of tremendous noise and excitement they were immediately removed and segregated. Both were sent up for a summary trial and since neither made any attempt to defend himself, both were sentenced to death. They died like heroes, mourned by all true patriots. There can be no doubt that Gossain's death had a decisive effect on the entire trial. He had already made several damaging statements which might have seriously jeopardised Sri Aurobindo's defence and created other grave complications. Gossain would certainly have been a key witness but with his death the Prosecution was debarred from producing his statements as evidence since the Defence would have no opportunity to cross-examine him on the witness stand. Thus, legally, the statements stood invalidated.

You may well ask: How could Kanai and Satyen get hold of the revolvers? Well, no one really knows but later investigations indicate that perhaps one of the revolutionaries of Chandernagore smuggled two revolvers into the jail and made them over to Barin. Whatever the means adopted, one cannot but admire the heroic resolution of those who silenced the traitor.

The preliminary trial came to an end on September 14. Of the thirty-nine prisoners three had lost their lives, Gossain, Kanai and Satyen. After hearing both the Prosecution and the Defence, the Magistrate committed the remaining thirty-six to trial by the Sessions Judge, Alipore, the next higher Court. All the accused were charged with 'organising a gang for the purpose of waging war against the Government by criminal force', a grave offence under the Indian Penal Code. In the case of Barin, Hemchandra Das, Ullaskar Dutt and others, additional charges were framed, those of conspiracy, complicity in plots for assassination and other murderous acts, illegal manufacture of explosives, etc. etc., charges which if proved, would call for the highest punishment. Sri Aurobindo was also specifically accused of some of these offences including conspiracy and complicity in terrorist plots. The stage was now set for the main trial to commence before the District and Sessions Judge for 24-Paraganas and Hooghly, Mr. Charles Porten Beachcroft.

As evidence 4000 documents, 300 to 400 exhibits including explosives, bombs and weapons were produced. Nearly 200 witnesses were examined. The case commenced on October 19, 1908, and went on until April 13, 1909 – 131 days. Judgement was delivered on May 6, 1909.

I shall make no attempt to take you through the ramifications of this tremendous legal battle on the outcome of which depended so many lives. It created an unparalleled sensation and reports of the trial were followed by people all over the country with breathless suspense. All I shall try to do is to give you a few of its main features and highlights.

It is a remarkable coincidence that the case should have come up for hearing in the court of Judge Beachcroft. He was a member of the ICS and had passed his preliminary examination in the same year as Sri Aurobindo, 1890. Sri Aurobindo had then secured a higher position than he in the examination. Thereafter both were scholars at Cambridge – Sri Aurobindo at King's College and Beachcroft at Clare College. Their paths must have met many times, particularly when they were taking the intermediate and final examinations for the ICS. Certainly they knew each other but they were not close friends; otherwise, Beachcroft might well have declined to try the case. But the fact that he knew Sri Aurobindo and was fully familiar with his background must have led Beachcroft to follow the case with more than usual attention and care. And there can be no doubt that he was a fair and fine judge, later rising to be a Judge of the Calcutta High Court. That his judgement was eminently sound is also shown by the fact that the Government, after careful consideration, decided not to appeal against it. Had there been a less impartial judge, the outcome could have been very different.

To fight their case, the Government engaged Eardley Norton, an eminent barrister from Madras, who was known as a formidable criminal lawyer with the reputation of a bully who could browbeat witnesses into submission and win his cases. In the early stages of the trial, a number of lawyers appeared on behalf of Sri Aurobindo and the other defendants but after it had reached the Sessions stage C.R. Das took charge of the Defence, particularly that of Sri Aurobindo. He was then a rising barrister with a growing reputation, had known Sri Aurobindo in England and was closely connected with him in the political field. At a great sacrifice he gave up all his other practice and conducted the Defence without charging any fees, toiling at it night and day with one-pointed zeal and perseverance. His masterly handling of the case set the seal on his reputation and he soon became one of the greatest lawyers of his day, and later a leader of the nation in the political sphere. Indeed, it can be said that the appearance of C.R. Das changed the course of the trial so far as it affected Sri Aurobindo, and in the famous speech Sri Aurobindo delivered at

Uttarpara, after his acquittal, indeed he says: 'When the trial opened in the Sessions Court, I began to write many instructions for my counsel as to what was false in the evidence against me and on what points the witnesses might be cross-examined. Then something happened which I had not expected. The arrangements which had been made for my defence were suddenly changed and another counsel stood there to defend me.... When I saw him I was satisfied, but I still thought it necessary to write instructions. Then all that was put away from me and I had the message from within, "This is the man who will save you from the snares put around your feet. Put aside those papers. It will not be you who will instruct him. I will instruct him."'

You can imagine the enormous expenses involved in fighting a long drawn-out legal battle of such magnitude. To meet these costs, a Defence Fund was started by Sarojini, Sri Aurobindo's sister and people from far corners of the country sent in their contributions, big and small, which were of great practical help to Sri Aurobindo's supporters in those difficult days.

There is one aspect of the trial or rather of the atmosphere of the court-room in which the trial was being held, that I would like to mention. As the proceedings went on day after day, the prisoners were brought daily to the courtroom from the jail to be present during the trial. They were placed behind a wire-network and policemen with fixed bayonets stood on guard throughout the room. Norton has stated that he used to keep a loaded revolver lying on his brief, as a precautionary measure. But in this tense atmosphere and whilst the courtroom drama was being enacted, the demeanour of the prisoners was an extraordinary sight. Sri Aurobindo sat quietly, detached and often completely self-absorbed; nor were the others in a flurry or fluster. Their appearance was cheerful and they seemed unconcerned about the future. In his *Karakahini* Sri Aurobindo writes: '...one could see a strange spectacle: while the trial was going on, and the fate of thirty or forty accused was being wrangled over, the result of which might have been hanging or transportation for life, some of these accused persons without as much as glancing at what was happening around them, were absorbed in reading the novels of Bankim Chandra, Vivekananda's *Raja Yoga*, or the Gita, the Puranas, or European Philosophy.'

At last the trial drew to a close. Had it not been for Sri

Aurobindo, the case would have been over long ago, for he was the one person, more than any other, whom the Prosecution was anxious to convict. The final speech for the Defence by C.R. Das spread over eight days. It is still recognised as a masterpiece of the art of legal advocacy and his inspired words towards the close of the speech when he addressed the Judge and Assessors have long been famous. He said: 'My appeal to you therefore is that a man like this who is being charged with the offences imputed to him stands not only before the bar in this Court but stands before the bar of the High Court of History. And my appeal to you is this: That long after this controversy is hushed in silence, long after this turmoil, this agitation ceases, long after he is dead and gone, he will be looked upon as the poet of patriotism, as the prophet of nationalism and the lover of humanity. Long after he is dead and gone his words will be echoed and reechoed not only in India, but across distant seas and lands. Therefore I say that the man in his position is not only standing before the bar of this Court but before the bar of the High Court of History.'

The judgement was due to be delivered on May 6, 1909. The Government had taken elaborate precautions to prevent any disorder or demonstrations on the day of the verdict. The prisoners were led into the courtroom, as usual, and at ten minutes to eleven, the Judge mounted the bench. Ten minutes later, he pronounced the sentence: Barin and Ullaskar were sentenced to death; ten others, including Hemchandra Das, were sentenced to transportation for life; seven others to transportation or imprisonment for varying periods. The remaining seventeen, whose names were not read out, were acquitted. Among them were Sri Aurobindo and Nolini Kanta Gupta.

Despite the severity of the sentences on the others (upon appeal the sentences on Barin and Ullaskar were reduced to transportation for life), there was widespread rejoicing at Sri Aurobindo's release. Along with the others who had been acquitted, Sri Aurobindo was taken straight to the house of C.R. Das where they were given a royal reception and garlanded by the ladies. There was much jubilation followed by a sumptuous meal. However, it is said that amidst all these rejoicings, Sri Aurobindo had 'the same wistful look in his eyes, outwardly unconcerned and unperturbed'.

I must turn now to Sri Aurobindo's experiences in the Alipore Jail and tell you something about them, for in a way they were even more important and significant than the dramatic events which took place outside.

From the very first hour of his year-long stay at the Jail Sri Aurobindo was placed in solitary confinement. In the *Karakahini* he writes: 'My solitary cell was nine feet long and five feet in width; it had no windows, in front stood strong iron bars, and this cage was my appointed abode. Outside was a small stone-paved courtyard and a high brick wall with a small wooden door. In that door at eye-level, there was a small hole or opening. After the door had been bolted the sentry peeped in from time to time in order to find out what the convict was doing. But my courtyard door remained open for most of the time.' In that small cell he had to eat, sleep and attend to Nature's calls. And yet, listen to the way he describes his predicament: 'Needless to say, because of all this arrangement in a small room, one had throughout to undergo considerable inconvenience, especially at meal times and during the nights. Attached bathrooms are, I know, oftentimes a part of western civilization, but to have, in a small cell, a bedroom, dining room and w.c. rolled into one – this is what is called too much of a good thing! We Indians are full of regrettable customs; it is painful for us to be so highly civilized.' Indeed the physical conditions under which he had to live were simply inhuman. It was in the thick of summer that he was arrested and that small cell was like an oven. The quality of the food was appalling: 'coarse rice, even that spiced with husk, pebbles, insects, hair, dirt and such other stuff; the tasteless lentil soup was heavily watered and the vegetables and greens were mixed with grass and leaves.' And even water was meagerly doled out. Sri Aurobindo was provided with a blanket, a plate and a bowl. 'My dear bowl,' Sri Aurobindo writes, 'was multi-purpose, free from all caste restrictions, beyond all discriminations; in my cell it helped in the act of ablution, later with the same bowl I rinsed my mouth and bathed, and a little later when I had to take my food, the lentil soup or vegetable was poured into the same container. I drank water out of it and washed my mouth. Such an all-purpose priceless object can be had only in a British prison.' But all our sense of indignation at such treatment is dissipated when we read his wonderful words: 'The description of the Alipore Government hotel which I have given here, and will elaborate later, is not for the purpose of advertising my own hardship; it is only to show what peculiar arrangements are made for undertrial prisoners in the civilised British Raj. What prolonged agony for the innocent! The causes of hardship I have described were no doubt there, but since my faith in divine mercy was strong I had to suffer only for the first few days; thereafter – by what means I shall mention later – the mind had risen above these sufferings and grown incapable of feeling any hardship. That is why when I recollect my prison life instead of anger or sorrow I feel like laughing.'

It was characteristic of Sri Aurobindo that amidst all the harshness and inhumanity of prison life he could still see that the fault lay in the system and not in the lack of human qualities in the jail officials. In the *Karakahini* he has given us very sympathetic sketches of the Jail Superintendent, Mr. Emerson, calling him 'an embodiment of Europe's nearly vanished Christian ideals', the assistant doctor, Baidyanath Chatterjee, and his superior officer Dr. Daly, an Irishman who had 'inherited many of the qualities of that liberal and sentimental race'. Indeed it was because of Dr. Daly that Sri Aurobindo was given permission after some time to take a stroll every morning and afternoon in the open space in front of his cell. He was also permitted to obtain clothes and books from home and accordingly asked his uncle, Krishna Kumar Mitra, to send him the *Gita* and the *Upanishads*.

We come now to the overwhelming spiritual experience Sri Aurobindo had in jail. He spoke of it in his Uttarpara Speech, to which I have referred earlier, and I shall be quoting from it extensively. But this experience did not come to him without a period of intense inner struggle. At Uttarpara he said: 'When I was arrested and hurried to the Lal Bazar *Hajat* I was shaken in faith for a while, for I could not look into the heart of His intention. Therefore I faltered for a moment and cried out in my heart to Him, "What is this that has happened to me? I believed that I had a mission to work for the people of my country and until that work was done, I should have Thy protection. Why then am I here and on such a charge?" A day passed and a second day and a third, when a voice came to me from within, "Wait and see." Then I grew calm and waited. I was taken from Lal Bazar to Alipore and was placed for one month in a solitary cell apart from men. There I waited day and night for the voice of God within me, to know what He had to say to me, to learn what I had to do. In this seclusion the earliest realisation, the first lesson came to me. I remembered then that a month or more before my arrest, a call had come to me to put aside all activity, to go into seclusion and to look into myself, so that I might enter into closer communion with Him. I was weak and could not accept the call. My work was very dear to me and in the pride of my heart I thought that unless I was there, it would suffer or even fail and cease; therefore I would not leave it. It seemed to me that He spoke to me again and said, "The bonds that you had not the strength to break, I have broken for you, because it is not my will nor was it ever my intention that that should continue. I have had another thing for you to do and it is for that I have brought you here, to teach you what you could not learn for yourself and to train you for my work." Then he placed the Gita in my hands. His strength entered into me and I was not only to understand intellectually but to realise what Sri Krishna demanded of Arjuna and what He demands of those who aspire to do His work.'

Then Sri Aurobindo goes on to speak of his experience: 'He made me realise the central truth of the Hindu religion. He turned the hearts of my jailors to me and they spoke to the Englishman in charge of the jail, "He is suffering in his confinement; let him at least walk outside his cell for half an hour in the morning and in the evening." So it was arranged, and it was while I was walking that His strength again entered into me. I looked at the jail that secluded me from men and it was no longer by its high walls that I was imprisoned; no, it was Vasudeva who surrounded me, I walked under the branches of the trees in front of my cell but it was not the trees, I knew it was Vasudeva, it was Sri Krishna whom I saw standing there and holding over me his shade. I looked at the bars of my cell, the very grating that did duty for a door and again I saw Vasudeva. It was Narayana who was guarding and standing sentry over me. Or I lay on the coarse blankets that were given me for a couch and felt the arms of Sri Krishna around me, the arms of my Friend and Lover. This was the first use of the deeper vision He gave me. I looked at the prisoners in the jail, the thieves, the murderers, swindlers, and as I looked at them I saw Vasudeva, it was Narayana whom I found in these darkened souls and misused bodies. Among these thieves and dacoits there were many who put me to shame by their sympathy, their kindness, the humanity triumphant over such adverse circumstances. One I saw among them especially, who seemed to me a saint, a peasant of my nation who did not know how to read and write, an alleged dacoit sentenced to ten years rigorous imprisonment, one of those whom we look down upon in our Pharisaical pride of class as *chhotalok*. Once more He spoke to me and said, "Behold the people among whom I have sent you to do a little of my work. This is the nature of the nation I am raising up and the reason why I raise them."'

And Sri Aurobindo continues: 'When the case opened in the Lower Court and we were brought before the Magistrate I was followed by the same insight. He said to me, "When you were cast into jail, did not your heart fail and did you not cry out to me, 'Where is Thy protection?' Look now at the Magistrate, look now at the Prosecuting Counsel." I looked and it was not the Magistrate whom I saw, it was Vasudeva, it was Narayana who was sitting there on the bench. I looked at the Prosecuting Counsel and it was not the counsel for the prosecution that I saw; it was Sri Krishna who sat there; it was my Lover and Friend who sat there and smiled. "Now do you fear?" he said, "I am in all men and I overrule their actions and their words. My protection is still with you and you shall not fear. This case which is brought against you, leave it in my hand. It is not for you. It is not for the trial that I brought you here but for something else. The case itself is only a means for my work and nothing more.... I am guiding, therefore fear not. Turn to your own work for which I have brought you to jail and when you come out, remember never to fear, never to hesitate. Remember that it is I who am doing this, not you nor any other. Therefore whatever clouds may come, whatever dangers and sufferings, whatever difficulties, whatever impossibilities, there is nothing impossible and nothing difficult. I am in the nation and its uprising and I am Vasudeva, I am Narayana, and what I will, shall be, not what others will. What I choose to bring about, no human power can stay."'

There is no need for me to comment on Sri Aurobindo's words – if you read them aloud you may feel something of the immense vibrations they contain. Sri Aurobindo himself has said that this was the realisation of the cosmic consciousness – of the Divine as all beings and all that is, *Vasudevah sarvamiti*, and it was the second of the four great realisations (of the first – the experience of Brahma-Nirvana at Baroda – I have already spoken) on which his yoga and spiritual philosophy are founded.

After sometime Sri Aurobindo was transferred from the solitary cell to a large hall in the jail where he lived with the other undertrial prisoners. Sri Aurobindo was then so intensely absorbed in his sadhana that he hardly took any part in the general talk, laughter and games in which the others would often be engaged. But now he had an opportunity to get acquainted with his fellow-accused, many of whom he had not met before. Of them he writes in *Karakahini*: 'Looking at these lads, one felt as if the large-hearted, daring, puissant men of an earlier age with a different training had come back to India.' In his Uttarpara speech also he spoke of them as 'young men of mighty courage'.

After the assassination of Naren Gossain, the authorities tightened up the security regulations in the Jail and Sri Aurobindo again occupied a solitary cell. But now he was so immersed in his sadhana that the prison became for him truly an ashram. During this period he had many extraordinary experiences, occult in nature, some of which he mentioned later. One of the most important of these experiences covered a period of two weeks when he heard constantly the voice of Vivekananda speaking to him in his solitary meditation and felt his presence. Sri Aurobindo told us: 'It was the spirit of Vivekananda which first gave me a clue in the direction of the Supermind. This clue led me to see how the Truth-Consciousness works in everything. He didn't say "Supermind" – "Supermind" is my own word....'

Another remarkable development was the sudden opening of the capacity for appreciating painting. He said: 'I knew something about sculpture, but was blind to painting. Suddenly one day in the Alipore Jail while meditating I saw some pictures on the walls of the cell and lo and behold, the artistic eye in me opened and I knew all about painting except of course the more material side of the technique.'

Once, as he was wondering during his sadhana, whether *siddhis* (powers) like levitation were possible at all, he found himself suddenly raised up in the air. On another occasion when he was practising raising his arms and leaving them in a suspended position without muscular effort, he went to sleep; the warden who saw the scene from outside was alarmed and reported that he was dead!

On still another occasion he experimented with fasting for eleven days to see what spiritual benefit accrued from it. Though he lost about ten pounds in weight, he had no adverse effects and could lift a pail of water above his head, which he normally could not do.

Yet another remarkable phenomenon was that his hair always glistened. One of his co-prisoners made bold to ask him: 'Do you use oil for your hair?' Sri Aurobindo stunned him with his reply: 'No, at present I do not take a bath. I am passing through some physical changes as a result of spiritual experiences. My hair draws fat from the body.'

Now, has science any explanation to offer about these extraordinary phenomena or will it dismiss them as grandmother's tales? I leave you to find your own answers but I think I have told you enough about Sri Aurobindo's experiences in the Jail for you to realise how profound were the changes they brought about in him. They remind me of these lines from *Savitri*:

A wide God-knowledge poured down from above,
A new world-knowledge broadened from within ...
The human in him paced with the divine.

Chapter VIII

"Karmayogin" – Chandernagore – Pondicherry
1909–1910

AFTER his acquittal, Sri Aurobindo wrote a letter to the Editor of the *Bengalee*, a popular daily newspaper of that time, to express his gratitude to all those who had sent in contributions to the fund opened by his sister Sarojini for his legal defence. The letter is beautifully worded, simple yet moving. Here is the text:

Sir,
    Will you kindly allow me to express through your columns my deep sense of gratitude to all who have helped me in my hour of trial? Of the innumerable friends known and unknown, who have contributed each his mite to swell my defence fund, it is impossible for me now even to learn the names and I must ask them to accept this public expression of my feeling in place of private gratitude; since my acquittal many telegrams and letters have reached me and they are too numerous to reply to individually. The love which my countrymen have heaped upon me in return for the little I have been able to do for them, amply repays any apparent trouble or misfortune my public activity may have brought upon me. I attribute my escape to no human agency, but first of all to the protection of the Mother of us all who has never been absent from me but always held me in Her arms and shielded me from grief and disaster, and secondarily to the prayers of thousands which have been going up to Her on my behalf ever since I was arrested. If it is

the love of my country which led me into danger, it is also love of my countrymen which has brought me safe through it.

Aurobindo Ghose

6, College Square, May 14, 1909

As a result of his profound spiritual experiences, Sri Aurobindo came out of the jail a completely changed person. But the situation outside had also changed radically. The *Bande Mataram* had come to a stop during his absence. Tilak had been sentenced to six years' imprisonment and banished to Burma. The Government had clamped down on the Nationalists and the revolutionaries with ruthless force. There was simmering discontent below the surface but it could not find expression except in stray acts of violence and terrorism.

On May 30, 1909, Sri Aurobindo delivered his historic speech at Uttarpara, from which I have already given you extracts relating to his spiritual experiences in jail. At Uttarpara ten thousand people listened to him in pin-drop silence in a spiritually surcharged atmosphere. He began by contrasting the situation before his arrest with what he now saw. He said: 'It was more than a year ago that I came here last. When I came I was not alone; one of the mightiest prophets of Nationalism sat by my side.... Now he is far away, separated from us by thousands of miles. Others whom I was accustomed to find working beside me are absent. The storm that swept over the country has scattered them far and wide.... When I went to jail the whole country was alive with the cry of Bande Mataram, alive with the hope of a nation, the hope of millions of men who had newly risen out of degradation. When I came out of jail I listened for that cry, but there was instead a silence. A hush had fallen on the country and men seemed bewildered; for instead of God's bright heaven full of the vision of the future that had been before us, there seemed to be overhead a leaden sky from which human thunders and lightnings rained. No man seemed to know which way to move, and from all sides came the question, "What shall we do next? What is there that we can do?" I too did not know which way to move, I too did not know what was next to be done. But one thing I knew, that as it was the Almighty Power of God which had raised that cry, that hope, so it was the same Power which had sent down that silence. He who was in the shouting and the movements was also in the pause and the hush. He has sent it upon us, so that the nation might draw back for a moment and look into itself and know His will. I have not been disheartened by that silence, because I had been made familiar with silence in my prison and because I knew it was in the pause and the hush that I had myself learnt this lesson through the long year of my detention.'

Then Sri Aurobindo related the experiences which were vouchsafed to him in the Jail and said that they had revealed to him the truth of the Hindu religion. He said: 'I realised what the Hindu religion meant. We speak often of the Hindu religion, of the Sanatana Dharma, but few of us really know what that religion is....

'...day after day, He showed me His wonders and made me realise the utter truth of the Hindu religion. I had had many doubts before. I was brought up in England amongst foreign ideas and an atmosphere entirely foreign. About many things in Hinduism I had once been inclined to believe that they were imaginations, that there was much of dream in it, much that was delusion and Maya. But now day after day I realised in the mind, I realised in the heart, I realised in the body the truths of the Hindu religion. They became living experiences to me, and things were opened to me which no material science could explain. When I first approached Him, it was not entirely in the spirit of the Bhakta, it was not entirely in the spirit of the Jnani. I came to Him long ago in Baroda some years before the Swadeshi began and I was drawn into the public field.

'When I approached God at that time, I hardly had a living faith in Him. The agnostic was in me, the atheist was in me, the sceptic was in me and I was not absolutely sure that there was a God at all. I did not feel His presence. Yet something drew me to the truth of the Vedas, the truth of the Gita, the truth of the Hindu religion. I felt there must be a mighty truth somewhere in this Yoga, a mighty truth in this religion based on the Vedanta. So when I turned to the Yoga and resolved to practise it and find out if my idea was right, I did it in this spirit and with this prayer to Him, "If Thou art, then Thou knowest my heart. Thou knowest that I do not ask for Mukti, I do not ask for anything which others ask for. I ask only for strength to uplift this nation, I ask only to be allowed to live and work for this people whom I love and to whom I pray that I may devote my life." I strove long for the realisation of Yoga and at last to some extent I had it, but in what I most desired I was not satisfied. Then in the seclusion of the jail, of the solitary cell I asked for it again. I said, "Give me Thy Adesh. I do not know what work to do or how to do it. Give me a message." In the communion of Yoga two messages came. The first message said, "I have given you a work and it is to help to uplift this nation. Before long the time will come when you will have to go out of jail; for it is not my will that this time either you should be convicted or that you should pass the time, as others have to do, in suffering for their country. I have called you to work, and that is the Adesh for which you have asked. I give you the Adesh to go forth and do my work." The second message came and it said, "Something has been shown to you in this year of seclusion, something about which you had your doubts and it is the truth of the Hindu religion. It is this religion that I am raising up before the world, it is this that I have perfected and developed through the Rishis, saints and Avatars, and now it is going forth to do my work among the nations. I am raising up this nation to send forth my word. This is the Sanatana Dharma, this is the eternal religion which you did not really know before, but which I have now revealed to you. The agnostic and the sceptic in you have been answered, for I have given you proofs within and without you, physical and subjective, which have satisfied you. When you go forth, speak to your nation always this word, that it is for the Sanatana Dharma that they arise, it is for the world and not for themselves that they arise...."

'...But what is the Hindu religion? What is this religion which we call Sanatana, eternal? It is the Hindu religion only because the Hindu nation has kept it, because in this Peninsula it grew up in the seclusion of the sea and the Himalayas, because in this sacred and ancient land it was given as a charge to the Aryan race to preserve through the ages. But it is not circumscribed by the confines of a single country, it does not belong peculiarly and for ever to a bounded part of the world. That which we call the Hindu religion is really the eternal religion, because it is the universal religion which embraces all others. If a religion is not universal, it cannot be eternal. A narrow religion, a sectarian religion, an exclusive religion can live only for a limited time and a limited purpose.'

These wonderful words from the Uttarpara Speech help us to understand the inspiration behind Sri Aurobindo's activities at this

time and his perceptions regarding the true meaning of nationalism and religion. From now on he relied increasingly on the inner
voice – the *adesh* or divine command from within – to regulate his
actions and at any moment of crisis, he instantly obeyed its
dictates. Also, mark that when he speaks of a Sanatana Dharma, it
is not of creed and dogmas, rites and rituals, that he speaks. As he
was to explain further in the *Karmayogin*: 'There is a mighty law of
life, a great principle of human evolution, a body of spiritual
knowledge and experience of which India has always been destined to be a guardian, exemplar and missionary. This is the
sanatana dharma, the eternal religion.'

In order to combat the gloom and despondency in the air Sri
Aurobindo launched the publication of two weekly journals, the
Karmayogin in English and the *Dharma* in Bengali. The first issue
of the *Karmayogin* came out on June 19, 1909, and that of the
Dharma on August 23. The *Karmayogin* described itself as 'a
weekly review of National Religion, Literature, Science, Philosophy etc.' The cover illustration was that of Sri Krishna and
Arjuna seated in their chariot on the battlefield of Kurukshetra,
and the two mottos on the top were 'Remember me and fight' and
'Yoga is skill in works.' Week after week Sri Aurobindo contributed articles of rare inspiration. The early issues also carried his
translations of the *Isha*, *Katha* and *Kena* Upanishads. There were
literary contributions as well – several of his poems, 'Baji
Prabhou', 'The Birth of Sin', 'Epiphany' and others appeared in
the paper for the first time; it also published his translation of the
first thirteen chapters of Bankim Chandra's *Anandamath*. In the
later issues can be found some remarkably constructive prose
contributions such as 'A System of National Education', 'The
National Value of Art', 'The Brain of India', etc. Both the
Karmayogin and *Dharma* soon acquired a wide readership and,
unlike the *Bande Mataram*, were financially self-supporting.

It must not be thought, however, that the *Karmayogin* refrained
from political writings. As in the *Bande Mataram*, there were tren-
chant comments on political developments but the stress was on
larger issues, moral and spiritual. The British Government, in an
effort to placate Indian feelings, had come forward with some half-
hearted proposals for political reforms, but as they did not really
transfer any political power to India Sri Aurobindo did not accept.
The Moderates in Bengal, under the leadership of Surendranath

Bannerjee, were anxious to come to an understanding with the Nationalist leaders so as to repair the split at Surat. Sri Aurobindo led the Nationalist delegates to a conference at Hoogly which was attended by the Moderates as well. He was also present at a few private meetings called by Surendranath to explore the possibilities of a rapprochement. However, these negotiations failed because Sri Aurobindo would in no way compromise on the issue of independence or accept the new constitution of the Congress. This again shows how steadfast he was in exercising his political will to establish independence as the one ideal to be followed and to plant this seed in the national consciousness.

The Government were in a quandary how to deal with Sri Aurobindo. They considered appealing to the High Court against the judgment of Beachcroft. After careful consideration, however, they dropped the idea as the appeal was not likely to succeed. A strong section of the bureaucrats was in favour of deportation but the Viceroy was against this extreme move lest it trigger off a violent reaction in India and provoke criticism in England. In fact Sister Nivedita warned Sri Aurobindo that the Government might deport him and he then told her that he would take steps to forestall their action. Accordingly Sri Aurobindo wrote a signed article in the *Karmayogin* in July 1909, calling it 'An Open Letter to My Countrymen' in which he exposed Government intentions and left his countrymen with what he called his 'last political will and testament' to guide them in his enforced absence. A masterly move, this must have effectively silenced those bureaucrats who were still thinking in terms of deporting him. Frustrated in these two directions, the Government continued to keep a close watch on the writings in the *Karmayogin* so as not to miss any opportunity of convicting Sri Aurobindo on a charge of sedition.

Meanwhile the political atmosphere remained murky and sullen. On December 25, 1909, Sri Aurobindo wrote another open letter, 'To My Countrymen', which appeared in the *Karmayogin*. In it he reviewed the political situation, referred to the failure in the negotiations between the Nationalists and the Moderates, strongly opposed the Morley-Minto Reforms which the Moderates were in favour of accepting and ended the letter by advocating a renewal of the passive resistance movement with a readiness to defy the Government if they resorted to ruthless repression. Again, it was a masterly example of political polemics.

At this time we have the remarkable instance of a prediction made by Sri Aurobindo regarding India's independence. This was in January 1910 when he gave an interview to a correspondent of the Tamil Nationalist weekly *India*. Sri Aurobindo said: 'Since 1907, we are living in a new era which is full of hope for India. Not only India, but the whole world will see sudden upheavals and revolutionary changes. The high will become low and the low high. The oppressed and the depressed shall be elevated. The nations and humanity will be animated by a new consciousness, new thought and new efforts will be made to reach new ends. Amidst these revolutionary changes India will become free.' These words were published with Sri Aurobindo's authorisation. I shall have occasion to remind you of the prediction later in our story.

On January 24, 1910, Shams-ul-Alam, Deputy Superintendent of the Police Intelligence Department, was shot down on the steps of the Calcutta High Court publicly and in daylight. You will remember no doubt the name of this detective about whom Sri Aurobindo has written with so much humour in his *Karakahini*. The very nature of this official's duties together with his ability and zeal had made him a marked man in the eyes of the revolutionaries. It became obvious that severe Government reprisals would follow this sudden assassination and the political situation became tense once again.

In the evenings Sri Aurobindo used to go to the *Karmayogin* office at 4 Shampukur Lane in the Shambazar area of Calcutta to attend to editorial work. One evening around the middle of February 1910, probably on the 15th, Sri Aurobindo went to the office as usual. Work over, he sat down with a few young associates in an automatic writing seance. Suresh Chakravarty (Moni) was one of the young men who was present on the occasion and I will now quote a passage in translation from his Bengali book of reminiscences which tells us of subsequent events. He writes: 'The atmosphere was filled with fun and laughter when Ram Majumdar, a staff member of the *Karmayogin*, suddenly entered and informed Sri Aurobindo that he had come to know from a high police official that a warrant of arrest had been issued against Sri Aurobindo. There was a tense moment of silence as we sat in perplexity. Then Sri Aurobindo calmly said: "I will go to Chandernagore." He stood up and came out of the house with Rambabu behind him. At a little distance were Biren and myself –

in this way a "dumb procession" was formed.
'Usually the police kept a watch over Sri Aurobindo's movements but that evening, when he came out of the office, there was
no vigil anywhere. After walking for about fifteen minutes we
reached a ghat of the river Ganges. Rambabu called out for a ferry
boat. Sri Aurobindo stepped into it – Biren and myself followed.
Then Rambabu went back. The boat started and we were afloat on
the Bhagirathi waters. It was a full-moon night; all around were
ripples as of a silver smile. Perhaps it was –
> The eleventh day of the moon,
> The sleepless moon
> Is ferrying all alone in the dream-sea!

'After a long night's crossing the boat reached Chandernagore
in the early morning. Sri Aurobindo sent Biren to Charu Chandra
Roy, well-known in revolutionary circles, to ask for shelter. But he
was singularly unhelpful and indeed suggested that Sri Aurobindo
should leave India and go to France! However the young revolutionary, Motilal Roy, came to know of Sri Aurobindo's arrival
and welcomed him in his own house. Now that a safe refuge had
been found, we returned to Calcutta in the same boat.'

Apropos of these events Sri Aurobindo later said: 'When I
heard of the arrest, I was thinking what should be done. Then all
on a sudden I got a clear command, "Go to Chandernagore." At
once I was ready, not from fright or despair, but that there should
be no hindrance to my yoga – that was why I came away. I gave up
political connections because I knew that the work I had started
would go ahead and its success was assured. My presence was not
needed for it. I requested Nivedita to take up charge of the
Karmayogin.'

Sri Aurobindo stayed at Chandernagore for about six weeks,
first at Motilal's house and then in a number of other locations to
avoid attracting attention from the police or the informers. He
demanded the strictest security precautions which Motilal did his
best to provide. In fact, throughout Sri Aurobindo's stay at
Chandernagore the Government had no scent of his whereabouts
although they were engaged in intensive searches for him
everywhere.

Sri Aurobindo has said hardly anything about this short period
of secluded life at Chandernagore except that 'he plunged entirely
into solitary meditation and ceased all other activities'. What little

we know is from Motilal who later wrote a book of memoirs. It was a period of intense sadhana for Sri Aurobindo. When he spoke it was as if somebody else was speaking through him. He would eat the food placed before him mechanically – even then he was deeply absorbed and ate very little. He meditated with his eyes open and saw various subtle forms and sights. Three deities appeared before him – Ila, Mahi (Bharati) and Saraswati whom he later recognised as Vedic Ishwaris. Motilal was himself now attracted to yoga and Sri Aurobindo gave him guidance – 'Surrender everything to God!' was his instruction.

Chandernagore was too dangerously near Calcutta for Sri Aurobindo to stay on there. Various plans for going elsewhere were being suggested when Sri Aurobindo again heard the Voice: 'Go to Pondicherry.' On his part, Sri Aurobindo once again followed this Voice without any hesitation or question. This is how the Divine guides and protects us when we take refuge in Him alone – *māmekam saranam vraja*, as the Gita says.

Plans for his departure to Pondicherry had to be made in great secrecy because of police surveillance. There were two stages of the journey. The first, and much the shorter passage, was from Chandernagore to Calcutta. Sri Aurobindo relied on Motilal to make the arrangements. He also sent word to Amar Chatterji, the young revolutionary from Uttarpara of whom I have spoken earlier, to give his assistance. As regards the second part of the journey, the longer and much more risky passage, he wrote to his maternal cousin Sukumar Mitra (Krishnakumar Mitra's son), to work out the details of a plan. Sukumar was also advised that Bijoy Nag, a young follower of Sri Aurobindo, would accompany him to Pondicherry. At the same time Sri Aurobindo sent a note to Suresh Chakravarty asking him to be ready to go to Pondicherry in advance.

Some of the persons who played a part in the exciting events that followed published their reminiscences in subsequent years. There are a few discrepancies in some of these accounts, possibly due to the fading memory of the authors, but the overall picture is clear enough and I shall be drawing on these writings to enable you to visualise the dramatic episodes.

First let us listen to Suresh: '...while I was living in a mess at No. 6 Crouch Lane, quite unexpectedly one day I received a small piece of paper, with a message in three or four lines of

Aurobindo's handwriting. It asked me to go to Pondicherry to arrange a house for him. My friend (who gave me the note) told me further that Sukumar, and Saurin Bose, Sri Aurobindo's wife's cousin, would make all the arrangements for my going to Pondicherry, the former secretly and the latter openly. All I had to do was to go to the Howrah station and get on the Madras Mail. My departure for Pondicherry was set for March 28.... Generally I never used to venture out before sundown but on the day of my departure I went out in the morning and had a hair-cut. I bought some new clothes too. I let it be known to everyone in the mess that I was going to my home-town Pabna in the evening by the Darjeeling Mail to attend a marriage.' I might mention here that Suresh was a very fair-complexioned young man and he purchased a suit of European clothes so as to pass off as an Anglo-Indian and not be suspected by the police.

To continue with Suresh's narrative, 'In those days the Madras Mail used to leave Howrah station in the evening. In the afternoon I put on my new clothes and left the house without any luggage. In my pocket I had a recently purchased money-bag containing three ten-rupee notes, a little change, and a piece of paper on which Aurobindo had written a few lines that were to be my letter of introduction to Pondicherry friends.... I reached Howrah station. The train was already at the platform. All around was the noisy hustle-bustle of the passengers. I found Saurin after much searching. He was waiting for me with a trunk and a small bedding-roll in front of a second-class compartment. After I took them from Saurin he gave me a second-class ticket (the second class, instead of third, being a cover) and a colourful paper-back novel by Guy Boothby entitled *Love Made Manifest*, recently bought from a book-stall for six annas....'

This is how young Suresh – he was barely eighteen at the time – left Calcutta. But his very youth and the fact that he was one of the few around Sri Aurobindo who did not have a police record gave him very suitable cover as an emissary. He duly arrived at Pondicherry on March 31, after changing trains at Madras. Later I shall pick up his trail at Pondicherry. Let me now return to Calcutta.

In his reminiscences, Sukumar Mitra writes: 'It was 1910, around the end of March. Unexpectedly I received a letter from Sri Motilal Roy of Chandernagore. He informed me of Auro-da's desire to leave Chandernagore and go to Pondicherry. All the arrangements for his departure were to be made by me. And I had to be most careful in keeping all this a secret.... I resolved to work with the utmost care and circumspection at every step and in every detail. At that time half a dozen plain-clothes detectives used to sit near the tank in front of our house and keep watch. They shadowed me as soon as I came out of the house.... Since the police openly picked me up and followed me from the moment I left the house, I felt it better not to be directly involved in making the arrangements but instead to get the work done by giving instructions to two men I trusted. Even so what I told one I did not pass on to the other, and I did not allow the two to meet.... I decided to send Aurobindo to Pondicherry by a French ship rather than by train, for to go by rail was, I decided, too dangerous. If he took the train he might be recognised during the long journey, for there were police spies on the alert at the stations. At that time a French shipping company called Messageries Maritimes operated from Calcutta. Ships of other companies also sailed from Calcutta to Colombo but they did not halt at Pondicherry. There was another advantage in travelling by a French ship, a political one. As soon as the ship went beyond the British Indian coast, the passengers would come under French jurisdiction. The security Aurobindo sought by going to Pondicherry would be his once he had travelled eighty miles south of Calcutta.'

The two persons chosen by Sukumar to assist him in carrying out the plan were Nagendrakumar Guharay and Surendrakumar Chakravarty, both trustworthy Swadeshi workers from Noakhali.

In later years Nagendrakumar wrote about these events and to his reminiscences he gave the title *Farewell to the god*. He writes: 'One day in the last week of March, Sukumar-da showed me two steel trunks in a room of his house (the *Sanjivani* office) and said that I should take them away and keep them at my mess. I lifted the trunks a little and realised that they were full. Jokingly I enquired whether they contained bombs and pistols. Sukumar-da smiled and said that whatever the contents, the trunks must be kept with me. So I took them to my mess at 44/1 College Street. He asked me to meet him again the following day.

'The next day when I met Sukumar-da at the appointed time, he wrote down the names and addresses of two men and, giving me the necessary money, asked me to buy two second class tickets on the Colombo steamer. I cannot remember exactly whether I bought the tickets for Pondicherry or Colombo. Sukumar-da recalls that the tickets were for Colombo. He says that he did this to divert the police for, in the event of an enquiry later, their attention would first be directed towards Colombo instead of Pondicherry. I cannot recall the name of the steamer company but Sukumar-da still remembers it. It was Messageries Maritimes. But I certainly haven't forgotten the name of the ship on which we would bid farewell to the god. A picture of that ship, the *Dupleix*, docked at Chandpal Ghat near the Eden Gardens of Calcutta still floats before my eyes. Sukumar-da had asked me to reserve a single cabin for two persons and I made the bookings accordingly. I then returned to the *Sanjivani* office and gave him the two tickets which he checked carefully. Handing them back to me he said, "Keep them with you for the time being – I will take them later."'

Under Sukumar's instructions Nagendrakumar had booked the passages in the names of Jatindra Nath Mitter of Uluberia (a town not far from Calcutta), and Bankim Chandra Bhowmik of Nilphamari, in Rangpur district, names to be assumed by Sri Aurobindo and Bijoy for the journey. Actually, they were not fictitious names and addresses but were taken by Sukumar from the subscribers' list of *Sanjivani*, his father's nationalist journal. This was done to mislead the police in case of any later investigations.

These arrangements took care of Sri Aurobindo's proposed journey from Calcutta to Pondicherry. The S.S. *Dupleix* was due to sail in the early hours of April 1, from Chandpal Ghat, Calcutta.

Sukumar now gave his attention to the problem of bringing Sri Aurobindo across from Chandernagore to Calcutta without arousing the suspicions of the police. He was determined to take the utmost precautions and decided that Sri Aurobindo should not be brought direct from Chandernagore to Calcutta so that the boatmen would be in the dark about his destination. So Sukumar planned the journey in several stages. Here let me explain that Chandernagore is situated on the western bank of the Ganges, whereas Calcutta is on the eastern side, about 35 km downstream from Chandernagore. Sukumar decided that the first stage of Sri Aurobindo's journey should be from Chandernagore to Agarpara, on the eastern side of the river, about halfway between Chandernagore and Calcutta. Whilst Sri Aurobindo made his journey,

Amar Chatterjee would hire a boat at Uttarpara, situated on the western bank, cross the river and pick up Sri Aurobindo from Agarpara. However, they would still not proceed direct from Agarpara to Calcutta. Instead, Amar and Sri Aurobindo would again cross the river and take up position at another ghat on the western side of the river, a few miles below Uttarpara. In the meantime Nagen and Suren, accompanied by Bijoy Nag, would hire a boat at Calcutta and proceed upstream to the appointed ghat on the opposite side of the river below Uttarpara. It was further decided that in event of any delay, Amar's boat would not be moored at the ghat, to avoid attention being drawn to it, but move towards the mid-river. Each boat would fly a banner of the same kind which would be their flag of identification. Once the two boats had established contact, Sri Aurobindo would be transferred to Nagen's boat which would bring the party direct to *Dupleix* at Chandpal Ghat. Sri Aurobindo and Bijoy would then board the ship from the river by a rope-ladder, instead of using the gangplank. The captain's permission to do so would be taken in advance and at that time the passengers' baggages would be deposited in the cabin reserved for them.

It was certainly an elaborate plan, perhaps over-elaborate, but Sukumar considered that a zig-zag route and various diversionary tactics were necessary so as to hoodwink the police. Also, it seemed a good idea for Sri Aurobindo to board the ship straight from the river, as the police usually kept a sharp look-out from the adjoining road when passengers entered the ship from the jetty.

On the morning of March 31, the day prior to the *Dupleix*'s date of sailing, Motilal Roy saw Sri Aurobindo off from the Borai-chanditola Ghat at Chandernagore. Motilal himself did not accompany Sri Aurobindo but deputed two of his trusted followers to be with him. In accordance with the plan, the boat moved downstream and crossed the river to reach Agarpara on the eastern bank.

In the meantime Amar Chatterjee had hired a boat at Uttarpara and, along with his right-hand man Manmath Biswas, set off for Agarpara. This journey was also uneventful and they had no trouble in making contact with Sri Aurobindo at Agarpara.

Now let us turn to the other participants in these exciting events and see what they were doing. On the same morning of March 31,

Sukumar sent word to Nagen, to come and see him. To quote from Sukumar's memoirs: 'I called Nagendra and asked him to put Aurobindo's two steel trunks in the reserved cabin on the *Dupleix*, show the two tickets to the captain and lock up the cabin. Nagendra loaded the trunks on to the ship and returned to inform me. I then called Surendranath Chakravarty and told him that before noon he would have to hire a boat to go northward up the Ganges. I gave him a banner I had ready and asked him to fix it high on the boat. I told him that a similar banner would be flying on a boat which he would come across near a ghat on the opposite side of Agarpara. He should meet this boat, transfer its passengers to his own boat and carry them to the *Dupleix* which would be moored at Chandpal Ghat. Surendrakumar did not ask any questions nor did he show any undue curiosity. He left to do his work as instructed.'

When Nagen came back after having deposited the two trunks in the ship's cabin, Sukumar instructed him also regarding the boat journey that he would have to make with Suren to pick up two persons from another boat and take them to the Colombo-bound ship. Recalling the events Nagen writes: 'I enquired of Sukumar-da "How am I going to recognise the men of the boat?" He replied, "I have explained everything to Suren." As Sukumar-da was saying this, all at once something flashed across my mind. I suddenly asked: "It isn't your Auro-da who is going, is it?" A little surprised he answered with a laugh, "Well, you have become very clever, haven't you? How did you know?" "It just occurred to me," I answered. "You guessed right", he said. "But be very careful that no one else finds out."'

Around midday Nagen and Suren set off in a boat which went up the river with the object of meeting the other boat that carried Sri Aurobindo, Amar and Manmath. All had worked out well so far. But now fate, or an unseen Hand, intervened. The two boats failed to establish contact either at the appointed ghat or in mid-river. There had probably been some delay in Nagen and Suren starting from Calcutta or the two boats might have passed each other without recognising the banner of identification which they were flying; whatever the reason, a very grave situation now developed.

Remember that Amar was neither aware of the arrangements

which had been made for boarding the *Dupleix* nor did he have the tickets. Detailed instructions as well as the tickets were being carried by Nagen and now the two parties had missed each other. The whole sequence of carefully prepared arrangements had gone awry.

Amar was now getting increasingly worried. He decided that he could wait no longer for Nagen to turn up and instructed the boatman to proceed towards Calcutta. He rightly concluded that he must meet Sukumar to find out what had gone wrong.

Meanwhile Nagen and Suren, equally perturbed at having searched for and failed to find Sri Aurobindo, also decided that they must return to Calcutta and report to Sukumar. Nagen writes in his reminiscences: 'We went straight to Sukumar-da's house and told him what had happened. He asked me to go at once to Chandpal Ghat and take the two trunks out of the ship's cabin. It was then about six in the evening. I again rushed to Chandpal Ghat. There was no end to my scurryings that day.... On the ship I learned that the ship's doctor had finished his examination of the passengers and gone home. My heart sank when I heard this. I thought, "All this labour and now our efforts are all wasted!"'

However, Nagen was resourceful enough to meet the captain, obtain the doctor's address (he was a European) and get the captain to agree that if the passengers could board the ship by 10 or 11 p.m. with the required medical certificates, they would be accepted. Then there was a stroke of good fortune. Nagen goes on to write: 'The coolie who took the two trunks down from the ship's cabin and put them on the hired horse-carriage told me that he knew the doctor-sahib's house and was acquainted with the sahib's servant. He could arrange everything. In the same breath he also made it clear that I would have to give him and the servant a fat tip to keep them happy. The coolie was a Bengali, a Calcutta man and very clever. From his behaviour and words I could see that he could get the job done. But the cloud of anxiety did not dissolve completely, because we did not know yet when and where this unforeseen game of hide-and-seek with the two passengers would end.'

To return now to Amar, Manmath and the precious human cargo they were carrying. Alighting at a ghat near Chandpal Ghat where the *Dupleix* was berthed, they hired a carriage, put Sri Aurobindo inside and rushed towards Sukumar's house in the

College Square area. Amar stopped the carriage some distance away from the house and sent Manmath to enquire at Sukumar's place. The situation was now full of danger. This was an area where plain-clothes policemen and informers were always on the lookout. Sri Aurobindo's face was well known. If by chance he were recognised and the police tipped off, the authorities would take swift action. To make matters worse, Manmath came back and reported that Sukumar was not in the house – he had apparently gone out in search of the missing party! There was nothing to be done except to wait. Amar recalling the events writes: 'My mind was restless as I sat with Aurobindo in the carriage worrying about where the others were. But he whose safety was causing me so much restlessness and agitation was himself untroubled, unshaken, motionless like a statue he sat there like a lifeless stone image.'

After some time Manmath tried again and on this occasion he succeeded in meeting Sukumar. The latter was aghast to hear that Sri Aurobindo was in that dangerous locality and asked that they immediately go back to the vicinity of Chandpal Ghat and wait there – he would arrange to send Nagen with the tickets etc. to them. Subsequent events have been vividly described by Nagen in his memoirs: 'By the time I arrived back at the mess with the two trunks, evening had advanced. I had asked the coolie to wait at the Ghat. Once again I rushed towards Sukumar-da's house. He was waiting for me in the outer room. I told him that I had removed the luggage from the ship's cabin. But before I could give him any other news he ordered me take the two trunks and the tickets back to the pier immediately. He said that Amar-babu had taken Aurobindo and Bijoy Nag there by carriage and they were waiting for me. I told him about the arrangements I had made for the medical examination and getting the health certificate. When I asked him for the necessary money he went in at once, got the money and gave it to me.

'Once again I took the two trunks from the mess and loaded them on a horse-carriage; taking the tickets along with me I rushed back to Chandpal Ghat. There I saw Aurobindo's carriage waiting by the roadside. Our coolie was sitting nearby. When he saw me he at once ran up and said, "Your babus have come. I've already told them of our arrangement. It's late. If you waste any more

time, the doctor sahib won't carry out the examination – he will
have gone to sleep.''...

'I sent my carriage away. The coolie put the two trunks on the
roof of Aurobindo's carriage with some other things.... I climbed
in and sat beside Amar-da. Aurobindo and Bijoy Nag were sitting
behind us. The coolie got up and sat next to the coachman. I don't
remember the name of the street on which the doctor's house was
situated but I recollect that it was in the European quarter on the
other side of Chowringhee.

'When we reached the doctor's residence, all four of us waited
on the verandah. The coolie called the servant and came to terms
with him. Before the doctor called in Aurobindo and Bijoy Nag, I
gave them their tickets and told them the names and addresses
under which they had been purchased. I recall that I gave the
money for the doctor's fees to Aurobindo but do not remember
the exact amount – perhaps thirty-two rupees.

'We had to stand and wait on the verandah for almost half-an-
hour before the doctor called Aurobindo and Bijoy Nag inside.
During this period the coolie did something amusing that we all
enjoyed a great deal. He came and whispered in my ear, "That
babu of yours – is he frightened? I guess he has never been near an
Englishman before. Tell him the doctor sahib is a good man, he
doesn't have to be afraid!'' The coolie had noticed the three of us
chatting off and on but, noticing that Aurobindo remained
completely silent and absorbed, he had reached his own conclusions! And, in a wink, he was before Aurobindo whispering to
him softly: "Babu, why are you afraid? The sahib is a very good
man, you don't have to be afraid.'' And as he spoke, he took hold
of Aurobindo's arms and shook them as if to make him alert. The
three of us silently enjoyed the whole episode, exchanging amused
glances and laughing to ourselves. Aurobindo too smiled gently.
The scene comes alive in my mind like a film even today.

'Hardly a moment later, the servant came and told us, "*Sahib
salaam diya*'' (the master bids you enter). Aurobindo and Bijoy
Nag were led into the doctor's room by the servant. They came out
ten or fifteen minutes later with certificates. I heard from Bijoy
Nag that after a moment or two of conversation the sahib had
realised that Aurobindo had been educated in England. When the
doctor asked about this, Aurobindo merely said, "Yes.''

'We climbed back into the carriage greatly relieved. It again sped towards Chandpal Ghat. We could not see the slightest trace of anxiety on Aurobindo's face. Later, we were to talk about this among ourselves and Amar-da rightly said: "The one for whom we were anxious was altogether calm like someone absorbed in the trance of samadhi." That Aurobindo was a man beyond anxiety or fear, that he was *abhi* [fearless] I had heard, but before this meeting I had not had the good fortune of seeing it for myself.

'It was almost eleven at night when the carriage reached Chandpal Ghat. After putting the luggage on the coolie's head the four of us boarded the *Dupleix* and entered the reserved cabin. The coolie arranged the luggage and then left. Bijoy Nag made Aurobindo's bed. Amar-da and I stood facing Aurobindo near the door. Amar-da took some currency notes from his shirt-pocket and gave them to Aurobindo saying that they were from Michhri-babu (Zamindar of Uttarpara). He accepted the notes without a word. Then Amar-da lowered his head, and touching his forehead with folded hands made *namaskar* to Aurobindo. I laid my forehead on Aurobindo's feet as an expression of my reverence, and in the touch of that divine body, I felt fulfilled.'

Early next morning, April 1, the *Dupleix* steamed out of Calcutta carrying Sri Aurobindo into the safety of the open seas and, four days later, on April 4, 1910, he reached Pondicherry where he was beyond the writ of British authority. His departure also marked the end of his physical association with his native province, for he left the shores of Bengal never to return.

How mysteriously does the Divine move in protecting those who surrender themselves to Him! Late in the afternoon of March 31, Sri Aurobindo's safety seemed to be in great jeopardy, for the carefully prepared plans for his getaway seemed to be wrecked. And yet, as we look back and reconstruct those distant events, it becomes clear that the delay in the two passengers boarding the ship actually proved a blessing in disguise. Had Sri Aurobindo reached the ship in time to be examined by the doctor, he would have faced much greater danger. It seems that those who made the plans so carefully had overlooked the fact that a Calcutta police-man was detailed, as a matter of routine, to be present at medical examinations. Sri Aurobindo could then have been easily recognised – with disastrous consequences. The records show that the police report for that evening merely stated that two ticket-holders with Bengali names did not turn up at the ship for the medical examination. It was not until April 4 that the police made further enquiries and learnt that two passengers had in fact embarked at the last moment and sailed away the next day. And because of the late hour at which Sri Aurobindo boarded the ship (it was about 11.00 p.m.) the police pickets had left so that there was no one to watch his arrival. In fact at every stage of the events which culminated in his final departure to Pondicherry one feels the presence of Sri Aurobindo's all-seeing Friend and Master controlling the events. And Sri Aurobindo's own comments on the *adesh* which he received are wonderfully revealing: 'As for Adesh, people speak of Adesh without making the necessary distinctions, but these distinctions have to be made. The Divine speaks to us in many ways and it is not always the imperative Adesh that comes. When it does it is clear and irresistible, the mind has to obey and there is no question possible, even if what comes is contrary to the preconceived ideas of the mental intelligence. It was such an Adesh that I had when I came away to Pondicherry.'

Even in this age of skepticism and materialism can one really deny that God exists, is near us, with us and leads us if only we are ready to surrender ourselves?

After Sri Aurobindo's departure to Pondicherry he ceased all public connection with politics for reasons I shall presently explain. Here I would like to pause briefly and sum up what Sri Aurobindo did for the nation during the four brief but tumultuous years (of which one was spent in jail). His first achievement was to awaken the nation from its torpor and slavish mentality under the British rule. His magnetic personality and his inspired writings in the *Bande Mataram* exercised a profound influence and I have already stressed that it was he who first demanded, in clear and explicit terms, that India must have complete political freedom. Next, he spiritualised politics, placing God at the head of the National movement as its leader, inspirer, force and strength. He saw the country, not as a political or geographical entity, but as the very body of the Divine Mother – this was the key to the inspiration he provided. Lastly, Sri Aurobindo developed the theory and practice of Passive Resistance as a means of giving a direction to the political struggle with the aim of achieving freedom. These ideas and programmes were imperfectly understood at that time but they influenced (sometimes unconsciously) subsequent political developments, such as the non-cooperation movement, with far-reaching results and eventual success.

Sri Aurobindo's sudden departure for Pondicherry and thereafter his complete severance with politics left a vacuum which was all the greater because of the powerful impact he had made earlier. The British did not believe that he had in fact withdrawn from politics but suspected that he was preparing for revolutionary action in secret. On the other hand those concerned with day-to-day politics deplored his retirement and thought that he was lost to India and the world, being interested only in his own spiritual salvation. So he was called a truant or an escapist. Even now there is insufficient understanding of what led to his decision. Yet Sri Aurobindo's own words in this connection leave little room for any misunderstanding. This is what he wrote in a letter to a disciple: 'I may also say that I did not leave politics because I felt I could do nothing more there; such an idea was very far from me. I came away because I did not want anything to interfere with my yoga and because I got a very distinct *adesh*. I have cut connections entirely with politics, but before I did so I knew from within that the work I had begun there was destined to be carried forward on lines I had foreseen by others and that the ultimate triumph of the movement I had initiated was sure without my personal action or presence. There was not the least motive of despair or sense of futility behind my withdrawal.'

There is another important consideration we should not overlook. Sri Aurobindo has stated that the very principle of his Yoga is 'not only to realise the Divine and attain to a complete spiritual consciousness, but also to take all life and all world activity into the scope of this spiritual consciousness and action and to base life on the Spirit and give it a spiritual meaning'. To say therefore that he had shunned the world is to misunderstand the nature and purpose of his Yoga. The vast range and significance of his spiritual force and action which he was now to radiate from Pondicherry – his 'Cave of Tapasya' – will unfold themselves more and more to us as we proceed further.

PART TWO

Sri Aurobindo as a student in England
c. 1884, age twelve

Sri Aurobindo as a Professor of English
in Baroda, 1906

Sri Aurobindo as an undertrial prisoner in
Alipur Jail, Calcutta, 1908-09

Sri Aurobindo in Pondicherry, c. 1918-20

Sri Aurobindo in Pondicherry, April 1950

Sri Aurobindo, Mahasamadhi (5 December 1950)

The Mother

The Darshan (April 1950)

Chapter IX

Pondicherry: Cave of Tapasya
1910–1914

SURESH Chakravarty, Sri Aurobindo's youthful emissary, stepped down at the Pondicherry railway station early in the morning of March 31, 1910. The long journey had been uneventful but he had done well in avoiding trouble on the way and the important task before him now was to establish contact with a group of revolutionaries who were bringing out a nationalist newspaper, *India*, from Pondicherry. This paper was originally published from Madras but had to shift to Pondicherry when its editor was jailed for sedition. You will recall that in January 1910 Sri Aurobindo had given an interview at Calcutta to one of its representatives and a link had then been formed with this South Indian group. Suresh was carrying a letter of introduction from Sri Aurobindo to Srinivasachari, a Tamil firebrand, who was the manager of the paper at Pondicherry.

Suresh succeeded in locating the small press which printed *India* and from there he was directed to Srinivasachari's residence. The latter was surprised to hear that a national leader of Sri Aurobindo's eminence had decided to come to Pondicherry, politically so isolated from the rest of India, but promised all assistance. Suresh explained that Sri Aurobindo would be arriving by steamer on April 4 and the first need was to fix a house for his stay. Srinivasachari gave his assurance that this would be done. However, two days passed and he did not seem at all concerned. After much prodding Suresh was at last shown a miserable garret in a house at the end of a blind alley in a particularly dirty part of the town. A more unsuitable place could hardly be found, but Suresh failed to persuade Srinivasachari to arrange for something better. Then, to add to his dismay, Suresh learnt that Srinivasachari and some of his friends were planning to give a rousing reception to Sri Aurobindo on his arrival with garlanding, speeches, etc. all in the best tradition. Suresh, despite his youth and inexperience, now fought back gallantly. With all the force at his command he pointed out that Sri Aurobindo was travelling incognito with the purpose of escaping the attention of the police and to give him a public reception would be to defeat his very purpose. When the plan for the reception was dropped, not without reluctance, Suresh breathed a sigh of relief.

At last the fourth of April arrived and the *Dupleix* reached Pondicherry at four in the afternoon. Because of the shallow water of the port, the ship had to anchor offshore. Srinivasachari, accompanied by Suresh, hired a boat and set off for the ship. As the boat neared, Suresh could see two figures on the deck and recognised them as Sri Aurobindo and Bijoy. You can well imagine how happy and relieved he must have felt. Soon he and Srinivasachari joined Sri Aurobindo in his cabin and, after a cup of tea, the four of them left the ship to be rowed back to the pier. Srinivasachari had arranged for a horse-carriage and left with Sri Aurobindo. With a guide to help him, Suresh followed with the luggage. Let me now quote from his memoirs: 'The house I was taken to by my Tamil guide was not the garret on that filthy blind-alley I had been shown the previous day. This was quite a big and respectable place on another street. Escorted by my guide, I went up to the third floor of this house and found the place neat, clean and uninhabited – just what was required. On entering a small room I saw Sri Aurobindo sitting in an easy-chair whilst Srinivasachari along with four or five others stood deferentially in front of him. All my doubts about the intelligence and ability of these people to find a suitable place for Aurobindo disappeared.... I found out from one of them – I don't remember who – that they had indeed at my request fixed up a house for Aurobindo, but they had some doubts whether I was a police spy or truly a messenger sent by Aurobindo. And so they had naturally withheld the information about the actual house from a possible police spy. They had decided to wait for the *Dupleix* to arrive on April 4, and if Aurobindo did not come by that ship then it would have been confirmed that I was indeed a police spy. In that case I would have been taught a lesson or two and packed off!'

When Srinivasachari heard that Sri Aurobindo was coming to Pondicherry he was both astonished and incredulous. These reactions are not surprising because Pondicherry then could lay claim to few favourable features. This is how Suresh describes his first impressions: 'I had heard of the beauty-loving French people and their remarkable capital of Paris,' he writes in his memoirs, 'but Pondicherry was a most ordinary town with very ordinary houses.' In his reminiscences, Nolini Kanta used even stronger words: 'The place was so quiet that we can hardly imagine now what it was really like. It was not quiet, it was dead; they used to call it a dead city... no wonder it was said, "Sri Aurobindo has chosen a cemetery for his sadhana."' And this cemetery, Nolini Kanta adds, 'had its full complement of ghouls'. These were the bands of ruffians – known locally as 'bandes' in French – who were in the pay of corrupt politicians and officials and terrorised the population, particularly during campaigns for political elections etc.

It would seem from these accounts that Pondicherry was hardly a propitious place in which to settle but, of course, Sri Aurobindo's decision to go there was not made after considering its merits or demerits; he simply obeyed the *adesh* he received and did so without the slightest question. This was the imperative inner reason which led him to Pondicherry. At first he did not perhaps intend to make a prolonged stay but as he advanced in his Yoga, Pondicherry grew to become the seat of his sadhana, the unshakable base for his *siddhi*, and he remained there for forty uninterrupted years. Initially he meant to find a place of shelter where he could continue his sadhana without interference by the British authorities but eventually, as Nolini Kanta says, 'It was he who gave shelter to Pondicherry within his own consciousness.' Let us remember, also, that appearances can be deceptive and to appraise Pondicherry only by its façade or recent past could well be misleading. In fact research has established that the origins of the city go back to antiquity and that at one time it was known as Vedapuri, a great centre of Vedic studies. According to tradition, Rishi Agastya came to the South to spread the Vedic lore and teach the Aryan discipline, and it was at Pondicherry that he founded a famous seat of Vedic learning; the great sage was known as the guardian spirit of the city. The parallelism here is striking. Sri Aurobindo also came from the North to the South and it was from Pondicherry that he was to give to the world a new interpretation of the Vedas, revealing their secret and showing that they carried the seeds of the spirituality of the future. Is this merely a coincidence or does it not serve to indicate that there are deep and occult forces which, unknown to us, operate behind the scenes to influence outward events and decisions?

The house to which Sri Aurobindo was taken from the ship belonged to Calve Shankara Chettiar, a well-to-do and prominent citizen of Pondicherry, who had generously made it available for Sri Aurobindo's stay. Years earlier Swami Vivekananda had also stayed here in the course of his tour of the South. It suited Sri Aurobindo's requirements admirably. He had a room on the top floor built on the rear portion of the house so that it could not be seen from the main road and escaped the attention of prying eyes. From the outset, Sri Aurobindo insisted on strict vigilance. Bijoy and Suresh were instructed to keep guard over the entrance and no visitors were allowed in without careful scrutiny. Indeed the two followers were so conscientious in carrying out their duties that for the first three months of their stay neither set foot outside the house.

There were good reasons for taking these precautions. The British had been thwarted in their efforts to seize Sri Aurobindo, but no one supposed that they would accept the situation lying down. The fact was that from about the middle of February 1910 the Government had lost track of Sri Aurobindo. There was much speculation about his whereabouts and, to add to the confusion, Sri Aurobindo himself had sent a little note from his hide-out at Chandernagore. It was published in the *Karmayogin* on March 26, 1910, just a few days before he left for Pondicherry and it read: 'We are greatly astonished to learn from the local Press that Sj. Aurobindo Ghose has disappeared from Calcutta and is now interviewing the Mahatmas in Tibet. We are ourselves unaware of this mysterious disappearance. As a matter of fact Sj. Aurobindo is in our midst, and if he is doing any astral business with Kuthumi or any of the other great Rishis, the fact is unknown to his other Koshas. Only as he requires perfect solitude and freedom from disturbance for his Sadhana for sometime his address is being kept a strict secret.'

Needless to say the Government were not amused to read this. At last they decided on taking legal action in order to force Sri Aurobindo's hands. You will remember that in July and December 1909 Sri Aurobindo had written two 'Open Letters' in the *Karmayogin*. After taking legal opinion, the Government came to the conclusion that the second letter, 'To My Countrymen', was seditious. In 1907 the charge against Sri Aurobindo in the *Bande Mataram* case had failed mainly because of the prosecution's inability to prove that Sri Aurobindo was actually the author of the seditious articles. On the present occasion the authorship was not in question as the open letters had been signed by Sri Aurobindo. So, confident of success, the Government launched a prosecution and on April 4, 1910, warrants of arrest were issued against Sri Aurobindo, writer of 'To My Countrymen' and Manmohan Ghosh, publisher and printer of the *Karmayogin*. Once again, it is a remarkable coincidence that the warrant against Sri Aurobindo should be issued on the very day he landed safely in Pondicherry, out of the clutches of British authority.

Sri Aurobindo came to know of the warrant later but meanwhile he insisted on vigilance because he knew the Government's intentions only too well. It is true that the Government of India had no authority over Pondicherry and could not arrest Sri Aurobindo there without the specific consent of the French Government. This was unlikely to be given as the Pondicherry Government jealously guarded their own authority and it was a point of honour for them to give protection to political refugees. However, the British were then a formidable power and they had a treaty of alliance with the French. Besides, the India Government had permission from the French to have their own contingent of CID men at Pondicherry and they spent money liberally in recruiting local spies to obtain information on the activities of the political absconders. Indeed it did not take the India Government long to find out that Sri Aurobindo was in Pondicherry. On April 9, a police detective at Madras, acting on information received from Pondicherry, reported to his superiors that the man they wanted seemed to have taken shelter in Pondicherry, having arrived by S.S. *Dupleix* and been received by Srinivasachari. It took a few more days to establish the identification and thereafter Sri Aurobindo and his companions came under the constant surveillance of the CID who would not again allow the 'most dangerous man in India' to slip away. Indeed it now became their endeavour to harass him as much as possible and the fact that a warrant had been issued against him meant that Sri Aurobindo could be arrested the minute he set foot on British territory.

There was another good reason for Bijoy and Suresh taking every care to see that Sri Aurobindo's privacy was not disturbed. His sadhana had entered upon a most intensive phase and Sri Aurobindo seldom left his own room, preferring to avoid visitors unless there were special reasons for meeting them. Apart from his two companions, only two other persons had more or less easy access to him. They were Srinivasachari and his close friend Subramania Bharati. The latter was then a young man of 28, not yet the most famous Tamil poet of his time, but already well known for his lyrics, impassioned patriotic poems and fearless criticism of the Government. As a result of his provocative writings he was forced to leave Madras and take refuge in Pondicherry where he was helping Srinivasachari to bring out *India*. Bharati, like so many sensitive young men of his generation, had been deeply influenced by the writings in the *Bande Mataram* and naturally the opportunity of meeting Sri Aurobindo in person was greatly welcome to him. From the beginning he was a regular visitor, usually coming after seven in the evening with Srinivasa-chari. Sri Aurobindo would then relax in their company and all sorts of subjects would be discussed. Stories and humorous anecdotes would be exchanged and the atmosphere was by no means serious all the time. Bharati listened avidly to Sri Aurobindo's comments and it is a great pity that he did not keep notes of these talks or leave behind a pen-picture of Sri Aurobindo at the time. With his great literary gifts, Bharati could have made them into a wonderful record for posterity.

During the early part of Sri Aurobindo's stay at Shankara Chettiar's house M. Paul Richard, a distinguished French intellectual visited him. Richard had come to Pondicherry to help a friend in his political campaign. Through Zir Naidu, a leading citizen of Pondicherry, Richard met Sri Aurobindo and they had wide-ranging discussions on two occasions. These meetings had a profound impact on Richard. Some years later when he went to Japan, he declared before an audience: 'The hour is coming of great things, of great events, and also of great men, the divine men of Asia. All my life I had sought for them across the world, for all my life I had felt they must exist somewhere in the world, that this world would die if they did not live. For they are its light, its heat, its life. It is in Asia that I found the greatest among them – the leader, the hero of tomorrow. He is a Hindu. His name is Aurobindo Ghose.'

An even deeper significance lay behind Richard's visit for he became the connecting link between his wife Mirra and Sri Aurobindo, paving the way for the former's arrival at Pondicherry four years later. In later years Mirra, referring to Richard's visit, said: 'In the year 1910 my husband came alone to Pondicherry where, under very interesting and peculiar circumstances he made the acquaintance of Sri Aurobindo. Since then we both strongly, wished to return to India – the country which I had always cherished as my true mother-country. And in 1914 this joy was granted to us.

'As soon as I saw Sri Aurobindo I recognised in him the well-known being whom I used to call Krishna.... And this is enough to explain why I am fully convinced that my place and my work are near him, in India.' Is it not marvellous that Mirra should have met Sri Aurobindo in the occult world long before she came to Pondicherry? Marvellous, yes, but not unbelievable, as I can give you another instance of how yogis who have access to the occult world can transcend space and time and foretell the future. The circumstances in this case were related by K.V. Rangaswamy Iyengar, a well-to-do zamindar who was a regular visitor at Shankara Chettiar's house and the facts were confirmed by Sri Aurobindo. Iyengar's family had been devoted to a famous South Indian Yogi, Nagai Japtha. At the time of his passing they were anxious to know whom they should follow in future for spiritual guidance. He had told them that a great Yogi would come to the South from the North and that Iyengar should seek his guidance. Asked how this Yogi could be recognised, the Guru had predicted that the *Uttara Yogi* would come to the South to seek protection so that he could continue practising his Yoga and that, secondly, he would be known by his 'three sayings.' Many years later, when Rangaswamy Iyengar met Sri Aurobindo at Shankara Chettiar's house he was amazed to recognise in him the *Uttara Yogi* mentioned by his Guru. About this Sri Aurobindo himself has written: 'The Yogi from the North (Uttara Yogi) was my own name given to me because of a prediction made long ago by a famous Tamil Yogi, that thirty years later (agreeing with my time of arrival) a Yogi from the North would come as a fugitive to the South and practise there an integral Yoga (Poorna Yoga), and this would be one sign of the approaching liberty of India. He gave three utterances as the mark by which this Yogi could be recognised and all these were found in the letters to my wife.'

At Shankara Chettiar's house Sri Aurobindo made some further experiments with automatic writing which he had tried out occasionally at Baroda and Calcutta. He did not use a planchette but generally just held a pen and, in his own words, 'a disembodied being wrote off what he wished, using my pen and hand.' In this fashion a whole book *Yogic Sadhan*, was written during evening seances at Chettiar's house. The book had nine chapters containing instructions and advice on yoga. Rangaswamy Iyengar was so impressed that he arranged for the publication of the book, bearing all the cost, and the name of the author was given as *Uttara Yogi*. However, Sri Aurobindo always said that he was not the author of *Yogic Sadhan* and disclaimed responsibility for its views. Although it ran into several editions Sri Aurobindo did not want it to remain in print and around 1927 it was withdrawn from circulation. Sri Aurobindo's final 'conclusion' about automatic writing was that 'though there are sometimes phenomena which point to the intervention of beings of another plane, not always or often of a high order, the mass of such writings comes from a dramatising element in the subconscient mind; sometimes a brilliant vein in the subliminal is struck and then predictions of the future and statements of things known in the present and past come up, but otherwise these writings have not a great value.' Note the detachment and objectivity with which these conclusions have been stated, like a scientist summing up the results of his investigations in a laboratory.

Sri Aurobindo tried out another experiment during this period. In the Alipore Jail he had gone on fast for ten days; he now carried the experiment further by fasting for twenty-three days at a stretch. Sri Aurobindo referred to this fast some years later when a disciple asked him whether it was possible to do completely without food. He said, 'When I fasted for about twenty-three days in Chettiar's house, I very nearly solved the problem. I could walk eight hours a day as usual. I continued my mental work and sadhana as usual and found that I was not in the least weak at the end of twenty-three days. But the flesh began to grow less and I did not find the clue to replacing the matter reduced in the body. Also, when I broke the fast, I did not observe the rule of people who undergo long fasts – beginning with a little food and so on. I began with the same quantity as I used to take before.' On another occasion he explained that such fasting was possible 'because one draws the energy from the vital plane instead of depending on physical substance'. Perhaps you have noted that even during the fast Sri Aurobindo 'could walk eight hours a day'. Indeed this habit of walking, which started at Baroda, grew with him and became a part of his Yoga. He rarely went out for his walk; it was his practice to walk for hours together in the house so much so that in one of his residences his feet rubbed away a part of the floor's surface, making a perceptible path from one end to the other. It was, he said, during these walks that he could bring down the highest Force.

Sri Aurobindo was living at Shankara Chettiar's house as his guest and obviously the arrangement could not continue indefinitely. In October 1910, he moved to a rented house on rue Suffren in the southern part of the town. It was a smaller house and belonged to one Sunder Chetty. Just before he changed residence, late in September, Saurin Bose (Mrinalini's cousin) came over from Calcutta to join Sri Aurobindo and in November Nolini Kanta Gupta arrived. There were now four young men around Sri Aurobindo: Bijoy, Suresh, Saurin and Nolini. The accommodation was barely sufficient for the five persons and from now on commenced a period of considerable financial hardship which continued over the next few years, sometimes assuming a very acute form.

In the meantime the news from Calcutta was far from favourable. In June 1910, the *Karmayogin* sedition case had come up for hearing before the Chief Presidency Magistrate. In the absence of Sri Aurobindo, the printer Manmohan Ghosh (no relation of Sri Aurobindo) was the main accused. The Magistrate found him guilty of the charge and sentenced him to six months' imprisonment.

However, in November there was a dramatic reversal of fortunes. When Nolini came, he brought the news that the appeal against the order of the Chief Presidency Magistrate had been heard by the High Court and that on November 7 it had delivered a most favourable judgement, setting aside the conviction of Manmohan Ghosh and ordering his release. As a result, the warrant against Sri Aurobindo stood withdrawn and his assets could no longer be seized. This was the Government's third attempt to incarcerate Sri Aurobindo and it had again failed. The High Court judgement completely vindicated Sri Aurobindo and it became clear that the bureaucracy had blundered in bringing the case against him. Also, the issue had earlier come up for debate in the House of Commons and the Government were then subjected to severe criticism. If Sri Aurobindo wished, he could now return to British India, for legally he was free to do so but, in fact, he had already taken the decision to remain in Pondicherry. On November 7, the very day on which the High Court gave its ruling, Sri Aurobindo had written a letter to the editor of *The Hindu*, the daily newspaper from Madras. In it he had announced publicly that 'I am and will remain in Pondicherry'; he also made his position clear by stating that he had come to Pondicherry 'in order to pursue my Yogic sadhana undisturbed by political action' and that he had 'retired for the time from political activity of any kind'.

In April 1911, after a stay of six months, Sri Aurobindo moved from Sunder Chetty's house to another house, belonging to one Raghava Chetty, on rue St. Louis. He was to stay here for the next two years. The house was slightly larger but living conditions were just as difficult. There was hardly any furniture, just a camp cot for Sri Aurobindo, a table and two chairs. Later a few chairs for visitors etc. were acquired. The young men cooked by turns and the food was spartan. One bath towel had to serve everybody, including Sri Aurobindo, and there were only two lamps in the house – one in Sri Aurobindo's room and another in the kitchen.

Despite these hardships, however, the young men soon had the measure of their surroundings. When they first came, they had assumed false names (except Suresh who had no police record) and locally they came to be known by these names. Thus Nolini's name was Manindranath Roy or Monsieur Roy to his friends and Bijoy continued to be Bankim Bhowmik, the passenger who came by the *Dupleix*. But, whatever their names, the young men soon won the esteem of the local people and also became very popular because of their prowess as footballers. Nolini, Suresh and Bijoy were all expert players, Nolini being particularly brilliant. They became members of a local club, the Cercle Sportif of Pondicherry; they soon formed a fine team and the boys of this club were the enlightened, nationalist element in the local population. In spite of Sri Aurobindo's statement in his letter to *The Hindu* that he had severed connections with politics, the Government of India had no intention of leaving him alone. They were obsessed with the idea that he was engaged in secret revolutionary action and no doubt they also smarted under the ignominy of successive 'defeats' Sri Aurobindo had inflicted on them. So the CID decided to strengthen their forces at Pondicherry and set up a permanent station there with a fairly large contingent of men to keep a watch over Sri Aurobindo and his companions as well as the other revolutionaries who had settled in Pondicherry. In his reminiscences Nolini Kanta gives an interesting account of their activities. He writes: 'They were of course plain-clothes men, for they had no right to wear uniform within French territory. They kept watch on our visitors and guests as well as ourselves. Soon they got into a habit of sitting on the pavement round the corner next to our house in groups of three or four. They chatted away the whole day and only now and again took down something in their notebooks. What kind of notes they took we found out later when, after India had become independent and the French had left, some of these notes could be secured from the police notes and confidential records. Strange records, these: the police reports were often based on pure fancy, and when they found it difficult to gather correct or precise information, they would just fabricate the news.'

However, the police and their nefarious agents did not stop at these mischievous, but relatively harmless fabrications. They thought of a far more sinister plan and entered into a conspiracy with a local politician, a rich businessman, a certain notorious character by the name of Nand Gopal Chetty, to kidnap Sri Aurobindo. The plan was to carry him out of the limits of French India and arrest him there on some trumped-up charge. Chetty had in his pay political *goondas* or 'bandes' to do such dirty work. News of the plan reached Sri Aurobindo through his young men who at once armed themselves with acid bottles etc. to 'welcome' the kidnappers. But none appeared on the scene. On the very day planned for the abduction, it was Nand Gopal Chetty himself who ran away from Pondicherry to Madras! He had come to know that a warrant of arrest had been issued against him by the Pondicherry Government and decided to beat an honourable retreat! The warrant was arranged by Chetty's political opponents – and a man like him had many enemies – who had been conspiring to get him arrested. So once again Providence intervened on behalf of Sri Aurobindo.

Some time after Sri Aurobindo moved into Raghava Chetty's house, Motilal Roy came over on a visit from Chandernagore but stayed in another house. He used to come and meet Sri Aurobindo regularly but, to avoid identification by the police, he never entered the house except by the back door and under cover of darkness. In his memoirs Roy has written about the acute financial difficulties which the household faced at the time and on his return to Chandernagore he arranged to send remittances from time to time. It was relatively safer to send money from Chandernagore. Remittances from British India were carefully noted by the CID and a sender could incur the wrath of the Government for aiding the revolutionaries.

Around July 1912 there was another conspiracy to implicate Sri Aurobindo in alleged revolutionary activities. The author of this plan was again another notorious character, a professional spy by the name of Mayuresan who worked hand in glove with the CID. By that time many Tamil revolutionaries had taken refuge in Pondicherry and a prominent figure among them was V.V.S. Aiyar who was close to Srinivasachari and also well known to Sri Aurobindo. Mayuresan got hold of some seditious pamphlets etc. and forged other documents such as letters and plans. He also produced some papers with the image of Kali and had some Bengali written on them to indicate that the *swadeshi* revolutionaries were involved with the Tamils in what appeared to be large-scale subversive activities. He then packed these in a tin which was dropped into the well at V.V.S. Aiyar's house. Having planted the 'evidence', Mayuresan now went to the French authorities and lodged an official complaint that the revolutionaries were engaged in carefully planned and extremely dangerous activities which would disturb peace and bring discredit to the French Government. He therefore asked that the houses of the revolutionaries be searched, particularly those of Aiyar and Sri Aurobindo. Unfortunately for Mayuresan, however, before the French police could take any action, the tin was discovered by Aiyar's maid-servant – she had gone to the well to draw water and the tin had come up with the bucket! She ran to her master with the find and when Aiyar saw the contents he at once consulted Srinivasachari and Bharati. The three of them then went to Sri Aurobindo who advised them to place the 'evidence' before the French authorities and explain the circumstances to them. Since Mayuresan's complaint had already been lodged, it was not difficult for the authorities to see through his game. However, in view of the official complaint, the formality of searching the houses had to be completed. The investigating Magistrate, or Juge d'Instruction as he was called, himself came to Sri Aurobindo's residence. Of course nothing incriminating was found and all that the Magistrate could discover was that the house contained hardly anything except books. And when he saw that some of the books in Sri Aurobindo's room were in Greek and Latin, he was overwhelmed with admiration and kept exclaiming: 'Il sait du latin, il sait du grec!' (He knows Latin, he knows Greek!) So the 'charmingly polite visit' came to a happy end. But the end for Mayuresan was not quite so happy. The revolutionaries filed a counter-complaint against him for perjury and for giving false information. As a result, a warrant of arrest was issued against him and, like Nand Gopal Chetty, he decided that it would be politic to run away from Pondicherry. He fled to the adjacent British town of Cuddalore and became, as Sri Aurobindo ironically said, a 'political refugee'!

A letter dated July 3, 1912 from Sri Aurobindo to Motilal Roy gives an indication of the financial position at the time. Sri Aurobindo wrote: '...I send enclosed a letter to our Marathi friend. If he can give you anything for me, please send it without the least delay. If not, I must ask you to procure for me by will-power or any other power in heaven or on earth Rs.50 at least as a loan.... The situation just now is that we have Rs.1.50 or so in hand. Srinivasa is also without money.... No doubt, God will provide, but He has contracted a bad habit of waiting till the last moment. I only hope He does not wish us to learn how to live on a minus quantity like Bharati.' The characteristic humour can hardly disguise the truly grim situation that prevailed.

It was probably during this period that the British put pressure on the French to deport the revolutionaries and the French seemed prepared to send them to Algeria or Indo-China, territories then under their control. Bharati and some other revolutionaries were excited at the prospect and came to Sri

Aurobindo for his views. Bharati said that the French seemed unwilling to shield them any longer in India and asked whether it would not be preferable in the circumstances to go elsewhere. Sri Aurobindo sat quietly for a few minutes and then said, 'Mr. Bharati, I am not going to budge an inch from Pondicherry. I know nothing will happen to me. As for yourself, you can do what you like.' Eventually the proposal was not pursued by the French any further.

Because of continuing financial pressure, Sri Aurobindo changed his residence in April 1913 to a house on Mission Street. The rent here was only Rs.15 per month and the facilities were minimal. Sri Aurobindo lived in this house for six months, but soon after the monetary situation improved and in October the household shifted to 41, rue François Martin, a much larger, well-lighted and ventilated house where Sri Aurobindo stayed until 1922. This was later known as the Guest House. Although the accommodation was more spacious, their way of life did not change. The young men continued sleeping on mats, there were not even shelves for the books which lay stacked on the floor, and even the canvas of Sri Aurobindo's camp-cot was torn so that he used to lie down carefully on the untorn side and sleep. However, life on the whole became easier, for around this time C.R. Das sent Rs.1000 for Sri Aurobindo's translation into English verse of Das's Bengali poems, *Sagar Sangeet.*

Towards the end of the year 1913 an incident occurred which showed how implacable the British were in their determination to spy on Sri Aurobindo's activities. A cousin of Bijoy Nag, Nagen had fallen ill at Calcutta and, with Sri Aurobindo's approval, he came over to Pondicherry to recuperate. Nagen brought with him a servant, Biren Roy, who was really more of a companion and was also a very good cook. Actually, Nagen's coming had eased the financial position for he was a man of means and he readily helped in securing the house on rue François Martin. By the time the shift was made Biren had proved himself a very useful member of the household.

One day, after the change of residence, the inmates saw that Biren had his head completely shaved. Suresh, who was not without his youthful whims, immediately decided to follow suit. Biren tried to dissuade him but Suresh was insistent and he too had his head shaved.

A day or two later, the inmates had gathered round Sri Aurobindo in the evening when there was a dramatic scene. Biren suddenly stood up and declared in highly emotional tones that he wanted to make a confession. The atmosphere at the time was rather gay and at first no one took him seriously. But Biren started shouting that he was a spy in the pay of the CID, a secret he could no longer keep to himself. Even then the young men thought that this was some kind of a joke and they started laughing. This upset Biren all the more and rushing out of the room he came back with some currency notes – Rs.100 or so – in his hand. This was the money he had received from the CID, he cried out, a proof of his connections with them, for who else could give him so much money. Then, full of remorse, he fell at Sri Aurobindo's feet, begged for his forgiveness and offered the money to him.

Everyone had now fallen silent, stunned by the confession. Slowly the full story came out. Biren had indeed been recruited by the CID who had thus succeeded in planting a spy in Sri Aurobindo's own household. However, having come in contact with Sri Aurobindo and his companions, Biren realised his enormous mistake and he wanted to leave. But the CID insisted on replacing him by a substitute. Since there would be problems of identification, with so many persons staying in the house, Biren was asked to shave off the hair on his head so that the substitute could identify him easily. When Suresh decided to cut his hair also, Biren was extremely upset for he thought that the young men had seen through his game and that the day of reckoning had come. Consumed by fear and remorse, he decided to make the confession. Nagen, Bijoy and the others were of course furious with Biren but Sri Aurobindo said nothing. He even allowed the culprit to stay on but Biren felt most uncomfortable and left after a few days. So ended yet another conspiracy against Sri Aurobindo, a failure like the preceding ones. One is reminded of a Hindi couplet which, in translation, runs: 'Even if there are as many enemies as there are stars in the sky, if the Grace of God is on a man, not a hair of his head can be touched.'

Sri Aurobindo's one-pointed sadhana was in no way disturbed by the vicissitudes of his early years in Pondicherry. Ever since his arrival, he was wholly absorbed in his Yoga. He was not following any of the traditional lines but, obeying the dictates of his inner Guide, was opening out a new path and sailing the uncharted seas of the Spirit. A letter dated July 1911, written a little more than a year after his arrival gives an indication of this new path and the magnitude of his spiritual endeavour. He writes: '...I am developing the necessary powers for bringing down the spiritual on the material plane, and I am now able to put myself into men and change them, removing the darkness and bringing light, giving them a new heart and a new mind.... What I perceive most clearly is that the principal object of my Yoga is to remove absolutely and entirely every possible source of error and ineffectiveness, of error in order that the Truth I shall eventually show to men may be perfect, and of ineffectiveness in order that the work of changing the world, so far as I have to assist it, may be entirely victorious and irresistible. It is for this reason that I have been going through so long a discipline and that the more brilliant and mighty results of Yoga have been so long withheld. I have been kept busy laying down the foundation, a work severe and painful. It is only now that the edifice is beginning to rise upon the sure and perfect foundation that has been laid.' Mark that he is writing here of 'the work of changing the world', not of attaining personal salvation or of escaping into a Paradise removed from this unhappy world which, according to his critics, were the reasons for his retiring to Pondicherry. And listen to these magnificent lines he was to write later in *Savitri*:

> Escape, however high, redeems not life,
> Life that is left behind on a fallen earth.
> Escape cannot uplift the abandoned race
> Or bring to it victory and the reign of God.
> A greater power must come, a larger light.

In another letter written in August 1912 to Motilal Roy, Sri Aurobindo was even more specific about his realisations and objectives. He wrote:

'15th August is usually a turning point or a notable day for me personally either in Sadhana or life, – indirectly only for others. This time it has been very important for me. My subjective Sadhana may be said to have received its final seal and something like its consummation by a prolonged realisation and dwelling in Parabrahman for many hours. Since then, egoism is dead for all in me except the Annamaya Atma, – the physical self which awaits one farther realisation before it is entirely liberated from occasional visitings or external touches of the old separated existence.

'My future Sadhana is for life, practical knowledge and Shakti, not the essential knowledge of Shakti in itself which I have got already, – but knowledge and Shakti established in the same physical self and directed to my work in life. I am now getting a clearer idea of that work and I may as well impart something of that idea to you; since you look to me as the centre, you should know what is likely to radiate out of that centre.

'1. To re-explain the Sanatana Dharma to the human intellect in all its parts, from a new standpoint... Sri Krishna has shown me the true meaning of the Vedas.... He has also shown me the meaning of all in the Upanishads that is not understood either by Indians or Europeans. I have therefore to re-explain the whole Vedanta and Veda in such a way that it will be seen how all religion arises out of it and is one everywhere. In this way it will be proved that India is the centre of the religious life of the world and its destined saviour through the Sanatana Dharma.

'2. On the basis of Vedic knowledge, to establish a Yogic Sadhana which will not only liberate the soul, but prepare a perfect humanity and help in the restoration of the Satya Yuga. That work has to begin now but it will not be complete till the end of the Kali.

'3. India being the centre, to work for her restoration to her proper place in the world; but this restoration must be effected as a part of the above work and by means of Yoga applied to human means and instruments, not otherwise.

'4. A perfect humanity being intended, society will have to be remodelled so as to be fit to contain that perfection.'

So completely absorbing was Sri Aurobindo's sadhana that he rarely moved out of his residence. But this did not mean that he cut himself off from all contacts in Pondicherry. Indeed many notable persons in the town were very much aware of his presence and held him in high esteem. How deep and genuine was this regard could be seen from an incident which occurred when the British once again tried one of their tricks. There was a law in French India known as the Alien's Act which required that a foreigner who wished to stay for any length of time in Pondicherry had to produce a 'good conduct' certificate from a high Government official of the place from which he came. Or else, he had to produce a similar certificate signed by five men of standing in Pondicherry. In this context Nolini Kanta writes in his memoirs: 'I need hardly say that the first alternative was for us quite impossible and wholly out of the question. We chose the second line and the five noble men who affixed their signatures were these: (1) Rassendren, (2) De Zir Naidu, (3) Le Beau, (4) Shankar Chettiar (in whose house Sri Aurobindo had put up on arrival), and (5) Murugesh Chettiar. The names of these five should be engraved in letters of gold. They had shown on that occasion truly remarkable courage and magnanimity. It was on the strength of their signatures that we could continue to stay here without too much trouble.'

In the evenings Sri Aurobindo usually spent some time with a few close associates who called on him. Amongst them Subramania Bharati and Srinivasachari continued to be regular visitors. Sri Aurobindo's young companions would join these gatherings and sometimes a special subject would be discussed and studied over a series of meetings. Let me give you another fine description from the pen of Nolini Kanta: 'At one time, one of our main subjects of study was the Veda. This went on for several months, for about an hour every evening, at the Guest House. Sri Aurobindo came and took his seat at the table and we sat around. Subramania Bharati and myself were the two who showed the keenest interest. Sri Aurobindo would take up a hymn from the Rigveda, read it aloud once, explain the meaning of every line and phrase and finally give a full translation. I used to take notes. There are many words in the Rigveda whose derivation is doubtful and open to differences of opinion. In such cases, Sri Aurobindo used to say that the particular meaning he gave was only provisional and that the matter could be finally decided only after considering it in all the contexts in which the word occurred. His own method of interpreting the Rigveda was this: on reading the text he found its true meaning by direct intuitive vision through an inner concentration in the first instance, and then he would give it an external verification in the light of reason, making the necessary changes accordingly.' During this period it was also Nolini's good fortune to learn Greek and Latin and some Italian from Sri Aurobindo. His method of teaching was unusual and Nolini writes: 'He never asked me to begin the study of a new language with primary readers or children's books. He started at once with one of the classics, that is, a standard work in the language. He used to say that the education of children must begin with books written for children, but for adults, for those, that is, who had already had some education the reading material must be adapted to their age and mental development. That is why, when I took up Greek, I began straightaway with Euripides' *Medea*, and my second book was Sophocles' *Antigone*.... I began my Latin with Virgil's *Aeneid*, and Italian with Dante.... I should tell you what one gains by this method, at least what has been my personal experience. One feels as if one took a plunge into the inmost core of the language, into that secret heart where it is vibrant with life, with the quintessence of beauty, the fulness of strength.'

By the end of the year 1913, arrangements were fairly well established in the new residence and in February 1914 Suresh, Saurin and Nolini left for Bengal on a visit, leaving Bijoy in charge of the household. However, by September they were back in Pondicherry. On August 4 war had broken out in Europe. In this grave situation the Government of India assumed special powers to deal with political dissidents and Nolini and Saurin were likely to be arrested if they stayed on in Bengal.

The fateful year 1914 was to see the beginning of immense and cataclysmic changes sweeping over the world. It was also to be a year of change for Sri Aurobindo. His period of 'silent Yoga' was coming to an end. On August 15, the new journal *Arya* commenced publication and through its pages Sri Aurobindo gave to the world a part of the Knowledge gained from his Yoga. There was another event of momentous significance: on March 29 Mirra Richard arrived in Pondicherry for the first time and met Sri Aurobindo. This was the beginning of a spiritual collaboration of utmost consequence.

Chapter X

Coming of the Mother – "Arya" Review – World War I

1914–1920

WITH the Mother's arrival, there was a mighty mingling of two vast streams of sadhana which Sri Aurobindo and the Mother were pursuing individually. These now joined forever to mark the beginning of a new era of spiritual creation: 'An hour began, the matrix of new Time.' To help you understand this, a brief sketch giving the background of the Mother's life is perhaps necessary.

Like Sri Aurobindo's, the Mother's life was not lived on the surface for men to see and yet its outward events are of absorbing interest, for they do not follow a stereotyped pattern. But they can hardly be compressed and described in a few words, and here I can give you just an outline; I hope, however, it will serve as an inducement to you to know more about her.

Mirra Alfassa was born on February 21, 1878, in Paris, the second child of Maurice Alfassa, a Turkish banker from Adrianople and his Egyptian wife, Mathilde Ismaloun of Cairo. Both the families were of aristocratic descent. Their first child, Matteo, was born in 1876. A year later the Alfassas moved to Paris to settle there permanently, in due course becoming French nationals.

Mirra grew up in Paris where she spent the first part of her life. Even at the age of five, she had deep and unusual spiritual experiences and knew that she would not live an ordinary life but had a great mission to fulfil. In preparation for this mission, she consciously pursued a life of inner development at an age when other children spend their time playing.

Perhaps because of her preoccupation with the inner life she was late in learning to read and write but when she did begin the progress was rapid and her thirst for learning, understanding and knowing things was endless. Also, she had the keenest powers of observation. 'From my earliest childhood I have not stopped observing things,' she once said, and it was not only the objective world that she observed, sometimes identifying her consciousness with what she saw but also her own inner movements. Indeed from her very childhood she practised yoga, although she did not then give it that name.

Yet she was not indifferent to external pursuits. At the age of eight she started playing tennis, a game she continued to play until late in life. She always tried to play against the best players she could find. 'I never won,' she said, 'but I learnt much.'

Mirra had a natural disposition for occult experiences and by the time she was twelve she was practising occultism as a conscious discipline. She would go out of her body and enter strange worlds which were not always pleasant. But she was fearless. Talking about her experiences of this time she later said, 'But I must say I had no fear – I feared nothing. One goes out of one's body, one is tied by something resembling an almost imperceptible thread – if the thread is cut, it is all over.'

As the years passed Mirra became increasingly aware of the mission she was to fulfil on earth. In later years she was once asked when and how she became conscious of this mission and in reply she stated:

'For the knowledge of the mission, it is difficult to say when it came to me. It is as though I was born with it, and following the growth of the mind and the brain, the precision and completeness of this consciousness grew also.

'Between eleven and thirteen a series of psychic and spiritual experiences revealed to me not only the existence of God but man's possibility of uniting with Him, of realising Him integrally in consciousness and action, of manifesting Him upon earth in a life divine. This, along with a practical discipline for its fulfilment, was given to me during my body's sleep by several teachers, some of whom I met afterwards on the physical plane.

'Later on, as the interior and exterior development proceeded, the spiritual and psychic relation with one of these beings became more and more clear and frequent; and although I knew little of the Indian philosophies and religions at that time, I was led to call him Krishna, and henceforth I was aware that it was with him (whom I knew I should meet on earth one day) that the divine work was to be done.' And you already know that as soon as she first saw Sri Aurobindo in Pondicherry she recognised him as the being she used to call Krishna.

In her sixteenth year Mirra joined a studio to learn drawing and painting, completing her training at the well-known Academie Julian. She became so accomplished a painter that her works were exhibited in the French Salon along with those of the great artists of the time – Renoir, Cézanne and others. She also developed a deep and abiding interest in music and played the organ with an inspired touch.

In October 1897 Mirra married Henri Morisset, a disciple of the painter Gustave Moreau. Their son, André, was born the following year in August. The next few years of her life were spent in a creative environment of highly gifted artists. It was an experience that enabled her to understand their ways of life and also gave her many insights into the creative process. She also read widely, knew thoroughly the museums, castles, and historical buildings of France and Italy and, generally, her culture acquired a breadth, refinement and diversity, altogether rare.

Through all these experiences her preoccupation with the inner life continued, but she never made the usual distinction between the spiritual and the mundane, separating the two into watertight compartments. 'All life is Yoga', Sri Aurobindo has said, and truly it was so with Mirra. She had by this time come across translations of some Indian scriptures and she was introduced to the Gita by a visiting Indian. It was a poor translation but Mirra was able intuitively to enter into its spirit. However, it was not on books or scriptures that she relied nor did she have a preceptor to guide her: she relied entirely on her own experiences which infallibly led her along the destined path.

During this period Mirra became the nucleus around whom a small group of spiritual seekers in Paris started meeting. The group was named *Idea*. Papers were read at the meetings and sometimes Mirra would discourse on her experiences. The members of this group were intensely interested in the future of humanity and in finding harmonious solutions to the immense problems that besieged it, but rejected the panaceas offered by the established religions. Indeed Mirra never had any belief in the conventional Gods of the religions, the One-God-on-high; it was the God *within* that she always sought. One of the members of her study group in Paris was Madame Alexandra David-Neel who became well known as a Tibetologist. In later years she used these words in speaking of the Mother of those early days:

'We spent marvellous evenings together with friends, believing in a great future. At times we went to the Bois de Boulogne gardens, and watched the grasshopper-like early aeroplanes take off.

'I remember her elegance, her accomplishments, her intellect endowed with mystical tendencies.

'In spite of her great love and sweetness, in spite even of her inherent ease of making herself forgotten after achieving some noble deed, she couldn't manage to hide very well the tremendous force she bore within herself.'

Around 1906 Mirra came in contact with Max Théon, a Polish exile who was a great adept in occultism. His wife Alma was also highly gifted spiritually. They lived in Tlemcen, a small town in Algeria on the border of the Sahara desert. This meeting with Théon strengthened Mirra's resolve to study occultism in greater depth and for the next two years she spent much of her time in Tlemcen. She went through a great many experiences there, a few of which she recounted in later years. These may be found among her writings. They reveal the existence of realms of consciousness, beings and forces which we ordinarily cannot even conceive of, and also how it is possible to bring such forces under control. However, the Mother always said that occult knowledge without spiritual discipline is a dangerous instrument, both for the one who uses it and for others, but so sure and strong were her own spiritual foundations that no harm could touch her during these years of study and experiment. I should also emphasise here that for the Mother occultism was a means of service to the Divine, never a mere play with invisible forces or a performance of so-called miracles.

By 1908 Mirra had settled down in Paris once again. In the same year her marriage with Henri Morisset was dissolved and she moved to a new apartment at 41, rue de Levis. It was the beginning of another period when she met many students and seekers, groups and individuals, who were in search of spiritual truth and helped them to face their problems of life and work. In 1910 she married Paul Richard, a brilliant intellectual who was deeply interested in both Western and Eastern spirituality. When Richard returned to Paris after his visit to India and she first heard of Sri Aurobindo from him, she felt irresistibly drawn to that country and felt that her destiny was linked with it.

Sometime during 1912 the Mother started keeping a kind of diary in which she wrote down her aspirations and experiences. From these diaries which continued over several years, a small selection was later translated into English, some of it by Sri Aurobindo himself, and published under the title *Prayers and Meditations*. As spiritual literature, it is an incomparable treasure but the Mother set such small store by her writings that the bulk of the diaries was destroyed by her.

In 1912 Mirra was closely associated with a group of seekers named *Cosmique*. It was a small group of about twelve persons who met once a week. A subject was given in advance and short papers on it were then read at the meeting. At the first gathering Mirra read out her paper. The subject was: What is the aim to be achieved, the work to be done, the means of achievement?

Here is the answer given by the Mother:

'The general aim to be achieved is the advent of a progressive universal harmony.

'In regard to the earth, the means of achieving this aim is the realisation of human unity by the awakening in all and the manifestation by all of the inner Divinity, who is one.

'In other words: to create unity by establishing the kingdom of God which is in all.

'Hence, the most useful work to be done is:

'1) For everyone individually the becoming aware in oneself of the divine Presence and one's identification with it.

'2) The individualisation of states of being which have so far never been conscious in man and, consequently, the putting the earth into touch with one of several sources of universal force which are yet sealed to it.

'3) To speak to the world, under a new form adapted to the present state of its mentality, the eternal word.

'4) Collectively, to found the ideal society in a place suited to the

flowering of the new race, that of "the Sons of God".'
Remember that the Mother had not yet met Sri Aurobindo nor
had she read any of his writings. Yet this programme was almost
on identical lines with the one being worked out by Sri Aurobindo
at that time in Pondicherry.

With the year 1914 the opportunity came at last for Mirra to visit
India. Paul Richard had decided to stand for a seat in the French
Parliament from Pondicherry, which was a separate constituency.
He had been in correspondence with Sri Aurobindo and doubtless
the prospect of meeting him again was also an important consideration for Richard – certainly it was paramount with Mirra.
On March 6, 1914, Paul and Mirra Richard boarded the Japanese ship *Kaga Maru*. They left the boat at Colombo and, crossing
over to the mainland, arrived by train at Pondicherry in the early
hours of March 29. At 3.30 in the afternoon the Mother met Sri
Aurobindo for the first time. Richard and Mirra came to his new
residence at 41, rue François Martin. Sri Aurobindo was expecting
them and received them at the top of the stairs. Mirra instantly
recognised him as the 'Krishna' she had met so often in her visions.

On the next day, March 30, Mirra wrote in her diary: 'It matters
little that there are thousands of beings plunged in the densest
ignorance, He whom we saw yesterday is on earth; his presence is
enough to prove that a day will come when darkness shall be
transformed into light, and Thy reign shall be indeed established
upon earth....'

Years later, Barin, Sri Aurobindo's younger brother, asked
him: 'The Mother has written in her *Prayers* what she felt after she
saw you. But what was your feeling when you saw the Mother?' Sri
Aurobindo paused for a moment and told him: 'That was the first
time I knew that perfect surrender down to the last physical cell
was humanly possible; it was when the Mother came and bowed
down that I saw that perfect surrender in action.'

The spiritual significance of this meeting between Sri Aurobindo
and the Mother is immeasurable and will reveal itself progressively
through developments and manifestations in time. Superficially, it
represented a meeting of the East and West but Sri Aurobindo
himself was an embodiment of the East-West synthesis and the
Mother a living expression of the finest flower of European culture
along with spiritual affiliations with the East. No, the significance
runs deeper. Once we asked Sri Aurobindo, 'The Mother's coming

must have greatly helped you in your work and in your sadhana, did it not?' He replied, 'Of course. All my realisations – Nirvana and others – would have remained theoretical as it were, so far as the outer world was concerned. It is the Mother who showed the way to a practical form. Without her, no organised manifestation would have been possible.' And this is echoed in the Mother's profound words: 'Without him I exist not, without me he is unmanifest.'

Richard and Mirra took up residence at 3, rue Dupleix, not far from Sri Aurobindo's house on rue François Martin. Mirra used to call on Sri Aurobindo daily in the afternoon between 4 and 4.30, bringing with her some sweets she had prepared for him. Later they would be joined by Richard who was busy with his election campaign. Once a week, on Sundays, Sri Aurobindo went across to the Richards in the evening for dinner. Nolini and the other young men would also come after their game of football. There was much to plan and discuss and sometimes the talks went on till late at night.

Sri Aurobindo gave his support to Richard in electioneering but knew that 'humanly speaking' he could hardly win. He had entered the field too late but, even otherwise, Pondicherry politics was so corrupt that an honest candidate had little chance of succeeding. So, not unexpectedly, the election went against Richard. In a letter to Motilal Roy at the time, Sri Aurobindo wrote that Richard's votes in some centres were got rid of 'by the simple process of reading Paul Bluysen (Richard's opponent) wherever Paul Richard was printed'! However, despite his defeat, Richard had succeeded in enlisting the support of many young men. And he decided to stay on in Pondicherry to work amongst them, and in order to give a positive shape to this work, he started a society called *l'Idée Nouvelle* (The New Idea) in which Sri Aurobindo and the Mother were both actively involved. For the Mother it was indeed a continuation of the work she had been doing in Paris. The object of the society was, in Sri Aurobindo's words, 'to group in a common intellectual life and fraternity of sentiment those who accept the spiritual tendency and idea it represents and who aspire to realise it in their own individual and social action'. All sectarian and political questions were consider- ed foreign to its idea and activities and the society had two rules only for its members: first, to devote some time every day for meditation and self-culture and, secondly, to use or create daily at least one opportunity of being helpful to others. The society had its headquarters at Pondicherry, with a reading room and a library, and had a branch at Karikal.

But Paul Richard's biggest contribution, by far, was to suggest and help in bringing out the *Arya*. Reminiscing about this, Sri Aurobindo recounted: 'Richard came and said, "Let us have a synthesis of knowledge." I said "All right. Let us synthesise."'

Even today, when Sri Aurobindo's writings are becoming more and more widely known throughout the world, not many know about the *Arya* and the stupendous achievement it represents. It was a monthly philosophical journal which came out uninterruptedly from August 1914 to January 1921 and it was in this review that Sri Aurobindo, within a period of six and a half years, published all his major works, with the exception of his epic poem *Savitri*. In June 1914, when the decision to bring out the journal was taken, Sri Aurobindo wrote to Motilal Roy: 'In this Review my new theory of the Veda will appear as also translation and explanation of the Upanishads, a series of essays giving my system of Yoga and a book of Vedantic philosophy (not Shankara's but Vedic Vedanta) giving the Upanishadic foundations of my theory of the ideal life towards which humanity must move. You will see so far as my share is concerned, it will be the intellectual side of my work for the world.'

The first issue of the *Arya* came out on August 15, 1914, Sri Aurobindo's forty-second birthday. On the cover page the names of Sri Aurobindo Ghose and Paul and Mirra Richard appeared as Editors. Simultaneously, a French publication called 'Revue de la Grande Synthèse', consisting mainly of translations from the *Arya* was brought out. In explaining the object of the *Arya* Sri Aurobindo wrote that it will be, firstly, 'a systematic study of the highest problems of existence' and, secondly, 'the formation of a vast synthesis of knowledge, harmonising the diverse religious traditions of humanity, occidental as well as oriental.' He wrote further that 'its object is to feel out for the thought of the future, to help in shaping its foundations and to link it to the best and most vital thought of the past.' Sri Aurobindo also explained the significance of the word 'Arya'. 'The word in its original use,' he wrote, 'expressed not a difference of race, but a difference of culture. For the Aryan peoples are those who had accepted a particular type of self-culture, of inward and outward practice, of ideality and aspiration.... Intrinsically, in its most fundamental sense, Arya means an effort or an uprising and overcoming. The Aryan is he who strives and overcomes all outside him and within him that stands opposed to the human advance. Self-conquest is the first law of his nature.' The word was later corrupted by Hitler who made it a symbol of racial superiority and arrogance, the Aryan representing the blond Nordic race who would be masters of the world. It was as if Sri Aurobindo anticipated the danger of such corruption and therefore wished to record the true meaning of the word.

The first issue of the *Arya* set its tone and character. It contained the opening chapter of *The Life Divine*, which still occupies the pride of place among Sri Aurobindo's prose writings, as well as the first instalments of two other major sequences, *The Secret of the Veda* and *The Synthesis of Yoga*. Paul Richard also contributed with *The Eternal Wisdom*, a selection of the finest thoughts of the world's seers, saints and savants, and the *Wherefore of the Worlds* in which he commenced a fundamental enquiry into the origin and evolution of the worlds. Mirra helped with the translations from the *Arya* for the French *Revue*, took care of the accounts, maintained in her own hand the subscribers' list (there were about 200 subscribers to begin with), saw the two reviews through the press.

In the meantime, the war was spreading in Europe affecting the lives of millions and it inevitably threw its shadow on Richard and Mirra for it soon became clear that they would have to return to France. Richard was in the Reserve list of the Army and Mirra had her own calls to duty. So, in spite of their deep commitment to the *Arya* and *l'Idée Nouvelle*, the decision to go had to be taken. In her diary entries we find expressions of Mirra's anguish but also of her unquestioning surrender to the Lord in trustfulness and readiness to accept whatever might come to her.

After a modest celebration of her birthday on February 21, 1915, Mirra and Richard left for France the next day and, with their departure, the entire burden of bringing out the *Arya* fell on Sri Aurobindo. However, although the French *Revue* had to be discontinued, there was no interruption in the publication of even a single issue of the *Arya*.

Let us now take a look at the major sequences that Sri

Aurobindo wrote for the *Arya*. These were:

> *The Life Divine* – August 1914 to January 1919
> *The Synthesis of Yoga* – August 1914 to January 1921
> *The Secret of the Veda* – August 1914 to July 1916 .
> *Isha Upanishad* – August 1914 to May 1915
> *Kena Upanishad* – June 1915 to July 1916
> *The Ideal of Human Unity* – September 1915 to July 1918
> *Essays on the Gita* (First Series) – August 1916 to July 1918
> *The Psychology of Social Development* – August 1916 to July 1918 (later published as *The Human Cycle*)
> *The Future Poetry* – December 1917 to July 1920
> *Essays on the Gita* (Second Series) – August 1918 to July 1920
> *The Renaissance in India* – August 1918 to November 1918
> *Is India Civilised?* – December 1918 to February 1919
> *A Rationalistic Critic of Indian Culture* – February 1919 to July 1919
> *A Defence of Indian Culture* – August 1919 to January 1921

The last three series were later published under one title as *The Foundations of Indian Culture*.

In 1918, at the end of the fourth year of the *Arya*, Sri Aurobindo reviewed all that had appeared in the journal up to then in order to bring out the underlying plan which was partly obscured by the fact that some of the sequences appeared simultaneously and all were written serially. I will give you some extracts from this review so that you may better appreciate his integral vision.

'We start from the idea', he wrote, 'that humanity is moving to a great change of its life which will even lead to a new life of the race, – in all countries where men think, there is now in various forms that idea and that hope, – and our aim has been to search for the spiritual, religious and other truth which can enlighten and guide the race in this movement and endeavour.... All philosophy is concerned with the relations between two things, the fundamental truth of existence and the forms in which existence presents itself to our experience. The deepest experience shows that the fundamental truth is truth of the Spirit; the other is the truth of life, truth of form and shaping force and living idea and action. Here the West and East have followed divergent lines. The West has laid most emphasis on truth of life and for a time came to stake

its whole existence upon truth of life alone, to deny the existence
of Spirit or to relegate it to the domain of the unknown and
unknowable; from that exaggeration it is now beginning to return.
The East has laid most emphasis on truth of the Spirit and for a
time came, at least in India, to stake its whole existence upon that
truth alone, to neglect the possibilities of life or to limit it to a
narrow development or a fixed status; the East too is beginning to
return from this exaggeration. The West is reawaking to the truth
of the Spirit and the spiritual possibilities of life, the East is
reawaking to the truth of Life and tends towards a new application
to it of its spiritual knowledge.'

In Sri Aurobindo's view, the antinomy created between the East
and the West is an unreal one. He writes: 'Spirit being the
fundamental truth of existence, life can be only its manifestation;
Spirit must be not only the origin of life but its basis, its pervading
reality and its highest and total result. But the forms of life as they
appear to us are at once its disguises and its instruments of self-
manifestation. Man has to grow in knowledge till they cease to be
disguises and grow in spiritual power and quality till they become
in him its perfect instruments. To grow into the fullness of the
divine is the true law of human life and to shape his earthly
existence into its image is the meaning of his evolution. This is the
fundamental tenet of the philosophy of the *Arya*.'

Sri Aurobindo then explained how this central truth has been
considered from different aspects in his writings. 'This truth', he
wrote, 'had to be worked out first of all from the metaphysical
point of view; for in philosophy metaphysical truth is the nucleus
of the rest, it is the statement of the last and most general truths on
which all the others depend or in which they are gathered up.
Therefore we gave the first place to the "Life Divine".' To quote
him further: 'It was necessary to show that these truths were not
inconsistent with the old Vedantic truths, therefore we included
explanations from this point of view of the Veda, two of the
Upanishads and the Gita. But the Veda has been obscured by the
ritualists and scholiasts. Therefore we showed in a series of
articles, initially only as yet, the way of writing of the Vedic
mystics, their system of symbols and the truths they figure. Among
the Upanishads we took the Isha and the Kena; to be full we
should have added the Taittiriya, but it is a long one and for it we
had no space. The Gita we are treating as a powerful application of

truth of spirit to the largest and most difficult part of the truth of life, to action, and a way by which action can lead us to birth into the Spirit and can be harmonised with the spiritual life. Truth of philosophy is of a merely theoretical value unless it can be lived, and we have therefore tried in the "Synthesis of Yoga" to arrive at a synthetical view of the principles and methods of the various lines of spiritual self-discipline and the way in which they can lead to an integral divine life in the human existence. But this is an individual self-development, and therefore it was necessary to show too how our ideal can work out in the social life of mankind. In the "Psychology of Social Development" we have indicated how these truths affect the evolution of human society. In the "Ideal of Human Unity" we have taken the present trend of mankind towards a closer unification and tried to appreciate its tendencies and show what is wanting to them in order that real human unity may be achieved.'

I hope you can now see more clearly the wonderful mosaic that constitutes Sri Aurobindo's writings. I would also ask you to read the series of essays he wrote during the closing years of the *Arya* on the foundations and main-springs of Indian culture and civilisation. Through these interpretations he has given us a vision of India which needs to be shared by his countrymen, if India is to help and play her rightful role in the advancement of humanity. Let me give you just one quotation from *The Renaissance in India*: 'Spirituality is indeed the master-key of the Indian mind; the sense of the infinite is native to it. India saw from the beginning, – and, even in her ages of reason and her age of increasing ignorance, she never lost hold of the insight, – that life cannot be rightly seen in the sole light, cannot be perfectly lived in the sole power of its externalities. She was alive to the greatness of material laws and forces; she had a keen eye for the importance of the physical sciences; she knew how to organise the arts of ordinary life. But she saw that the physical does not get its full sense until it stands in right relation to the supra-physical; she saw that the complexity of the universe could not be explained in the present terms of man or seen by his superficial sight, that there were other powers behind, other powers within man himself of which he is normally unaware, that he is conscious only of a small part of himself, that the invisible always surrounds the visible, the supra-sensible the sensible, even as infinity always surrounds the finite. She saw too that man has the power of exceeding himself, of becoming himself more entirely and profoundly than he is, – truths which have only recently begun to be seen in Europe and seem even now too great for its common intelligence. She saw the myriad gods beyond man, God beyond the gods, and beyond God his own ineffable eternity; she saw that there were ranges of life beyond our life, ranges of mind beyond our present mind and above these she saw the splendours of the spirit. Then with that calm audacity of her intuition which knew no fear or littleness and shrank from no act whether of spiritual or intellectual, ethical or vital courage, she declared that there was none of these things which man could not attain if he trained his will and knowledge; he could conquer these ranges of mind, become the spirit, become a god, become one with God, become the ineffable Brahman. And with the logical practicality and sense of science and organised method which distinguished her mentality, she set forth immediately to find out the way. Hence from long ages of this insight and practice there was ingrained in her her spirituality, her powerful psychic tendency, her great yearning to grapple with the infinite and possess it, her ineradicable religious sense, her idealism, her Yoga, the constant turn of her art and her philosophy.' It has been a long quotation but, carried away by its magnificence, I did not know where to stop!

How is it possible, you may now ask, for one person, howsoever gifted, to write on such diverse subjects, all concerned with the highest reaches of human vision and thought, month after month without the inspiration flagging, without any discontinuity in the arguments and in a language which one of his English disciples Arjava (J.A. Chadwick) aptly described as 'global', a word which was new when Arjava used it? Moreover, Sri Aurobindo did not write in book form, at leisure and with the advantage of making changes and corrections as necessary, but in serial instalments as if he were writing a novel for a popular magazine! I, for one, do not know of any comparable instance in the sphere of journalism, literature or philosophy. There is another question: How could Sri Aurobindo, who never made a deep study of philosophy write a philosophical masterpiece such as *The Life Divine*? Sri Aurobindo himself has given us the answer to these questions. Nothing that he wrote, he explained, was the result of strenuous individual effort or intense intellectual activity, but was the outcome of the Yogic

Force he had developed through his sadhana. Once, in a mood of doubt and scepticism, I wrote to him that too much is made of Yoga-Force and that for any real and remarkable achievement the main issue is to be born with the capacity and then to have the determination to develop it; and I concluded, '...then Force or no Force, one will have the result. Well?' In his characteristic way, he parried my question with one of his own: 'How was it that I who was unable to understand and follow a metaphysical argument and whom a page of Kant or Hegel or Hume or even Berkeley left either dazed and uncomprehending and fatigued or totally uninterested because I could not fathom or follow, suddenly began writing pages of the stuff as soon as I started the *Arya* and am now reputed to be a great philosopher? Kindly reflect a little and don't talk facile nonsense. Even if a thing can be done in a moment or a few days by Yoga which would ordinarily take a long, "assiduous, sincere and earnest" cultivation, that would of itself show the power of the Yoga force. But here a faculty that did not exist appears quickly and spontaneously or impotence changes into highest potency or an obstructed talent changes with equal rapidity into fluent and facile sovereignty. If you deny that evidence, no evidence will convince you, because you are determined to think otherwise.' Also, in a letter to another disciple, Dilip Kumar Roy, he wrote: 'And philosophy! Let me tell you in confidence that I never, never, never was a philosopher – although I have written philosophy which is another story altogether. I knew precious little about philosophy before I did the Yoga and came to Pondicherry – I was a poet and a politician, not a philosopher. How I managed to do it and why? First, because Richard proposed to me to co-operate in a philosophical review – and as my theory was that a Yogi ought to be able to turn his hand to anything, I could not very well refuse; and then he had to go to the war and left me in the lurch with sixty-four pages a month of philosophy all to write by my lonely self. Secondly, because I had only to write down in the terms of the intellect all that I had observed and come to know in practising Yoga daily and the philosophy was there automatically. But that is not being a philosopher!' And the Mother has explained: 'Sri Aurobindo began writing the *Arya* in 1914. It was neither a mental knowledge nor even a mental creation which he transcribed: he silenced his mind and sat at the typewriter, and from above, from the higher planes, all that had to be written came down, all ready, and he had only to move his fingers on the typewriter and it was transcribed. It was in this state of mental silence which allows the knowledge – and even the expression – from above to pass through that he wrote the whole *Arya*, with its sixty-four printed pages a month. This is why, besides, he could do it, for if it had been a mental work of construction it would have been quite impossible.'

One more word about the *Arya*. When it was being planned, Richard reckoned on getting as a start 200 subscribers in France for the French edition and Sri Aurobindo wrote to Motilal Roy about the English edition: 'Let us try 250 subscribers to start with, with the ideal of having 800 to 1000 in the first year. If these subscribers can be got before the Review starts, we shall have a sound financial foundation to start with. The question is, can they be got?' In the event, even 250 subscribers could not be secured from Bengal and, after the Richards' departure, the French *Revue* had to be discontinued. However, although the original targets could not be achieved, the *Arya* did not incur any financial loss but, in fact, earned a surplus which was a considerable help towards meeting Sri Aurobindo's establishment expenses. Sri Aurobindo did not expect a large public response and wrote in a letter that 'the *Arya* presents a new philosophy and a new method of Yoga and everything that is new takes time to get a hearing.' There were, however, a few deserving readers who recognised the great truths which were being formulated in the *Arya* and which, with the passage of time, have gained increasing acceptance. Moreover, the fact that the *Arya* appeared at a time when the First World War broke out cannot be dismissed as a mere coincidence. In the subtle world of thought the *Arya* represented a counterpoise of spiritual knowledge and harmony against the vibrations let loose by the senseless destruction of the war.

With France and England fighting side by side as allies in Europe, relations between the Governments of French and British India improved with the result that the latter made renewed efforts to deal with the *swadeshi* revolutionaries in Pondicherry who were a thorn in their flesh. There was an attempt at this time to get the French Government to agree to extradite Sri Aurobindo. The Mother was then still in Pondicherry. Years afterwards we heard from her that, on coming to know of this threat, she wrote to her brother who was then a highly placed Government official in Paris (later he became the Governor of one of the French colonies) to see if he could intervene in any way. He succeeded in preventing Sri Aurobindo's dossier from reaching the higher authorities and eventually the matter went no further. However, throughout the war years, the Government of India kept a specially close watch on the *swadeshis*. You will remember that, shortly after the outbreak of the war, Nolini, Saurin and Suresh had returned to Pondicherry from their visit to Bengal. Bijoy now wished to pay a brief visit also, although Sri Aurobindo warned him of the danger; and it turned out that, immediately he crossed the border, he was arrested and kept in jail for the duration of the war.

After arriving in France the Mother became seriously ill, her physical body reflecting the sufferings of the war-ravaged world. In April she left Paris and went to Lunel in the South of France where she spent the next six months. Her diary entries reveal that even during her illness she continued through her sadhana to exert an occult influence on men and events. There was some correspondence between Sri Aurobindo and her during this period, touching generally upon their common spiritual quest and goal and the inevitable struggles and vicissitudes of their unprecedented Yoga. Perhaps it was at this time that there was a suggestion that their Yoga could be better pursued in a place less exposed to British interference than Pondicherry, for in a letter to the Mother on May 6, 1915, Sri Aurobindo wrote: 'The whole earth is now under one law and answers to the same vibrations and I am sceptical of finding any place where the clash of the struggle will not pursue us. In any case, an effective retirement does not seem to be my destiny. I must remain in touch with the world until I have either mastered adverse circumstances or succumbed or carried on the struggle between the spiritual and the physical so far as I am destined to carry it on....

'One needs to have a calm heart, a settled will, entire self-abnegation and the eyes constantly fixed on the beyond to live undiscouraged in times like these which are truly a period of universal decomposition. For myself, I follow the Voice.... The result is not mine and hardly at all now even the labour.' He wrote again on May 20: 'Heaven we have possessed, but not the earth; but the fullness of the Yoga is to make, in the formula of the Veda, "Heaven and Earth equal and one."'' These words are almost repeated in the Mother's diary entry on July 31: 'The heavens are definitely conquered, and nothing and nobody could have the power of wresting them from me. But the conquest of the earth has still to be made; it is being carried on in the very heart of the turmoil....' On July 28, in another letter, Sri Aurobindo drew a parallel between the spiritual conflict within and the world conflict without: 'Everything internal is ripe or ripening, but there is a sort of locked struggle in which neither side can make a very appreciable advance (somewhat like the trench warfare in Europe), the spiritual force insisting against the resistance of the physical world, that resistance disputing every inch and making more or less effective counter-attacks.... And if there were not the strength and Ananda within, it would be harassing and disgusting work; but the eye of knowledge looks beyond and sees that it is only a protracted episode.'

The strength and Ananda did indeed prevail, for an aura of great peace and serenity surrounded Sri Aurobindo. Outwardly his life followed a more or less regular routine. He read the *Hindu* in the mornings, met special visitors before lunch, wrote out his articles for the *Arya* whenever he could find time, received his close associates (Bharati, Srinivasachari and a few others) in the evenings and had dinner usually at nine. To the small group of young men who lived with him he was friend, comrade, teacher, chief and Guru but his own relations with those around him in the house were more of a friend and companion than of a Guru. In his behaviour with others he treated everyone as his equal including the servants. Once, it appears, his foot touched a young associate accidentally; immediately he sat up and said: 'I beg your pardon.' On another occasion, a press compositor had brought the proofs late because of his drunkenness and when he was being berated by one of the inmates, Sri Aurobindo came out and said: 'You have no right to interfere in his personal life. It is meaningless to give him advice. He has perfect freedom to drink. What you should tell him is to observe the terms of his service and bring the proofs regularly.'

During this period the number of visitors started increasing. A Danish painter, Johannes Hohlenberg, came and did a portrait of Sri Aurobindo. In 1916 Khaserao Jadhav, Sri Aurobindo's old friend from Baroda came specially to meet him. A young but regular visitor was K. Amudan, whom Sri Aurobindo later gave the name 'Amrita', who first came in 1913 when he was still a school boy. Soon he was an ardent disciple and by 1919 he had become a member of the household. When the Ashram came into being, he was to render invaluable service and was one of the Mother's most devoted workers. Another notable visitor was T.V. Kapali Sastry, an extraordinary scholar and initiate. He used to read the *Arya* from cover to cover as soon as an issue came out and, having fallen under its spell, he called on Sri Aurobindo in 1917. An adept in various branches of learning – Veda, Tantra, Ayurveda, Astrology etc., he was also a philosopher and poet. Later he joined the Ashram and was a widely respected figure.

Let me now return to France briefly. In November 1915 the Mother left Lunel and came back to her home in Paris. But this was to be a short stay. Richard was given an important assignment in Japan. Mirra decided to accompany him and on March 13, 1916, they set sail from London. The Mother was to stay in Japan for the next four years. Here it will not be possible to dwell on her many experiences in Japan and I shall merely mention that they were a perfect preparation for the great work ahead of her on her return to India. Incidentally, when Rabindranath Tagore visited Japan in 1919 he met the Mother. The poet was so impressed by her personality that he requested her to come to Shantiniketan and take charge of the institution. The Mother could not accept the offer as she knew that although her field of work was India, the centre was not Shantiniketan.

Before leaving for Japan, the Mother had sent some funds for the purpose of starting the 'Aryan Stores' to be managed by Saurin. It was expected to provide a modest income for Sri Aurobindo's household. The store was opened in September 1916 and Sri Aurobindo was present at the opening ceremony. However, this business experiment did not make much headway and the financial position continued to be difficult throughout these years. On a deeper plane, these difficulties were only an outer sign of the larger struggle against anti-divine forces which had ranged themselves to thwart Sri Aurobindo's sadhana. In Sri Aurobindo's view, money is a universal force which in its origin and true action belongs to the Divine but it has been usurped for the purposes of ego and held by hostile influences and perverted to their purpose. In the course of a conversation Sri Aurobindo once said: 'As the money-power today is in the hands of the hostile forces, naturally, we have to fight them. Whenever they see that you are trying to oust them they will try to thwart your efforts. You have to bring a higher power than these and put them down.'

After reaching Japan it seems that the Mother wrote to Sri Aurobindo mentioning some difficulties or recoils in a particular phase of her sadhana. In a long reply dated June 26, 1916, Sri Aurobindo explained the special difficulties which were inherent in their Yoga and in the course of this letter he wrote: 'The ordinary Yoga is usually concentrated on a single aim and therefore less exposed to such recoils; ours is so complex and many-sided and embraces such large aims that we cannot expect any smooth progress until we near the completion of an effort, – especially as all the hostile forces in the spiritual world are in a constant state of opposition and besiege our gains; for the complete victory of a single one of us would mean a general downfall among them. In fact by our own unaided effort we could not hope to succeed. It is only in proportion as we come into a more and more universal communion with the Highest that we can hope to overcome with any finality.... The final goal is far but the progress made in the face of so constant and massive an opposition is the guarantee of its being gained in the end. But the time is in other hands than ours. Therefore I have put impatience and dissatisfaction far away from me.'

In 1917 Sri Aurobindo had another visitor, B. Shiva Rao, who was the secretary of Mrs. Annie Besant, leader of the Home Rule Movement at that time. More than fifty years later, Shiva Rao wrote an interesting account of that meeting: 'The Home Rule Movement was at that time quickly gathering support and vitality mainly as a result of the war-time internments. Some of us who were on the staff of *New India* went out on trips to build up a campaign of organisation. One of these trips took me to Pondicherry where Sri Aurobindo had made his home after leaving Bengal in 1910. Even in those early days there was an atmosphere of great peace and serenity about him which left on me a deep, enduring impression. He spoke softly, almost in whispers. He thought Mrs. Besant was absolutely right in preaching Home Rule for India, as well as in her unqualified support of the Allies in the First World War against Germany....'

In 1918, when it was apparent that the war was coming to an end, the British Government announced the Montagu-Chelmsford Reforms which were meant as a step towards self-government for

India. In response to a request from Mrs. Besant for an opinion on the reform proposals, Sri Aurobindo wrote a letter which was published in *New India* on August 10, 1918. He described the proposal as a 'cleverly constructed Chinese puzzle' and added that 'even a three days' examination has failed to discover in them one atom of real power given to these new legislatures.... On the other hand, new and most dangerous irresponsible powers are assumed by the Government. How, under the circumstances, is acceptance possible?' He concluded: 'The struggle cannot be avoided; it can only be evaded for the moment, and if you evade it now, you will have it tomorrow or the day after, with the danger of its taking a more virulent form.' The letter was not signed by Sri Aurobindo but appeared under the name, 'An Indian Nationalist'. As a rule, he refrained from making public pronouncements on the issues of the day. His Yoga had now assumed vast dimensions and he preferred to concentrate his Force on planes, occult or hidden from us, to bring about the changes he sought.

I shall give you an example of his pre-vision of events to come. In December 1918, Ambalal B. Purani (you may remember his name – he was an early disciple of Sri Aurobindo, who later became one of his personal attendants and also his biographer) came to Pondicherry for the first time. Sri Aurobindo knew about this young man through his elder brother Chhotalal, to whom Sri Aurobindo had given a revolutionary programme in 1908 at Baroda. Ambalal himself was an ardent nationalist and revolutionary but after reading the *Arya* he was also interested in sadhana and wrote to Sri Aurobindo. Sri Aurobindo gave Purani an interview which he has recounted fully in his biography of Sri Aurobindo. I shall give you extracts from it, for it is indeed a remarkable record.

After Purani had described his efforts at sadhana and the organisation their group had set up for revolutionary work, the dialogue was as follows:

Purani: Sadhana is all right, but it is difficult to concentrate on it so long as India is not free.

Sri Aurobindo: Perhaps it may not be necessary to resort to revolutionary activities to free India.

Purani: But without that how is the British government to go from India?

Sri Aurobindo: That is another question; but if India can be free without revolutionary activity, why should you execute the plan?

It is better to concentrate on yoga – spiritual practice.

Purani: But India is a land that has sadhana in its blood. When India is free, I believe thousands will devote themselves to yoga. But in the world today who will listen to the truth or spirituality of slaves?

Sri Aurobindo: India has already decided to win freedom and so there will certainly be found leaders and men to work for that goal. But all are not called to yoga. So, when you have the call, is it not better to concentrate upon it?...

Purani: But even supposing that I admit and agree to sadhana, that is, yoga, as being of greater importance and even intellectually understand that I should concentrate upon it, my difficulty is that I feel intensely that I must do something for the freedom of India. I have been unable to sleep soundly for the last two years and a half. I can remain quiet if I make a very strong effort. But the concentration of my whole being turns towards India's freedom. It is difficult for me to sleep till that is secured.

Sri Aurobindo remained silent for two or three minutes. It was a long pause. Then he said: 'Suppose an assurance is given to you that India will be free?'

'Who can give such an assurance?' I could feel the echo of doubt and challenge in my own question.

Again he remained silent for three or four minutes. Then he looked at me and added: 'Suppose I give you the assurance?'

I paused for a moment, considered the question within myself, and said: 'If you give the assurance, I can accept it.'

Sri Aurobindo: Then I give you the assurance that India will be free.

As the year 1918 was drawing to a close, the sad news of Mrinalini's death at Calcutta reached Sri Aurobindo. She had fallen a victim to the virulent influenza epidemic which ravaged the world after the war and died suddenly on December 17, 1918. We heard later that a framed photograph of Mrinalini in Sri Aurobindo's room fell down during a spell of rain and storm at this time.

Mrinalini had received permission from Sri Aurobindo to come to Pondicherry and was in fact making preparations to do so when death intervened. During her years of separation from Sri Aurobindo she had borne her trials with great fortitude and steadfast devotion to her husband.

There is a letter dated February 19, 1919 from Sri Aurobindo to his father-in-law, Bhupal Chandra Bose, which allows us a glimpse of the depths of Sri Aurobindo's feelings. It reads:

'My dear father-in-law,
      I have not written to you with regard to this fatal event in both our lives; words are useless in face of the feelings it has caused, if even they can ever express our deepest emotions. God has seen good to lay upon me the one sorrow that could still touch me to the centre. He knows better than ourselves what is best for each of us, and now that the first sense of the irreparable has passed, I can bow with submission to His divine purpose. The physical tie between us is, as you say, severed; but the tie of affection subsists for me. Where I have once loved, I do not cease from loving. Besides she who was the cause of it, still is near though not visible to our physical vision.
      'It is needless to say much about the matters of which you write in your letter. I approve of everything that you propose. Whatever Mrinalini would have desired, should be done, and I have no doubt that this is what she would have approved of. I consent to the *chudis* [bangles] being kept by her mother; but I should be glad if you would send me two or three of her books, especially if there are any in which her name is written. I have only of her her letters and a photograph.'

With the end of the war on November 11, 1918, the world started slowly getting back to normalcy and the way became clear for the Mother to leave Japan. However, it was not until 1920 that she was able to complete her preparations for returning to India, and with her 'second coming' our story enters a new phase.

Chapter XI

Beginnings of the Ashram
1920–1926

ON APRIL 24, 1920, the Mother arrived at Pondicherry for the second time, never to depart again. Paul Richard came with her and she was also accompanied by Miss Dorothy Hodgson, an English lady who had known the Mother in France and had stayed with her in Japan. Dorothy later came to be known as 'Datta', shortened from Vasavadatta, the name given to her by Sri Aurobindo.

After staying for a few days in hotels, they moved to a rented house at 1, rue St. Martin, called the 'Bayoud House'. Sri Aurobindo was still residing at the 'Guest House' in rue François Martin. Soon the relationship resumed the pattern of 1914-1915. Richard and Mirra would visit Sri Aurobindo in the afternoon or evening, while Sri Aurobindo with his young men called on the Richards every Sunday evening and dined with them. When she came to the Guest House, the Mother generally kept herself in the background and it was only gradually that the inmates of the house began to feel her presence. The significance of the day of her arrival, April 24, and its importance in the Yoga of Sri Aurobindo came to be increasingly recognised with the passage of time, culminating in the anniversary becoming one of the four days in the year when Sri Aurobindo and the Mother gave *darshan* to their disciples in the Ashram and to visitors who received permission to come for the occasion.

With the end of the war, the British Government pushed through the Montagu-Chelmsford Reforms by passing the

Government of India Act of 1919. The effect of these reforms was, as Sri Aurobindo had pointed out earlier, to leave real authority exactly where it had always been – in the hands of the British. Nevertheless there were many Indians who were in favour of giving the Act a trial. Indeed there was a dearth of political leadership at the time and the atmosphere was one of angry frustration and humiliation arising out of the Jallianwalla Bagh massacres on April 13, 1919. Mrs. Besant's Home Rule Movement had run its course and Gandhiji had yet to assume his position of influence and command over the Congress. Tilak had returned to India after his long incarceration in Mandalay and was trying to revive and reorganise the Nationalist forces. Late in 1919 he asked one of his lieutenants, Joseph Baptista, to request Sri Aurobindo to accept the editorship of a paper they proposed to bring out as the authentic voice of the Nationalists. In a long reply dated January 5, 1920, Sri Aurobindo wrote: 'Your offer is a tempting one, but I regret I cannot answer it in the affirmative.' Giving the reasons for declining the offer, Sri Aurobindo first expressed the doubt whether the Government would leave him free to pursue his activities and he thought that, in the event of a clash, he would be interned or imprisoned. 'Now I have too much work on my hands,' he wrote, 'to waste my time in the leisured ease of an involuntary Government guest.' He then went on to explain: 'But even if I were assured of an entirely free action and movement, I should yet not go just now. I came to Pondicherry in order to have freedom and tranquillity for a fixed object having nothing to do with present politics – in which I have taken no direct part since my coming here, though what I could do for the country in my own way I have constantly done, – and until it is accomplished, it is not possible for me to resume any kind of public activity. But if I were in British India, I should be obliged to plunge at once into action of different kinds. Pondicherry is my place of retreat, my cave of tapasya, not of the ascetic kind, but of a brand of my own invention. I must finish that, I must be internally armed and equipped for my work before I leave it.'

A few months afterwards there was another attempt, more determined this time to bring Sri Aurobindo back into the political arena. On August 1, 1920, Lokmanya Tilak died. In response to a request from Bepin Chandra Pal, Sri Aurobindo wrote a magnificent tribute to the departed leader. It was published in Pal's paper, the *Independent*, and commenced with the memorable words: 'A great mind, a great will, a great and pre-eminent leader of men has passed away from the field of his achievement and labour.' The Nationalists now looked to Sri Aurobindo to assume their leadership and Dr. B.S. Munje, an influential congressman who had the support of the Nationalists and who was known to Sri Aurobindo earlier, came to Pondicherry to meet him. In the course of long talks Munje pressed Sri Aurobindo to accept the Presidentship of the ensuing Nagpur session of the Congress in December 1920, but Sri Aurobindo declined. Later Dr. Munje sent a telegram to renew the offer and Sri Aurobindo replied on August 30, 1920, giving a number of reasons for not being able to accept it. 'The central reason however,' he wrote, 'is this that I am no longer first and foremost a politician, but have definitely commenced another kind of work with a spiritual basis, a work of spiritual, social, cultural and economic reconstruction of an almost revolutionary kind, and am even making or at least supervising a sort of practical or laboratory experiment in that sense which needs all the attention and energy that I can have to spare.'

There is another remarkable letter from Sri Aurobindo during this period, which throws light on his views of yoga, politics and similar subjects. He wrote in April 1920 to his younger brother, Barin, who had been released earlier from the Andamans, following an amnesty to political prisoners by the Government after the armistice. On returning to Bengal, Barin visited a number of spiritual centres, including the Prabartak Sangha of Motilal Roy at Chandernagore, but apparently he was disappointed with what he saw. So he wrote to Sri Aurobindo seeking initiation into his yoga, but also expressing his doubts as to his fitness. Sri Aurobindo's long reply was written in Bengali, a rare feat for him, and I shall give you some extracts from it in translation. He wrote: 'First, about your yoga. You want to give me the charge of your yoga, and I am willing to accept it. But this means giving it to Him who, openly or secretly, is moving me and you by His divine power. And you should know that the inevitable result of this will be that you will have to follow the path of yoga which He has given me, the path I call the Integral Yoga.... What I started with, what Lele gave me, what I did in jail – all that was a searching for the path, a circling around looking here and there, touching, taking up, handling, testing this and that of all the partial yogas, getting a more or less complete experience of one and then going off in pursuit of another. Afterwards, when I came to Pondicherry, this unsteady condition ceased. The indwelling Guru of the world indicated my path to me completely, its full theory, the ten limbs of the body of yoga. These ten years he has been making me develop it in experience; it is not yet finished.... For the present, I can only say that its fundamental principle is to make a synthesis and unity of integral knowledge, integral works and integral devotion, and, raising this above the mental level to the supramental level of the Vijnana, to give it a complete perfection. The defect of the old yoga was that, knowing the mind and reason and knowing the Spirit, it remained satisfied with spiritual experience in the mind. But the mind can grasp only the fragmentary; it cannot completely seize the infinite, the undivided. The mind's way to seize it is through the trance of samadhi, the liberation of moksha, the extinction of nirvana and so forth. It has no other way. Someone here or there may indeed obtain this featureless liberation, but what is the gain? The Spirit, the Self, the Divine is always there. What the Divine wants is for man to embody Him here, in the individual and the collectivity – to realise God in life. The old system of yoga could not synthesise or unify the Spirit and life; it dismissed the world as an illusion or a transient play of God. The result has been a diminution of the power of life and the decline of India....'

Sri Aurobindo then explained the significance and need for a *deva-sangha* or spiritual community: 'Then about Motilal's group. What Motilal got from me is the first foundation, the base of my yoga – surrender, equality etc. He has been working on these things; the work is not complete.... I have spoken in my English writings of the "divine life". Nolini has translated this as *deva-jivana*. The community of those who want the *deva-jivana* is the *deva-sangha*. Motilal has begun an attempt to establish this kind of community in seed-form in Chandernagore and to spread it across the country. If the shadow of the fragile ego falls upon this sort of endeavour, the community turns into a sect.... You will perhaps ask, "What is the need of a *sangha*? Let me be free and fill every vessel. Let all become one, let all take place within that vast unity." All this is true, but it is only one side of the truth. Our business is not with the formless Spirit only; we have to direct life as well. Without shape and form, life has no effective movement.

It is the formless that has taken form, and that assumption of name and form is not a caprice of Maya. The positive necessity of form has brought about the assumption of form. We do not want to exclude any of the world's activities. Politics, trade, social organisation, poetry, art, literature – all will remain. But all will be given a new life, a new form.'

Regarding Barin's fitness for yoga and his comment that he was 'not a god, only some much-hammered and tempéred steel', Sri Aurobindo wrote: 'No one is a god, but each man has a god within him. To manifest him is the aim of the divine life. That everyone can do. I admit that certain individuals have greater or lesser capacities. I do not, however, accept as accurate your description of yourself but whatever the capacity, if once God places his finger upon the man and his spirit awakes, greater or lesser and all the rest make little difference. The difficulties may be more, it may take more time, what is manifested may not be the same – but even this is not certain. The god within takes no account of all these difficulties and deficiencies; he forces his way out. Were there few defects in my mind and heart and life and body? Few difficulties? Did it not take time? Did God hammer at me sparingly – day after day, moment after moment? Whether I have become a god or something else I do not know. But I have become or am becoming something – whatever God desires. This is sufficient. And it is the same with everybody; not by our own strength but by God's strength is this yoga done.'

On the subject of politics Sri Aurobindo's words are revealing: 'Why did I leave politics? Because our politics is not the genuine Indian thing; it is a European import, an imitation of European ways. But it too was needed. You and I also engaged in politics of the European style. If we had not done so, the country would not have risen, and we would not have had the experience or obtained a full development. Even now there is a need for it, not so much in Bengal as in the other provinces of India. But now the time has come to take hold of the substance instead of extending the shadow. We have to awaken the true soul of India and to do everything in accordance with it. For the last ten years I have been silently pouring my influence into this foreign political vessel, and there has been some result. I can continue to do so wherever necessary. But if I took up that work openly again, associating with the political leaders and working with them, it would be

supporting an alien law of being and a false political life.'
Towards the end of the letter Sri Aurobindo warned against
some failings and weaknesses in the Bengali temperament, viz.
a proneness to 'emotional excitement' and a tendency to 'pick up
things the easy way – knowledge without thought, results without
labour, spiritual perfection after an easy discipline'. Then comes a
magnificent passage: 'I do not wish to make emotional excitement,
feeling and mental enthusiasm the base any longer. I want to make
a vast and strong equality the foundation of my yoga; in all the
activities of the being, which will be based on that equality I want a
complete, firm and unshakable power; over that ocean of power I
want the radiation of the sun of Knowledge and in that luminous
vastness, an established ecstasy of infinite love and bliss and
oneness. I do not want tens of thousands of disciples. It will be
enough if I can get as instruments of God one hundred complete
men free from petty egoism. I have no confidence in guruhood of
the usual type. I do not want to be a guru. What I want is for
someone, awakened by my touch or by that of another, to
manifest from within his sleeping divinity and to realise the divine
life. Such men will uplift this country.'

A few words about Motilal Roy and the Prabartak Sangha may
not be out of place here. From the time Motilal gave shelter to Sri
Aurobindo at Chandernagore, he enjoyed Sri Aurobindo's trust
and confidence. On his part, Motilal visited Pondicherry as often
as he could during the difficult period of Sri Aurobindo's early stay
and helped by sending money etc. from Chandernagore. There is
no doubt that Sri Aurobindo put a special force on Motilal to
mould him into a fit instrument for the work in Bengal. In 1914, a
beginning was made when Motilal Roy gathered together a small
group at Chandernagore to give a concrete form to Sri
Aurobindo's conception of a spiritual commune. Motilal drew his
inspiration from Sri Aurobindo who gave him detailed instructions
from time to time. A Bengali fortnightly journal, *Prabartak*, was
started in September 1915 and later an English weekly, the
Standard Bearer. Sri Aurobindo wrote occasionally for both the
journals. The Sangha at first made good progress – its watchwords
were 'Commune, Culture and Commerce' – and visitors who came
to Chandernagore spoke highly of the organisation which became
quite well known, filling a vacuum in the spiritual and cultural life
of Bengal at that time. So long as Motilal Roy remained in touch

with Pondicherry and was receptive to Sri Aurobindo's spiritual force, the Sangha moved in the right direction; but afterwards it changed its course. In 1921 Motilal came to Pondicherry with his wife for an intensive pursuit of sadhana but he could not adjust himself to the changes he saw and was unable to settle down. After a period of vacillation he eventually left on August 10, in spite of Sri Aurobindo's advice to him to stay on. This hurried departure practically marked the end of Sri Aurobindo's association with Motilal and the Prabartak Sangha. In the course of a conversation with his disciples in 1926, Sri Aurobindo said: 'At the time I had some construction in my mind. Of course, there was something behind it which I knew to be true. Even then I was not sure that it would work out successfully. Anyway, I wanted to give it a trial and gave that idea to Motilal. Then he took up the idea and, as you know, he took it up with all his vital being and in an egoistic way. So the vital forces found their chance. They tried to take possession of the work and the workers.'

Like Motilal Roy, Paul Richard found himself unable to bear the pressures of sadhana and take the path of complete self-surrender. Perhaps his approach was too mental or vitalistic. In any case, he decided that he could not stay on indefinitely in Pondicherry and he left after a few months never to return. Yet he retained his profound admiration for Sri Aurobindo.

After his departure, Mirra and Datta continued to stay at Bayoud House but it was an old building and particularly vulnerable during the cyclonic storms which swept over Pondicherry from time to time. On November 24, 1920, there was a great tempest followed by heavy rainfall. Nolini Kanta writes in his reminiscences: 'The house [where the Mother was staying] was old and looked as if it was going to melt away. Sri Aurobindo said, "Mirra cannot be allowed to stay there any longer. She must move into our place." That is how the Mother came into our midst and stayed on for good, as our Mother.'

The Mother gradually took charge of the household arrangements, after moving into the 'Guest House' with Datta. The young inmates were at first somewhat nonplussed and uneasy at this sudden 'invasion' by the two European ladies, as it was a jolt to their rather bohemian way of life. Initially there was some resistance but the Mother's loving kindness and her unobtrusive ways soon won them over and they learned to accept the changes that came about. Purani, who had first come in 1918, came again in 1921, and on this occasion he noted: 'The house had undergone a great change. There was a clean garden in the open courtyard, every room had simple and decent furniture, – a mat, a chair and a small table. There was an air of tidiness and order. This was no doubt the effect of Mother's presence.'

The real change, however, was not so much in the outward mode of living but, as Nolini Kanta has recounted in his reminiscences, 'Our life itself took on a different turn with the arrival of the Mother. How and in what direction? It was like this. The Mother came and installed Sri Aurobindo on his high pedestal as Master and Lord of Yoga. We had hitherto known him as a dear friend and close companion, and although in our mind and heart he had the position of a Guru, in our outward relations we seemed to behave as if he were just like one of ourselves. He too had been averse to the use of the words "guru" and "Ashram" in relation to himself, for there was hardly a place in his work of new creation for the old traditional associations these words conveyed. Nevertheless, the Mother taught by her manner and speech and showed us in actual practice, the meaning of disciple and Master; she has always practised what she preached. She showed us, by not taking her seat in front of or on the same level as Sri Aurobindo, but by sitting on the ground, what it meant to be respectful to one's Master, what was real courtesy. Sri Aurobindo once said to us, perhaps with a tinge of regret, "I have tried to stoop as low as I can, and yet you do not reach me."'

During his visit in 1921, Ambalal Purani noticed an even more remarkable change than the one he had seen before. He writes: 'But the greatest surprise of my visit in 1921 was the "darshan" of Sri Aurobindo. During the interval of two years his body had undergone a transformation which could only be described as miraculous. In 1918 the colour of the body was that of an ordinary Bengali – rather dark, though there was a lustre on the face and the gaze was penetrating. Now on going upstairs to see him I found his cheeks wore an apple-pink colour and the whole body glowed with a soft creamy white light. So great and unexpected was the change that I could not help exclaiming: "What has happened to you?" Instead of giving a direct reply he parried the question; as I had grown a beard he asked: "And what has happened to you?" But afterwards in the course of our talk he explained to me that when the Higher Consciousness, after descending to the mental level, comes down to the vital and even below the vital, then a transformation takes place in the nervous and even in the physical being....'

I shall now turn to an incident, or rather a series of incidents, which took place towards the end of 1921 in what later came to be called the 'Guest House'. In describing the events I will not use my own words. Many years later, in the course of her 'Wednesday classes' for the students and sadhaks of the Ashram, the Mother gave a detailed account of what had happened and I shall quote extensively from her narration.

'We had a cook called Vatel. This cook was rather bad-tempered and didn't like being reproved about his work. However, he was in contact with some Musulmans who had, it seems, magical powers – they had a book of magic and the ability to practise magic. One day, this cook had done something very bad and had been scolded [by Datta] – and he was furious. He had threatened us saying: "You will see, you will be compelled to leave this house." We had taken no notice of it.

'Two or three days later, I think, someone came and told me that stones had fallen in the courtyard – a few stones, three or four; bits of brick. We wondered who was throwing stones from the next house. We did exactly what we forbid children to do: we went round on the walls and the roofs to see if we could find someone or the stones or something – we found nothing.

'That happened, I believe, between four and five in the afternoon. As the day declined, the number of stones increased. The next day, there were still more. They started striking specially the door of the kitchen and one of them struck Datta's arm as she was going across the courtyard. The number increased very much.... I must tell you that this Vatel had informed us that he was ill and for the last two days – since the stones had started falling – he hadn't come. But he had left with us his under-cook, a young boy of about thirteen or fourteen, quite fat, somewhat lifeless and a little quiet, perhaps a little stupid. And we noticed that when this boy moved around, wherever he went the stones increased. The young men who were there... shut the boy up in a room, with all the doors and windows closed; they started making experiments like the spiritists: "Close all the doors, close all the windows." And there was the boy sitting there inside and the stones began falling, with all the doors and windows closed! And more and more fell, and finally the boy was wounded in the leg. Then they started feeling the thing was going too far.

'I was with Sri Aurobindo: quietly we were working, meditating together. The boys cast a furtive glance to see what was going on and began warning us, for it was perhaps time to tell us that the thing was taking pretty serious proportions. I understood immediately what the matter was.

...Then I said: "All right, send the boy out of the house immediately. Send him to another house, anywhere, and let him be looked after, but don't keep him here, and then, that's all. Keep quiet and don't be afraid." I was in the room with Sri Aurobindo and I thought, "We'll see what it is." I went into meditation and gave a little call. I said: "Let us see, who is throwing stones at us now? You must come and tell us who is throwing stones."...I saw three little entities of the vital, those small entities which have no strength and just enough consciousness confined to one action – it is nothing at all, but these entities are at the service of people who practise magic. When people practise magic, they order them to come and they are compelled to obey. There are signs, there are words. So, they came, they were frightened – they were terribly frightened! I said, "But why do you fling stones like that? What does it mean, this bad joke?" They replied, "We are compelled. We are compelled... It is not our fault, we have been ordered to do it, it is not our fault."

'I really felt so much like laughing but still I kept a serious face and told them, "Well, you must stop this, you understand!" Then they told me, "Don't you want to keep us? We shall do all that you ask." "Ah!" I thought, "let us see, this is perhaps going to be interesting." I said to them, "But what can you do?" – "We know how to throw stones." – "That doesn't interest me at all. I don't want to throw stones at anyone...but could you perchance bring me flowers? Can you bring me some roses?" Then they looked at each other in great dismay and answered, "No, we are not made for that, we don't know how to do it." I said, "I don't need you, go away and take care specially never to come back, for otherwise it would be disastrous!" They ran away and never came back.

'There was one thing I had noticed: it was only at the level of the roof that the stones were seen – from the roof downwards, we saw the stones; just till the roof, above it there were no stones. This meant that it was like an automatic formation. In the air nothing could be seen: they materialised in the atmosphere of the house and fell.

'And to complete the movement, the next morning – all this happened in the evening – the next morning I came down to pay a visit to the kitchen – there were pillars in the kitchen – and upon one of the pillars I found some signs with numbers as though made with a bit of charcoal, very roughly drawn – I don't remember the signs now – and also words in Tamil. Then I rubbed out everything carefully and made an invocation, and so it was finished, the comedy was over.

'However, not quite. Vatel's daughter was *ayah* in the house, the maid-servant. She came early in the afternoon in a state of intense fright saying, "My father is in the hospital, he is dying; this morning something happened to him; suddenly he felt very ill and he is dying, he has been taken to the hospital, I am terribly frightened." I knew what it was. I went to Sri Aurobindo and said to him, "You know, Vatel is in the hospital, he is dying." Then Sri Aurobindo looked at me and smiled: "Oh! just for a few stones!"

'That very evening Vatel was cured. But he never started anything again.'

In explaining how the stones materialised and could be seen, the Mother said: 'There are beings who have the power of dematerialising and rematerialising objects. These were quite ordinary pieces of bricks but they materialised only in the field where the magic acted. The magic was practised for this house, specially for its courtyard, and the action of vital forces worked only there. That was why when I sent away the boy and he went to another house, not a single stone hit him any more. The magical formation was made specially for this house and the stones materialised in the courtyard. And as it was something specially directed against Datta, she was hit on the arm.... There was something else. We came to know later to which magician Vatel had gone. He was very well known here. Vatel asked him to make stones fall in our house. The magician said: "But that's the house Sri Aurobindo lives in. No, I am not going to meddle in this business." However, he could not resist the lure of money, but he said, "In a circle of 25 metres around Sri Aurobindo the stones will not fall." That is why not a single stone came near us!'

I have given you the Mother's narration in some detail because the facts provide a striking illustration of what is called Black Magic. Our ordinary intelligence is quite baffled when it comes across such phenomena and tends to disbelieve them. But they are true enough and they are by no means mysterious or inexplicable to those who have the knowledge of occult science. You may recall Hamlet's words to Horatio in Shakespeare's play, apropos of the Ghost which appeared before them: 'There are more things in heaven and earth, Horatio, than are dreamt of in your philosophy.'

From January 1, 1922, the Mother took full charge of the management of the household. The number of residents, including Sri Aurobindo and the Mother, had now increased to nine. In addition to the four companions who initially came with Sri Aurobindo, K. Amrita became an inmate in 1919, followed by Barin, who arrived after his exchange of letters with Sri Aurobindo, and by Datta who came with the Mother. With the increase in the number of inmates it became necessary to find additional accommodation. In September 1922 Sri Aurobindo, the Mother, Datta and a few others moved to a house in rue de la Marine. This building, which later came to be known as the 'Library House', now forms the south-western part of the complex of constructions which constitute the main buildings of Sri Aurobindo Ashram. The other house in rue François Martin was retained; some visitors as well as inmates were housed there and it acquired the name 'Guest House'.

As the number of residents grew, the nucleus of a small spiritual community formed itself without any preconceived planning; it developed as an organic growth with Sri Aurobindo as its centre. His own personal routine did not follow a rigid or inflexible pattern binding on everyone, although everything was subordinated to the needs of Sri Aurobindo's sadhana. In general, however, the mornings (usually after breakfast between 9 and 11) were set aside for interviews with visitors whose numbers continued to increase. Around four in the afternoon there was collective meditation (this practice had commenced in 1921, after the Mother's arrival) in which Sri Aurobindo and the Mother participated and which practically all the inmates attended. Later in the evening, the disciples and permitted visitors gathered together for a sitting during which Sri Aurobindo replied to questions and took part in the discussions that followed. This was a very informal gathering with no fixed time and depended on Sri Aurobindo's leisure; in fact these 'Evening Talks' were a continuation of the earlier sittings which used to be held in the first floor verandah of the Guest House from 1918 onwards. In the Library House also there was a verandah on the first floor where the sittings took place. The disciples and the visitors sat on the floor; for Sri Aurobindo there was a chair and a small table in front of it. With an air of expectancy the gathering waited for Sri Aurobindo to come. Purani writes: 'He came dressed as usual in a dhoti, part of which was used by him to cover the upper part of his body. Very rarely did he come out with a chaddar or shawl, and then it was "in deference to the climate" as he sometimes put it. At times for minutes he would be gazing at the sky from a small opening at the top of the grass-curtains that covered the verandah in 9, rue de la Marine. How much these sittings were dependent on him may be gathered from the fact that there were days when more than three-fourths of the time passed in complete silence without any outer suggestion from him.... The whole thing was so informal that one could never predict the turn the conversation would take. The whole house therefore was in a mood to enjoy the freshness and the delight of meeting the unexpected. There were peals of laughter and light talk, jokes and criticism which might be called personal, – there was seriousness and earnestness in abundance.'

Purani became an inmate early in 1923 and from then on he kept detailed notes of the Evening Talks. Although not intended for publication, these later appeared in book form and provide fascinating glimpses of Sri Aurobindo's views on an immense variety of subjects including sadhana, politics, art, literature, education, medicine, etc. However, it is important to remember that the record of these talks was not seen by Sri Aurobindo, and Purani himself writes in his Introduction to *Evening Talks*: 'What was said in the small group informally was not intended by Sri Aurobindo to be the independent expression of his views on the subjects, events or the persons discussed. Very often what he said was in answer to the spiritual need of the individual or of the collective atmosphere. It was like a spiritual remedy meant to produce certain spiritual results, not a philosophical or meta-physical pronouncement on questions, events or movements. The net result of some talks very often was to point out to the disciples the inherent incapacity of the human intellect and its secondary place in the search for the ultimate Reality.'

During the first years of her stay in the Library House the Mother continued to keep herself in the background. However, her presence and influence were increasingly felt by the disciples not only in their community life but in matters of sadhana also. The disciples could see for themselves how frequently her advice was sought by Sri Aurobindo and how closely she was consulted by him in matters of yoga. Nolini Kanta writes in his reminiscences: 'In the beginning, Sri Aurobindo would refer to the Mother quite distinctly as Mirra. For sometime afterwards (this may have extended over a period of years) we could notice that he stopped at the sound of M and uttered the full name Mirra as if after a slight hesitation. To us it looked rather queer at the time, but later we came to know the reason. Sri Aurobindo's lips were on the verge of saying "Mother"; but we had yet to get ready, so he ended with Mirra instead of saying Mother. No one knows for certain on which particular date, at what auspicious moment, the word "Mother" was uttered by the lips of Sri Aurobindo but that was a divine moment in unrecorded time....' Gradually as Sri Aurobindo's sadhana grew more and more in its intensity, it was he who receded into the background and the disciples learnt increasingly to turn to the Mother for inspiration and guidance.

Let me now tell you briefly about some of the visitors who met Sri Aurobindo during this period. They came from all walks of life: some were followers or associates from his political days; others came as intending disciples, and yet others who knew not why they came were drawn by the aura of his magnetic personality. I shall mention only a few of these visits and only those where there is a sufficient record of the meeting or interview to throw light on Sri Aurobindo's views or to reveal a facet of his personality.

Towards the end of 1920, Sarala Devi, a niece of Rabindranath Tagore, met Sri Aurobindo on two days. She was a well-known litterateur and was then deeply concerned with Gandhiji's non-cooperation movement. Purani has provided a record of the interview from which I shall give you a few excerpts:

SARALA DEVI: Is it true that you are against the non-cooperation movement?

SRI AUROBINDO: I am not against it; the train has arrived, it must be allowed to run its own course. The only thing I feel is that there is a great need of solidifying the national will for freedom into stern action.

SARALA DEVI: Non-cooperation has declared war against imperialism.

SRI AUROBINDO: Yes, it has, but I am afraid it is done without proper ammunition, and mobilisation and organisation of the available forces.

SARALA DEVI: Why don't you come out and try to run your own train?

SRI AUROBINDO: I must first prepare the rails and lay them down, then only can I get the train to arrive....

SARALA DEVI: Don't you think that sufficient work has been done in the country to start the fight?

SRI AUROBINDO: Until now only waves of emotion and a certain all-round awakening have come but the force which could stand the strain when the government would put forth its force in full vigour is still not there....

SARALA DEVI: I find many people ridicule non-cooperation. ...What is your frank personal opinion?

SRI AUROBINDO: We have qualified sympathy with the movement; sympathy is there because we have the same objective; it is qualified because we feel the basis is not sound.... Some students from Madras came here the other day and told me that they wanted to non-cooperate because the government was unjust. Asked whether they would put up with a just British government they could not reply. India must want freedom because of herself, because of her own Spirit.... Our basis must be broader than that of mere opposition to the British government. All the time our eyes are turned to the British and their actions. We must look to ourselves irrespective of them and having found our own nationhood make it free.

Sarojini, Sri Aurobindo's sister, came in 1921. Sri Aurobindo went to the railway station to receive her as well as to see her off. He gave her the publication rights of his book *War and Self-determination* to help her.

Around this time, there came an unusual visitor. One day, a tall well-dressed sannyasi appeared, complete with long matted hair, iron tongs and a staff, and accompanied by a few *chelas*. He begged for Sri Aurobindo's darshan. When there was some hesitation in meeting his request, he muttered softly to one of those present to inform Sri Aurobindo that Gabriel had come. When this was conveyed to Sri Aurobindo, he is said to have exclaimed, in astonishment 'Good Lord!' For Gabriel was the code name he had himself given to Amarendranath Chatterjee, the young revolutionary who was personally initiated by him into the movement. You will also recall that Amar was one of those who were closely associated with Sri Aurobindo's get-away from Chandernagore. The visitor was then taken to Sri Aurobindo and there was a happy reunion. Amar was a revolutionary much wanted by the police and in order to escape from their clutches he had assumed the garb of a sannyasi. He took the name Swami Kevalananda and wandered all over the country, collecting some disciples in the process. Sri Aurobindo advised him to return to Bengal and, in the changed circumstances after the war, to disclose his identity but refrain from revolutionary activities. The next morning 'Gabriel' left, to carry out Sri Aurobindo's instructions.

During 1922 C.R. Das wrote to Sri Aurobindo urging him to re-enter politics and assume the leadership of the Congress which was then in the throes of a controversy between the 'changers' and 'non-changers' over the question of seeking election to the enlarged legislative councils provided under the new Government of India Act. Sri Aurobindo's reply, sent through his brother Barin in November, was on the lines of his earlier letters to Baptista and Dr. Munje. 'I have become confirmed in a perception,' he wrote, '...that the true basis of work and life is the spiritual, – that is to say a new consciousness to be developed only by Yoga. I see more and more manifestly that man can never get out of the futile circle the race is always treading until he has raised himself to a new foundation.... I am determined not to work in the external field till I have the sure and complete possession of this new power of action, – not to build except on a perfect foundation.' In June 1923 C.R. Das, who was then on a political tour of South India, came to Pondicherry and met Sri Aurobindo. Das, Motilal Nehru and like-minded leaders had by then broken away from the Congress to found the Swaraj Party and participate in the elections to the legislative assemblies. C.R. Das requested Sri Aurobindo to give his support to the new party. Sri Aurobindo declined to do so openly but assured Das of his spiritual help. It seems that at this time C.R. Das also sought to be initiated into Sri Aurobindo's Yoga but Sri Aurobindo did not agree to accept him as a disciple. Commenting on this many years later Sri Aurobindo said: 'He was the last of the old group. He came here and wanted to be a disciple. I said he wouldn't be able to go through in Yoga as long as he was in the political movement. Besides, his health was shattered.' Indeed Das had not many more years to live and he passed away on June 16, 1925. Sri Aurobindo paid a memorable tribute to his old associate: 'Chittaranjan's death is a supreme loss. Consummately endowed with political intelligence, magnetism, personality, force of will, tact of the hour and an uncommon plasticity of mind, he was the one man after Tilak who could have led India to Swaraj.'

G.V. Subbarao, a political leader from Andhra, met Sri Aurobindo in October 1923 and the visit is interesting because of a vivid pen-picture which Subbarao drew subsequently. He wrote: 'Sri Aurobindo was dazzling bright in colour – it was said that, in his earlier years, he was more dark than brown – and had a long, rather thin beard which was well dressed with streaks of white strewn here and there. The figure was slender and not much taller than Gandhiji's but a bit more fleshy. The eyes were big and elongated to a point and their looks were keen and piercing like shells. He was dressed in fine cotton – not khaddar evidently. He had only two clothes on, one a dhoti and the other an upper cloth worn in the traditional fashion of an *Upaveetam*, i.e. right arm and shoulder exposed....

'His voice was low, but quite audible and musical. He was fast in his flow of speech, clear like a crystal and analytical to a degree. In a fifteen-minute talk, he gave me his philosophy in a nutshell. He was simple and courteous, outspoken and free in his interrogation. It seemed as though he could know a man by the sweep of his eyes, and read men's minds from a survey of their photographs. He appeared as one highly cognisant of the value of time.... He was kind throughout, as to a child, but I could discern enough in his demeanour to conclude that he could be stern and imperious when required.'

A notable visitor in January 1924 was Dilip Kumar Roy. Son of the famous poet and dramatist, Dwijendra Lal Roy, Dilip had already made a name for himself as a singer, and with his many talents he could have had a glittering career, but there was a restless urge in him which drew him to the spiritual path. Sri Aurobindo gave him a long interview which has been faithfully recorded in Roy's well-known book, *Among the Great*. It is worth reading in full and I will refrain from giving you extracts except to quote his first impressions when he was taken to Sri Aurobindo: 'A radiant personality! sang the very air about him. A deep aura of peace encircled him, an ineffable yet concrete peace that drew you at once into its magic orbit. But it was the eyes that fascinated me most – shining like beacons.' Dilip Roy was later to join the Ashram and as a disciple he had a specially close relationship with Sri Aurobindo.

Sometime during this period Gandhiji sent his son Devdas to meet Sri Aurobindo and know his mind on the problems before the country. It seems that the interview was not a success. When Devdas asked for Sri Aurobindo's views on non-violence, he posed the counter-question: 'Suppose there is an invasion of India by the Afghans, how are you going to meet it with non-violence?' It also appears that Devdas asked – perhaps not in very good taste – why Sri Aurobindo was 'attached to smoking'? And the answer he received was: 'Why are you attached to non-smoking?' It was difficult for Devdas Gandhi to appreciate that Sri Aurobindo had practised and perfected *samata*, equality, as part of his sadhana and there was no field of life where it was not applied. Even when there happened to be no salt in the food, he would say nothing. Later, if anyone complained, he would merely remark: 'Yes, today there was no salt.' As for smoking, in 1926 Sri Aurobindo gave it up at one effortless stroke.

The following year in January 1925, two other political leaders, Lala Lajpat Rai and Purushottamdas Tandon came to meet Sri Aurobindo. Lajpat Rai, a stalwart of the Nationalist movement, had a private interview with Sri Aurobindo for 45 minutes. Then they were joined by Tandon and others. The following excerpt from A.B. Purani's record of the conversation is of interest.

Sri Aurobindo: How are things getting on at Allahabad?

P. T.: We are trying to carry out Mahatmaji's programme.

Lajpat Rai: Are you really trying to carry it out? (*turning to Sri Aurobindo*) They are trying to capture local bodies.

P. T.: I am not in favour of that programme, because it will lead in the end to lust for power and then personal differences and jealousies would also creep in. We cannot, in that case, justify the high hopes which people have about our work.

LAJPAT RAI: They expect you to usher in the golden age.

SRI AUROBINDO: But why do you give them such high hopes?

LAJPAT RAI: In the democratic age you have to.

SRI AUROBINDO: Why?

LAJPAT RAI: If you want to get into the governing bodies you must make big promises; that is the nature of democracy!

SRI AUROBINDO: Then, why democracy at all? The lust for power will always be there. You can't get over it by shutting out all positions of power; our workers must get accustomed to it. They must learn to hold the positions for the nation. This difficulty would be infinitely greater when you get Swaraj. These things are there even in Europe. The Europeans are just the same as we are. Only, they have got discipline – which we lack – and a keen sense of national honour.

As I have mentioned, many people came to Sri Aurobindo, some with a genuine seeking to follow his Yoga. Even so, only a few were accepted as disciples, for Sri Aurobindo laid stress on the special difficulties of the path and the need for complete self-surrender. Of those who were accepted I shall mention only two who were outstanding as disciples. Champaklal, a young man of eighteen from Gujarat, first came in 1921. He then went back but returned in 1923, this time to stay for good. He later served both the Mother and Sri Aurobindo as a personal attendant with rare dedication and devotion. Towards the end of 1925, a young Frenchman, Phillippe Barbier Saint-Hilaire, came to meet Sri Aurobindo. He was a brilliant graduate of the prestigious École de Polytechnique in Paris and, had he wished, could have been an engineer of the first rank. But his spiritual quest led him first to Japan and then to a lamasery in Mongolia. There also he did not find what he was seeking; so he came to Pondicherry. He met Sri Aurobindo and never left. When he was accepted as a disciple Sri Aurobindo gave him a new name, 'Pavitra'. Subsequently he served the Mother as her secretary for foreign correspondence etc. and also played a leading role when the International Centre of Education was established at the Ashram.

By 1926 the number of inmates had increased to 25; they came mostly from Bengal, Gujarat and the South, whilst two, Datta and

Pavitra, came from countries beyond the shores of India. The foundations of the Ashram had begun to be laid.

We come now to the great day, November 24, 1926, known as the Day of *Siddhi*. For sometime past the disciples could see that Sri Aurobindo was more and more absorbed in his sadhana. Often he would be late in coming for the evening talks – on one occasion he came at two o'clock in the morning! The feeling grew among the disciples that some Higher Power would soon descend and the expectation was strengthened by the various references Sri Aurobindo made in his talks to its distinct possibility. In the course of a talk on his birthday in 1925, Sri Aurobindo mentioned that the universal conditions were more ready now for the coming down of the Supermind. He said:

'Firstly, the knowledge of the physical world has increased so much that it is on the verge of breaking its own bounds.

'Secondly, there is an attempt all over the world towards breaking the veil between the outer and the inner mental, the outer and the inner vital and even the outer and the inner physical. Men are becoming more "psychic".

'Thirdly, the vital is trying to lay its hold on the physical as it never did before.... Also, the world is becoming more united on account of the discoveries of modern science.... Such a union is the condition for the highest Truth coming down and it is also our difficulty. Fourthly, the rise of persons who wield tremendous vital influence over large numbers of men.

'These are some of the signs to show that the universal condition may be more ready now.'

On the other hand, Sri Aurobindo also stressed that there was still great resistance in the earth atmosphere to the Truth descending and said: 'I find that the more the Light and Power are coming down the greater is the resistance. You yourself can see that there is something pressing down. You can also see that there is tremendous resistance... I am not doing an isolated yoga.... If I were seeking my own liberation and perfection, my yoga would have been finished long ago.'

Let me return to November 24, 1926. There were 24 disciples who had the good fortune to be present on that momentous day. Purani was one of them and I shall quote from his *Life of Sri Aurobindo* to give you an eye-witness account:

'From the beginning of November 1926 the pressure of the

Higher Power began to be unbearable. Then at last the great day, the day for which the Mother had been waiting for so many long years, arrived on 24th November. The sun had almost set, and everyone was occupied with his own activity – some had gone out to the seaside for a walk – when the Mother sent word to all the disciples to assemble as soon as possible in the verandah where the usual meditation was held. It did not take long for the message to go round to all. By six o'clock most of the disciples had gathered. It was becoming dark. In the verandah on the wall near Sri Aurobindo's door, just behind his chair, a black silk curtain with gold lace work representing three Chinese dragons was hung. The three dragons were so represented that the tail of one reached up to the mouth of the other and the three of them covered the curtain from end to end. We came to know afterwards that there is a prophecy in China that the Truth will manifest itself on earth when the three dragons (the dragons of the earth, of the mid-region and of the sky) meet. Today on 24 November the Truth was descending and the hanging of the curtain was significant.

'There was a deep silence in the atmosphere after the disciples had gathered there. Many saw an oceanic flood of Light rushing down from above. Everyone present felt a kind of pressure above his head. The whole atmosphere was surcharged with some electrical energy. In that silence, in that atmosphere full of concentrated expectation and aspiration, in the electrically charged atmosphere, the usual, yet on this day quite unusual, tick was heard behind the door of the entrance. Expectation rose in a flood. Sri Aurobindo and the Mother could be seen through the half-opened door. The Mother with a gesture of her eyes requested Sri Aurobindo to step out first. Sri Aurobindo with a similar gesture suggested to her to do the same. With a slow dignified step the Mother came out first, followed by Sri Aurobindo with his majestic gait. The small table that used to be in front of Sri Aurobindo's chair was removed this day. The Mother sat on a small stool to his right.

'Silence absolute, living silence, not merely living but over-flowing with divinity. The meditation lasted about forty-five minutes. After that one by one the disciples bowed to the Mother.

'She and Sri Aurobindo gave blessings to them. Whenever a disciple bowed to the Mother, Sri Aurobindo's right hand came forward behind the Mother's as if blessing him through the

Mother. After the blessings in the same silence there was a short meditation.

'In the interval of silent meditation and blessings many had distinct experiences. When all was over they felt as if they had awakened from a divine dream. Then they felt the grandeur, the poetry and the absolute beauty of the occasion. It was not as if a handful of disciples were receiving blessings from their Supreme Master and the Mother in one little corner of the earth. The significance of the occasion was far greater than that. It was certain that a Higher Consciousness had descended on earth. In that deep silence had burgeoned forth, like the sprout of a banyan tree, the beginning of a mighty spiritual work. This momentous occasion carried its significance to all in the divine dynamism of the silence, in its unearthly dignity and grandeur and in the utter beauty of its every little act. The deep impress of divinity which everyone got was for him a priceless treasure.

'Sri Aurobindo and the Mother went inside. Immediately Datta was inspired. In that silence she spoke: "The Lord has descended into the physical today."'

What, you may ask, is the significance of the *Siddhi* Day, the Day of Victory as the Mother called it? Well, mental explanations of a spiritual event, specially one of such magnitude, can never be really adequate, and it is best to listen to Sri Aurobindo's own words. In a letter to me he wrote: '24th November 1926 is the day when Sri Krishna descended into the body. His descent means the descent of the Overmind God which will prepare the descent of the Supermind.' To another disciple he wrote: '24th was the descent of Krishna into the physical. Krishna is not the supramental Light. The descent of Krishna would mean the descent of the Overmind Godhead preparing, though not itself actually, the descent of the Supermind and Ananda. Krishna is the Anandamaya; he supports the evolution through the Overmind leading it towards the Ananda.'

Sri Aurobindo tells us that between Mind and Supermind there are various intermediate planes or ranges of consciousness, each with its characteristic Light, Power and Knowledge, and the Overmind is the highest of these ranges. He said that the Overmind has to be reached and brought down before the Supramental Descent is at all possible. The 'Descent of Krishna' signified the fullness of the Overmental realisation, the Descent of the Divine into the very physical consciousness of Sri Aurobindo, and it was the culmination of all his previous realisations. It marked a decisive stage in his sadhana and paved the way for the Supramental Descent – the goal of Sri Aurobindo's Yoga.

Outwardly, too, there was a great change. Sri Aurobindo announced that he would go into complete seclusion to concentrate on his Yoga. Henceforward the Mother would take up the direct charge of the community of sadhaks – their inner sadhana as well as the outer organisation. It is so that November 24, 1926, is regarded as the day when the Sri Aurobindo Ashram was founded.

Chapter XII

The Integral Yoga and the Ashram
1927–1938

DURING the weeks and months that followed the *Siddhi* Day, the Ashram went through a remarkable phase, known as its 'brilliant period'. Nolini Kanta writes in his reminiscences: 'The Mother would now sit down daily for her meditations with all of us together, in the evening after nightfall. She made a special arrangement for our seating. To her right would sit one group and to her left another, both arranged in rows. The right side of the Mother represented Light, and the left was Power. Each of us found a seat to her right or left according to the turn of our nature or the inner being.... The Mother's endeavour at that time was for a new creation, the creation here of a new inner world of the Divine Consciousness. She had brought down the Higher Forces, the Gods, into the earth atmosphere, into our inner being and consciousness.' In one of her talks in later years the Mother herself referred to this period and said: '[After 24 November 1926] suddenly, immediately, things took a certain form: a very brilliant creation was being worked out in extraordinary details, with marvellous experiences, contact with divine beings, and all sorts of manifestations usually considered miraculous. Experiences followed one upon another, indeed, things were unfolding altogether brilliantly and... I must say, in an extremely interesting way.' However, when she spoke to Sri Aurobindo about the prospect of this new creation, Sri Aurobindo said: 'Yes, this is an Overmind creation.... You will perform miracles which will make you famous throughout the world, you will be able to turn all events on earth topsyturvy.... It will be a *great* success.... And it is not success we want; we want to establish the Supermind on earth. One must know how to renounce immediate success in order to create the new world, the supramental world in its integrality.' So the Mother discontinued the experiment. There was another factor which influenced the decision. Many of the sadhaks could not bear the pressure of the descents brought down by the Mother. In this context Sri Aurobindo once wrote to a disciple: 'In those days when the Mother was either receiving the sadhaks for meditation or otherwise working and concentrating all night and day without sleep and with very irregular food, there was no ill-health and no fatigue in her and things were proceeding with a lightning swiftness.... Afterwards, because the lower vital and the physical of the sadhaks could not follow, the Mother had to push the Divine Personalities and Powers, through which she was doing the action, behind a veil and come down into the physical human level and act according to its conditions.'

Meanwhile the number of inmates in the Ashram continued to increase. From twenty-five in 1926 it went up to thirty-six in 1927 and to eighty by the end of the following year; within the next five years, the number nearly doubled itself. This continuous growth meant an enormous increase in the Mother's work, not only in guiding the sadhana of the growing number of disciples but also in directing the physical organisation of the Ashram. More houses had to be rented, facilities had to be expanded and an increasing number of Services such as Building Service, Electric Service, Domestic Service, Laundry, etc. had either to be started or enlarged. The work given to each disciple was meant to be carried out by him as part of his sadhana, as Karma Yoga, and he was encouraged to take his problems and difficulties to the Mother. Also, those who were given charge of the Service Departments were required to prepare monthly reports which were submitted to the Mother and Sri Aurobindo for their perusal. As the Ashram grew, the number of visitors also increased and they were invariably impressed to see the quiet efficiency with which everything was carried out and the smooth coordination of all the Ashram activities. From its very day of inception, the Ashram bore the imprint of the Mother's organisational genius. Indeed this was not an Ashram in the usual sense of the term; its members were not sannyasis, pursuing a life of meditative retirement, and each sadhak was expected to do some work in the Ashram as part of his spiritual preparation. Commenting on the character of the Ashram, Sri Aurobindo wrote: 'This Ashram has been created with another object than that ordinarily common to such institutions, not for the renunciation of the world but as a centre and field of practice for the evolution of another kind and form of life which would in the final end be moved by a higher spiritual consciousness and embody a greater life of the spirit.'

Here you may ask: what was the basis adopted for selecting the inmates – how could one become a disciple? A difficult question to answer in a few words. The sadhaks came from all walks of life – some were engineers, doctors or administrators; others were intellectuals or scholars; and some others were apparently very ordinary persons who could not be conveniently fitted into a conventional category. Sri Aurobindo once told a disciple that the Mother's choice of sadhaks was not exclusively governed by their spiritual advancement or intellectual brilliance: 'She selects different types.... She wants to observe how the Divine works in different types.' And in a letter Sri Aurobindo wrote: 'It is necessary or rather inevitable that in an Ashram which is a "laboratory"... for a spiritual and supramental yoga, humanity should be variously represented. For the problem of transformation has to deal with all sorts of elements favourable and unfavourable. The same man indeed carries in him a mixture of these two things. If only sattwic and cultured men come for yoga, men without very much of the vital difficulty in them, then, because the difficulty of the vital element in terrestrial nature has not been faced and overcome, it might well be that the endeavour would fail.... Those in the Ashram come from all quarters and are of all kinds; it cannot be otherwise.' Indeed the Ashram community soon acquired a cosmopolitan cast with men and women represented from different parts of India and also from other countries. It must not be thought, however, that each disciple was an 'ideal' type, and indeed there were many who had their full share of human weaknesses and frailties. Once, in a despondent mood, I wrote to Sri Aurobindo: 'Looking around and at one's self, one heaves a sigh and says – What disciples we are, of what a Master! I wish you had chosen or called some better stuff....' His reply, brief and characteristic, is highly significant: 'As to the disciples, I agree! – Yes, but would the better stuff, supposing it to exist, be typical of humanity? To deal with a few exceptional types would hardly solve the problem. And would they consent to follow my path – that is another question. And if they were put to the test, would not the common humanity suddenly reveal itself – that is still another question.'

Sri Aurobindo's decision in 1926, to retire into complete seclusion was a severe blow to some of the older sadhaks who were accustomed to meeting him every day or at least whenever the need arose. They felt as if abandoned and, unable fully to accept the Mother as their Guru, a few of them (including Barin, his brother) left the Ashram. But Sri Aurobindo would not relent and break the rule he had imposed. To one disciple he wrote: 'You consider that the Mother can be of no help to you.... If you cannot profit by her help, you would find still less profit in mine. But, in any case, I have no intention of altering the arrangement I have made for all the disciples without exception that they should receive the light and force from her and not directly from me and be guided by her in their spiritual progress. I have made the arrangement not for any temporary purpose but because it is the one way, provided the disciple is open and receives, that is true and effective.' Also, in reply to queries from disciples regarding the Mother's spiritual stature and her role in the Yoga, he wrote some wonderfully revealing letters which form part of the book, *The Mother*. It is small in size but a masterpiece and the elevated magnificence of its language acts as a *mantra*.

In the case of outside visitors, however, Sri Aurobindo did make one or two exceptions and on May 29, 1928, he had a brief meeting with Rabindranath Tagore. The Poet was then on his way to Europe by sea and he disembarked at Pondicherry to meet Sri Aurobindo. Shortly afterwards, Rabindranath wrote an account of the meeting in Bengali and followed it up with an English version which appeared in *The Modern Review*. The Poet wrote: 'At the very first sight I could realise that he had been seeking for the soul and had gained it, and through this long process of realisation had accumulated within him a silent power of inspiration. His face was radiant with an inner light and his serene presence made it evident to me that his soul was not crippled and cramped to the measure of some tyrannical doctrine, which takes delight in inflicting wounds upon life....

'I felt that the utterance of the ancient Hindu Rishi spoke from him of that equanimity which gives the human soul its freedom of entrance into the All. I said to him, "You have the Word and we are waiting to accept it from you. India will speak through your voice to the world, 'Hearken to me.' "...

'Years ago I saw Aurobindo in the atmosphere of his earlier heroic youth and I sang to him,

"Aurobindo, accept the salutation from Rabindra."

'Today I saw him in a deeper atmosphere of a reticent richness of wisdom and again sang to him in silence,

"Aurobindo, accept the salutation from Rabindra."'

For many years very little had been written about Sri Aurobindo and he had receded from the public view. This appreciation by Tagore, whose name was widely known in the country, attracted a good deal of attention. On reading it many felt that Sri Aurobindo was not, after all, an 'extinct volcano'!

A disciple once asked Sri Aurobindo why it was necessary for him to be so strict about his seclusion. His reply was: 'It was meant as a temporary necessity: for, if I had to do all the work that the Mother was doing, my "real" work would have remained undone for want of time.' We should therefore try to understand for ourselves the nature of this 'real' work. And since the work he was engaged in was yogic in character, a few words about yoga may be helpful. To render it into the simplest terms, yoga means union, union with God, the Divine. To see Him, to be with Him and, in Sri Ramakrishna's words, to be able to speak to Him – this is our life's highest aim and purpose. All the ways and practices which lead to this union, are called paths of yoga. Many indeed are the ways and the means, but the aim is always the union of the soul of man with the Divine, the Self, God, Brahman, or whatever name we give to that One Reality.

It is possible for the soul of man to unite with the Divine because the soul – the psychic being, as Sri Aurobindo calls it – is a portion of the Divine and it is through this union that man can gain true Knowledge, 'knowledge by identity', in Sri Aurobindo's words Ordinarily, i.e. in our ordinary state of consciousness, we are unaware of our psychic being or of the Divine Consciousness and live in a state of ignorance and separation which are the real causes' of our sorrow and suffering. The aim of yoga is to remove this lid of ignorance and the veil of separation so that the soul may live in oneness with the Divine in a state of knowledge and bliss.

In many of the traditional paths of yoga, it is considered necessary to renounce the world, to become a sannyasi, in order to find God because the world is looked upon as unreal, an illusion or Maya, and the aim is to realise the pure Spirit which is the sole Reality. In Sri Aurobindo's view, this ascetic renunciation is not necessary – Spirit and Matter, 'the two poles of existence', are not mutually exclusive or antagonistic, for Spirit is involved in Matter and is progressively manifesting itself in the material world through the evolutionary process. Sri Aurobindo teaches us that our world is the scene of an ascending evolution which goes from the stone to the plant, from the plant to the animal, and from the animal to man. But man, the mental being, is himself a transitional being, not the final end and summit of evolution. In the next step, man will develop a new and higher spiritual consciousness which Sri Aurobindo has called the Supramental consciousness. In *The Life Divine* he writes:

'As the impulse towards Mind ranges from the more sensitive reactions of Life in the metal and the plant up to its full organisation in man, so in man himself there is the same ascending series, the preparation, if nothing more, of a higher and divine life. The animal is a living laboratory in which Nature has, it is said, worked out man. Man himself may well be a thinking and living laboratory in whom and with whose conscious co-operation she wills to work out the superman, the god. Or shall we not say, rather, to manifest God? For if evolution is the progressive manifestation by Nature of that which slept or worked in her, involved, it is also the overt realisation of that which she secretly is. We cannot, then, bid her pause at a given stage of her evolution, nor have we the right to condemn with the religionist as perverse and presumptuous or with the rationalist as a disease or hallucination any intention she may evince or effort she may make to go beyond. If it be true that Spirit is involved in Matter and apparent Nature is secret God, then the manifestation of the divine in himself and the realisation of God within and without are the highest and most legitimate aim possible to man upon earth.'

You can now see why renunciation of the world has no place in Sri Aurobindo's yoga. What must be renounced, rejected completely, is the hold of egoism and of the lower movements of nature in man – the instincts, sensations, desires and passions of various kinds, the likings and dislikings, vanity, anger and a host of other things which bind man to his lower nature. Only then can the individual soul in man awaken, the inmost psychic being come into the forefront, governing and purifying his external mind, life and body, and lead him to a union with the Divine.

This individual realisation of the soul is the indispensable first step in Sri Aurobindo's Yoga, difficult and arduous as it is. But he bids us ascend further. The second step is the realisation of the universal or cosmic Self which is one in all and the perception of the One and Divine infinitely everywhere, 'sarvam khalvidam brahma', verily, all this that is is the Brahman. And still there is a third and final step: to rise beyond the individual and the universal to the Transcendent through the Supramental consciousness and to bring down the powers of the Supramental into mind, life and body for a total and perfect transformation.

We need not go into details here. In his *Synthesis of Yoga* and other writings Sri Aurobindo has dealt extensively with the stages involved and the psychological and other disciplines which we have to follow if we seek these realisations. He has called this sadhana the Integral Yoga. It combines many of the elements of the older yogas, the paths of Karma, Bhakti and Jnana, but also goes beyond them. There is one point, however, which I should like to stress here. Sri Aurobindo has repeatedly emphasised that there are no short-cuts in his Yoga. To seek the final stage of his Yoga without going through the earlier stages is not only futile but foolhardy and dangerous. And the Mother has said that to do the Integral Yoga one must first resolve to surrender entirely to the Divine: there is no other way – *it is the only way*. Then comes the practice, growth and perfection of the five psychological virtues – Sincerity, Faith, Devotion, Courage and Endurance. Truly, it is not an easy path.

We can now come back to the subject of the 'real' work Sri Aurobindo was engaged in: this was to bring down the Light and Power of the Supermind into the earth-consciousness through himself. Sri Aurobindo and the Mother represented in themselves the highest and deepest spiritual aspirations of humanity. As leaders of the evolution, it was their divine work to hasten the evolutionary process, to manifest the Supermind as its next decisive step. Sri Aurobindo has called the Supermind the 'Truth-Consciousness'. He writes: 'The essential character of Supermind is a Truth-Consciousness which knows by its own inherent right of nature, by its own light: it has not to arrive at knowledge but possesses it.' And again: 'Mind is an instrument of the Ignorance trying to know – Supermind is the Knower possessing knowledge.... It is a dynamic and not only a static Power, not only a Knowledge, but a Will according to Knowledge – there is a supramental Power or Shakti which can manifest direct its world of Light and Truth in which all is luminously based on the harmony and unity of the One, not disturbed by a veil of ignorance or any disguise.' However, let me say here straightaway that the mind by itself cannot understand the Supermind. This is not surprising: after all, the animal, with its vital instincts and sensations, cannot follow the workings of man's mind. The Supermind represents a level and realm of consciousness radically different from and superior to Mind, just as, in the evolutionary process, Mind is a higher range of consciousness than Life. Sri Aurobindo tells us that in its passage to the Supermind the mind must learn to fall into silence and then progressively open itself to the ranges of the Higher Consciousness.

As the disciples gradually came to know that Sri Aurobindo had retired into complete seclusion in order to concentrate on his task of hastening the Supramental Descent, their minds were beset with many questions. From 1930 onwards they were given the freedom to write letters to Sri Aurobindo (I shall come back to this subject later) and many put all sorts of questions regarding the Supermind. Some were born of mere curiosity and Sri Aurobindo discouraged these, although he never admonished the disciples. But where the questions genuinely sought an answer, Sri Aurobindo invariably sent a reply which varied in manner and content according to the disciple's capacity to understand. Sri Aurobindo was once asked in what way his Yoga was 'new' and whether it had been tried in earlier times. He advised the disciples not to lay stress on the 'newness' or novelty of the Integral Yoga but rather on its truth. However, to clarify the disciples' conceptions, Sri Aurobindo wrote:

'It is new as compared with the old yogas:

'1. Because it aims not at a departure out of world and life into Heaven or Nirvana, but at a change of life and existence, not as something subordinate or incidental, but as a distinct and central object. If there is a descent in other yogas, yet it is only an incident on the way or resulting from the ascent – the ascent is the real thing. Here the ascent is the first step, but it is a means for the descent. It is the descent of the new consciousness attained by the ascent that is the stamp and seal of the sadhana....

'2. Because the object sought after is not an individual achievement of divine realisation for the sake of the individual, but something to be gained for the earth-consciousness here, a cosmic, not solely a supra-cosmic achievement. The thing to be gained also is the bringing in of a Power of Consciousness [the supramental] not yet organised or active directly in earth-nature, even in the spiritual life, but yet to be organised and made directly active.

'3. Because a method has been preconized for achieving this purpose which is as total and integral as the aim set before it, viz. the total and integral change of the consciousness and nature, taking up old methods but only as a part action and present aid to others that are distinctive. I have not found this method (as a whole) or anything like it professed or realised in the old yogas. If I had, I should not have wasted my time in hewing out a road and in thirty years of search and inner creation when I could have hastened home safely to my goal in an easy canter over paths already blazed out, laid down, perfectly mapped, macadamised, made secure and public. Our yoga is not a retreading of old walks, but a spiritual adventure.'

This led to a further round of questions: if great men in the past did not have this vision, if even an Avatar like Krishna had not attempted to bring down the Supermind, was it not somewhat presumptuous of Sri Aurobindo to try and do so? These questions brought forth a magnificent reply: 'It is not for personal greatness that I am seeking to bring down the Supermind. I care nothing for greatness or littleness in the human sense. I am seeking to bring some principle of inner Truth, Light, Harmony, Peace into the earth-consciousness; I see it above and know what it is – I feel it ever gleaming down on my consciousness from above and I am seeking to make it possible for it to take up the whole being into its own native power, instead of the nature of man continuing to remain in half-light, half-darkness. I believe that the descent of this Truth opening the way to a development of divine consciousness here to be the final sense of the earth evolution. If greater men than myself have not had this vision and this idea before them, that is no reason why I should not follow my Truth-sense and Truth-vision. If human reason regards me as a fool for trying to do what Krishna did not try, I do not in the least care. There is no question of X or Y or anybody else in that. It is a question between the Divine and myself – whether it is the Divine Will or not, whether I am sent to bring that down or open the way for its descent or at least make it more possible or not. Let all men jeer at me if they will or all Hell fall upon me if it will for my presumption, – I go on till I conquer or perish. This is the spirit in which I seek the Supermind, no hunting for greatness for myself or others.' Still another question came up: How could he be so sure that the Supermind will in fact descend? Sri Aurobindo replied: 'If I believe in the probability and not only possibility, if I feel practically certain of the supramental Descent (I do not fix a date), it is because I have my grounds for the belief, not a faith in the air. I know that the supramental Descent is inevitable – I have faith in view of my experience that the time can be and should be now and not in a later age.' There was a further misconception that Sri Aurobindo had to remove. Some disciples thought that the descent of the Supermind would result in miraculous changes and at once usher in the Golden Age. Sri Aurobindo wrote: 'All that is absurd. The descent of the supramental means only that the Power will be there in the earth-consciousness as a living force just as the thinking mental and higher mental are already there.' In another letter he wrote: 'The whole of humanity cannot be changed at once. What has to be done is to bring the Higher Consciousness down into the earth-consciousness and establish it there as a constant realised force, just as mind and life have been established and embodied in Matter, so as to establish and embody the supramental Force.'

Yet such explanations and clarifications touch merely the surface of his sadhana of this period. Sri Aurobindo seldom wrote of the experiences he was going through and in any case these would have been largely unintelligible to the disciples. Only in a few letters did he indicate the immense difficulties which lay in the path of his Supramental Yoga. In one letter he wrote: 'My whole life has been a struggle with hard realities, from hardships, starvation in England and constant dangers and fierce difficulties to the far greater difficulties continually cropping up here in Pondicherry, external and internal. My life had been a battle from its early years and is still a battle: the fact that I wage it now from a room upstairs and by spiritual means as well as others that are external makes no difference to its character. But, of course, as we have not been shouting about these things, it is natural, I suppose, for others to think that I am living in an august, glamorous, lotus-eating dreamland where no hard facts of life or Nature present themselves. But what an illusion all the same!' There is another revealing letter in which he explains to a disciple why it was necessary for him and the Mother to confront and conquer these tremendous difficulties. He writes: 'As for the Mother and myself, we have had to try all ways, follow all methods, to surmount mountains of difficulties, a far heavier burden to bear than you or anybody else in the Ashram or outside, far more difficult conditions, battles to fight, wounds to endure, ways to cleave through impenetrable morass and desert and forest, hostile masses to conquer – a work such as, I am certain, none else had to do before us. For the Leader of the Way in a work like ours has not only to bring down and represent and embody the Divine, but to represent too the ascending element in humanity and to bear the burden of humanity to the full and experience, not in a mere play or Lila but in grim earnest, all the obstruction, difficulty, opposition, baffled and hampered and only slowly victorious labour which are possible on the Path. But it is not necessary nor tolerable that all that should be repeated over again to the full in the experience of others. It is because we have the complete experience that we can show a straighter and easier road to others – if they will only consent to take it.'

In one of his finest poems, 'A God's Labour' – written in 1935, Sri Aurobindo has given us a glimpse of the unprecedented *tapasya* he underwent for mankind. Here are a few stanzas from the poem:

> He who would bring the heavens here
>   Must descend himself into clay
> And the burden of earthly nature bear
>   And tread the dolorous way. ...
>
> I have been digging deep and long
>   Mid a horror of filth and mire
> A bed for the golden river's song,
>   A home for the deathless fire. ...

A voice cried, 'Go where none have gone!
   Dig deeper, deeper yet
Till thou reach the grim foundation stone
   And knock at the keyless gate.'

I saw that a falsehood was planted deep
   At the very root of things
Where the grey Sphinx guards God's riddle sleep
   On the Dragon's outspread wings. ...

I have delved through the dumb Earth's dreadful heart
   And heard her black mass' bell.
I have seen the source whence her agonies part
   And the inner reason of hell. ...

A little more and the new life's doors
   Shall be carved in silver light
With its aureate roof and mosaic floors
   In a great world bare and bright.

I shall leave my dreams in their argent air,
   For in a raiment of gold and blue
There shall move on the earth embodied and fair
   The living truth of you.

I think I have said enough for you to realise that Sri Aurobindo
did not go into seclusion for attaining his personal salvation in
solitude, indifferent to the fate of the world. This misconception
still persists but, as you have seen, it is far from the truth. His daily
routine included reading newspapers and journals and he was
always in touch with the currents of world-movements and their
reflections in outward events. And, whenever called for, he
applied his Yogic Force so as to change the drift of events or
circumstances. He told us that he was constantly working on
India's movement for freedom. And he once explained to me in a
letter: '...behind events in the world there is always a mass of
invisible forces at work unknown to the outward minds of men,
and by Yoga, (by going inward and establishing a conscious
connection with the cosmic Self and Force and forces) one can
become conscious of these forces, intervene consciously in the

play, to some extent at least determine things in the result of the play.'

Besides, there were two other ways in which he maintained contact with the outer world – through *darshan* and through his correspondence with the disciples. I shall dwell on them separately.

After 1926, on three days in the year, February 21 (the Mother's birthday), August 15 (Sri Aurobindo's birthday) and November 24 (the day of *Siddhi*), Sri Aurobindo and the Mother gave a joint *darshan* to the disciples and to some visitors who had obtained prior permission to come for the occasion. These three days were known as *darshan* days and I cannot describe the eagerness and expectancy with which we used to look forward to them. Each *darshan* was a special occasion for the sadhak, an exceptional moment of spiritual communion and communication with the Master and the Mother when he could offer himself anew to them and receive their blessings. For Sri Aurobindo and the Mother it was an occasion to look into the innermost being of each disciple to see his spiritual progress. Besides, Sri Aurobindo said that at the time of the *darshans* there were special descents of spiritual Force, Light, Peace, etc. which could help the disciples in their sadhana if they were receptive. Many indeed had unusual experiences and some would have the vision of divine manifestations emanating from Sri Aurobindo and the Mother. Also, for a visitor, a *darshan* could in a few moments of silent contact change the whole course of his life. Indeed the *darshan* was an unforgettable experience – *ascharyavat*, a thing of wonder. Clad in a fine dhoti, a chaddar across his body, Sri Aurobindo appeared august and vast, with an amiable smile playing on his lips; while the Mother sitting on his right in a beautiful sari, with her irresistible smile beckoned everyone to their Divine Presence. A marvellous vision!

I shall turn now to Sri Aurobindo's correspondence with his disciples: it is a very big subject and I can but touch on it. Between 1930 and 1938 a considerable part of Sri Aurobindo's time was given to this correspondence and sometimes he would spend eight or nine hours, mostly during the night, writing letters to the disciples. I had once sent him a typescript containing some criticism of our poetry by a visiting Englishman and requested him to give his comments on it. As his reply was delayed I wrote to him: 'What has happened to my typescript? Hibernating?' He wrote back in the humorous tone he often used with me: 'My dear sir, if you saw me nowadays with my nose to paper from afternoon to morning, deciphering, deciphering, writing, writing, writing, even the rocky heart of a disciple would be touched and you would not talk about typescripts and hibernation. I have given up (for the present at least) the attempt to minimise the cataract of correspondence; I accept my fate like Ramana Maharshi with the plague of Prasads and admirers, but at least don't add anguish to annihilation by talking about typescripts.'

There are many reasons for Sri Aurobindo giving so much of his time to these letters. Both he and the Mother encouraged the disciples to write freely and regularly about their difficulties and problems in sadhana and to raise other questions which vexed or perplexed them. Writing these letters helped the disciples to face their problems and to define their questions, and this also served to break down the barriers they sometimes created between themselves and the Guru. Through his replies Sri Aurobindo sent his Force and Light and the letters were the means or channels of his direct help to the disciples in their practice of yoga. In replying to letters on sadhana, Sri Aurobindo usually consulted the Mother as she was more directly in touch with the sadhaks; each reply was directed to the inner need of the sadhak and was in a language which never went beyond his capacity to understand. On other subjects Sri Aurobindo wrote according to the mental equipment of the disciple. To those with a strong intellectual bent of mind or where the questions raised were of general importance, Sri Aurobindo's replies were closely reasoned, often running into several pages, and provided illuminating answers which reflected his vast knowledge and integral vision. These letters find a place amongst his finest writings.

All this led to an immense volume of letters and, equally, to their immense variety. Of the thirty volumes of his writings which were published as the Sri Aurobindo Birth Centenary Library (SABCL), three entire volumes with a total of 1800 pages comprise his letters. And there are hundreds yet unpublished. The published letters have been grouped into four parts and each part into several sections. The first part alone contains the following sections from which you can get an idea of the range of subjects covered:

The Supramental Evolution
Integral Yoga and Other Paths
Religion, Morality, Idealism and Yoga
Planes and Parts of the Being
The Divine and the Hostile Powers
The Purpose of Avatarhood
Rebirth
Fate and Free-Will, Karma and Heredity, etc.

The second, third and fourth parts consist of letters concerned more directly with sadhana and there is no aspect of Integral Yoga which Sri Aurobindo has left uncovered. These letters form a perfect supplement to his major works such as *The Life Divine* and *The Synthesis of Yoga*. From another point of view, there can be no better introduction to Sri Aurobindo's writings than these letters. As you read them you will feel as though they were directly addressed to you and you will get the most clear answers to the many questions which inevitably crop up in our mind from time to time.

There are two other categories of letters to which I should make at least a passing reference. Occasionally in his letters Sri Aurobindo wrote about some incident in his own life or drew upon his personal experiences to explain or illustrate the subject matter of the letter. Sometimes he would also write to correct misstatements about himself which appeared in others' writings. These letters have been grouped together and appear in a separate volume of the SABCL. We cannot be sufficiently grateful for these occasional reminiscences and revelations, for they form the main source of the little knowledge that we have about his life and experiences. Then there are Sri Aurobindo's letters on Art, Literature and, in particular, on Poetry. Sri Aurobindo is the supreme Poet of Yoga, and he encouraged his disciples also to write poetry. The inspiration and help he provided and the atmosphere prevailing in those days in the Ashram brought out the latent poet in many disciples who had earlier neither the capacity for writing poems nor even an inclination towards it. I was myself one of those who came under the spell of the Muse, although I had never before written a line of poetry. J.A. Chadwick (Arjava) was another and I can give many more instances. At Cambridge Chadwick had been a brilliant scholar of mathematical philosophy and had little interest in poetry. At the Ashram he blossomed into a fine poet and wrote some exquisite poems which were published after his untimely death. Sri Aurobindo asked the disciples who wrote poetry to submit their compositions to him without hesitation and in letter after letter he would give his comments, unstinted in his praise where it was due, and yet pointing out the weaknesses and imperfections, sometimes even rewriting the whole poem. In this way he taught us prosody and the finer points of poetic diction and rhythm. It was an education in itself, but Sri Aurobindo taught us to write poetry as part of our sadhana, not for the sake of name or fame. Besides, in his letters he would occasionally make passing comments on poems and poets, both past and present. Even these casual observations are gems of literary criticism and always throw a new light on the subject.

Apart from the range and variety of subjects in these letters, their language has a special quality. From the excerpts I have already given, you may have noticed its luminous clarity (Chadwick once remarked that it had 'light without heat – like his eyes!') which goes straight to the mind and heart of the reader. And its perfect finish is all the more amazing when we consider the incredible speed with which Sri Aurobindo wrote. Sri Aurobindo never 'wrote down' to the disciples nor did he deliver sermons from a lofty height. The tone is invariably courteous and compassionate with hardly ever a harsh word even where the disciple is gravely at fault.

I shall end this subject on a personal note. I first came to the Ashram in 1930, left after a short stay and then returned in February 1933 to join the Ashram permanently. From around April 1933 to November 1938 I wrote to Sri Aurobindo almost daily. I used to put my questions in a notebook and Sri Aurobindo usually answered them in the margin – at times, the longer answers followed at the end. Gradually I came to use three notebooks: personal, medical and literary, for I had by then been given charge of the Ashram dispensary and had to attend to the inmates' ailments; also, with his encouragement, I had started writing poetry. This long Guru-shishya correspondence has now been published (excerpts had earlier appeared in separate books and in the SABCL) almost in its entirety and in chronological order. It consists of two volumes running into 1200 pages.

When I came to the Ashram I cared very little for God and had no faith. A medical man, materialist by education, I started the sadhana without having any idea about it, as Stendhal's Fabrice joined the army in utter ignorance of what war was like. If you read my correspondence with Sri Aurobindo you will see how he took in hand this raw and sceptical fellow and carried him along the path of sadhana, changed his entire way of thinking and opened his eyes to new realms of creative poetry and literature. But in this I was not alone, for Sri Aurobindo did the same for many other disciples, although I might have been a more difficult case! However, as our correspondence progressed, I was thrilled to notice that a new tone and manner was coming into his letters to me, a note of easy familiarity, of intimacy even, with shafts of humour lighting up the whole letter. This was certainly unusual and I did not fail to grasp my good fortune with both hands. I started writing to him much more freely and his replies continued in the same vein. It had a marvellous effect. I soon lost all my reservations, my fear and awe of him, and I wrote to him on every subject which occurred to me, putting all sorts of questions to him, and with a sense of freedom which I could not have imagined before. Friends would sometimes caution me against my boldness but Sri Aurobindo never objected nor did he rebuke me and his indulgence towards me was another way of showing his regard for individual liberty, his readiness to look at the whole life from the sublime to the trivial, and his incomparable tolerance and compassion. It is also an illustration of his way of dealing with each sadhak according to his nature and on the basis of his individual relationship with the Guru. In this way our correspondence flourished for a period of five and a half years. In the process it revealed a side of Sri Aurobindo's nature which dispels once for all the notion that he was always aloof and grave. I had written to him once: 'Your grandeur, your Himalayan austerity frightens us.' And his reply was: 'O rubbish! I am austere and grand, grim and stern! Every blasted thing that I never was! I groan in un-Aurobindian despair when I hear such things. What has happened to the commonsense of all you people? In order to reach the Overmind it is not at all necessary to take leave of this simple but useful quality.'

I have already given you quite a few examples of Sri Aurobindo's humour in his letters and two more instances must suffice for the present.

29-4-35

NIROD (N): I am plunged in a sea of dryness and am terribly thirsty for something. Along with it, waves of old desires. Any handy remedy?

SRI AUROBINDO: Eucharistic injection from above, purgative rejection below; liquid diet, psychic fruit juice, milk of the spirit.

30-4-35

N: Your prescription, Sir, is splendid, but the patient is too poor to pay. I feel I am the least fitted for the path. The God-seekers whose lives I have read reveal what a great thirst they had for the Divine!

SRI AUROBINDO: And what deserts they had to pass through without getting their thirst satisfied? The lives left out that?

N: Whatever you may say, Sir, the path of Yoga is absolutely dry and especially that of Integral Yoga!

SRI AUROBINDO: One has to pass through the desert sometimes – doesn't follow that the whole path is like that.

N: For this yoga, one must have the heart of a lion, the mind of a Sri Aurobindo and the vital of a Napoleon.

SRI AUROBINDO: Good Lord! Then I am off the list of the candidates – for I have neither the heart of a lion nor the vital of a Napoleon.

N: You may say that when the psychic comes to the front, the path becomes a Grand Trunk Road of Roses. But it may take years and years!

SRI AUROBINDO: Does not matter how long it takes – it crops up one day or another.

N: And who knows one may not simply pine away in the dry desert before that?

SRI AUROBINDO: No necessity to carry out any such disagreeable programme.

N: Have I the necessary requirements for the sadhana? The only thing I seem to have is a deep respect for you, which almost all people have today.

SRI AUROBINDO: It is good that, for accuracy's sake, you put in the 'almost'.

N: I made the unhappy discovery that it is surely from a financial pressure outside that I jumped for the Unknown and the Unknowable.

SRI AUROBINDO: It must have been a stupendous pressure to produce such a gigantic leap.

N: No escape now. Let me be roasted for somebody's toast. Pardon my vagaries.

SRI AUROBINDO: All this simply means that you have, metaphorically speaking, the hump. Trust in God and throw the hump off.

1-5-35

N: 'Trust in God'? Personal or Impersonal? Tell me instead, 'Trust in Me', that would be comforting, tangible and practical.

SRI AUROBINDO: All right. It comes to the same thing in the upshot.

5-9-36

N: Again I have a blessed boil inside the left nostril – painful. I feel feverish. A dose of Force, please!

SRI AUROBINDO: As the modernist poet says

O blessed blessed boil within the nostril,

How with pure pleasure dost thou make thy boss thrill!

He sings of thee with sobbing trill and cross trill,

O blessed, blessed boil within the nostril.

I hope this *stotra* will propitiate the boil and make it disappear, satisfied.

6-9-36

N: What a powerfully effective 'stotra'! The boil couldn't but burst.... I couldn't make out one word. Is it 'make thy *bows* thrill'?

SRI AUROBINDO: I thought you'd boggle over it. 'Boss' man 'boss' = yourself as owner, proprietor, patron, capitalist of the boil.

As I read and read again my correspondence with him, my abiding feeling is one of infinite gratitude: gratitude for the endless trouble he took over me even in small things, for helping, guiding and sustaining me through all my difficulties and failings in sadhana, and for sharing his divine laughter with me.

We come now to an event with deep and occult implications, the full significance of which may not be easy to understand. The outward occurrence is clear enough, grim and completely unexpected though it was. In the early hours of November 24, 1938, around 2 a.m. and only a few hours before the *darshan* was due to commence, Sri Aurobindo met with a serious accident in his room. He was on his way to the bathroom when he stumbled over a tiger's skin on the floor and fell, his right knee striking the head of the tiger. He tried to get up but failing to do so lay down quietly expecting that the Mother would come in soon. She was resting in her room when she received a strong vibration which made her feel that something had happened to Sri Aurobindo. She went quickly to his room and found him lying on the floor. Her intuition and her considerable knowledge of medical science made her suspect a fracture. She rang the emergency bell. A.B. Purani, who was on the ground floor below preparing hot water for Sri Aurobindo's bath, ran up to find the Mother at the head of the staircase. He was told of the accident and asked to summon a doctor. Fortunately, Dr. Manilal, a disciple and an experienced doctor, had come for the *darshan* from Gujarat and he was immediately available. He came at once, made a quick examination and said that he suspected a fracture. The Mother then asked Purani to get further assistance. When I came up with the other doctors, we saw that Dr. Manilal was still busy examining the leg. The Mother was sitting by Sri Aurobindo's side, fanning him gently. I could not believe what I saw: on the one hand Sri Aurobindo lying helplessly, on the other a deep divine sorrow on the Mother's face. But I soon regained my composure and helped the doctor in the examination. My medical eye could not help taking in at a glance Sri Aurobindo's entire body and appreciating the robust manly frame. His right knee was flexed, his face bore a perplexed smile as if he did not know what was the matter with him; the chest was bare, well-developed, and the snow-white dhoti now drawn up contrasted with the shining golden thighs. A sudden fugitive vision of the Golden Purusha of the Vedas!

During the medical examination Sri Aurobindo uttered very few words, and then only to answer the doctor's questions. Finally, Dr. Manilal pronounced that there was a fracture of the thigh bone. Sri Aurobindo simply heard the verdict and made no comment.

Meanwhile more than two hours had passed and the shattering news had flown all over the Ashram. The hopes and aspirations of hundreds of people were suddenly set at naught. The disciples gathered in the courtyard of the Ashram in great anxiety and then departed with a fervent prayer for Sri Aurobindo's speedy recovery. One of the visitors for the *darshan* was Miss Wilson, President Woodrow Wilson's daughter who had come all the way from America. She accepted Fate's decree with a calm submission. The Mother, out of compassion for the disappointed devotees, gave *darshan* to all in the evening, wiping away their gloom with the sunshine of her smile.

Since medical facilities at Pondicherry were inadequate, it was decided to call in Dr. Rao from the nearby town of Cuddalore in British India. He was the Superintendent of the Hospital there and known to us. In the meantime the injured leg was put in a cast of plaster as a first aid. Sri Aurobindo lay completely immobile on the bed. He disclosed to us later that it was a period of excruciating pain and said: 'The pains I had experienced so far were of an ordinary nature which I could transform into *ananda*. But this was intense. And since it came swiftly and suddenly, I could not change it into *ananda*. But when it settled down into a steady sensation I could.'

Dr. Rao arrived and after hearing the full account suggested that an orthopaedic surgeon from Madras, Dr. Narasimha Ayer, be called for consultation. With the Mother's approval Dr. Rao left for Madras to bring the specialist over.

It was evening by the time Dr. Rao returned with Dr. Ayer. They had also in the meantime arranged for a radiologist to attend and he too arrived after a few hours. The X-ray pictures revealed an impacted fracture of the right femur above the knee, two fragments firmly locked together. The specialist remarked that it was a very serious accident and had the fragments projected backwards, the consequences would have been disastrous. His advice was to avoid any drastic treatment, to put the limb in plaster and exert a steady traction by means of splints. The advice was accepted and the limb put into traction from the end of the bed. It would be necessary for Sri Aurobindo to stay in bed for a number of weeks and the specialist would pay a second visit later to consider the future course.

I should mention here that after the specialist had completed his investigations, the Mother put many intricate questions to him on the various possibilities, the prognosis, the lines of treatment, etc. and Dr. Ayer was lost in admiration of her knowledge of medical matters. Sri Aurobindo, on the other hand, listened carefully to all that was said but uttered not a single word. He was quite content to leave things entirely in the Mother's hands and accepted whatever she decided for him. I was much intrigued by this passive role. One who had been sending me sound medical advice about patients had not a word to say about himself on such a crucial matter. To me this has always been a living example of complete self-surrender.

The Mother now directed me to form a team of attendants who would be constantly available to serve Sri Aurobindo's needs. Champaklal, previously Sri Aurobindo's only personal attendant, and Purani, because of his long association with Sri Aurobindo, naturally came into the team along with Dr. Becharlal, an experienced Ashram doctor and Mulshankar, a young sadhak who assisted us at the dispensary. One more hand was still needed. The Mother was looking through the window shutters of Sri Aurobindo's room when she saw Dr. Satyendra standing in front of his Dental Clinic. 'Take Satyendra,' she told me and so the team was completed. Dr. Manilal postponed his departure for Gujarat and, being an experienced medical man with an equable temperament, he was a great help. Attendance by the entire team was required only at particular times, for instance when Sri Aurobindo's body needed some adjustment after a long stay in one position. Otherwise, we divided our duties, although ready to be summoned whenever needed. In this way circumstances broke down the barriers of Sri Aurobindo's seclusion and brought about a new pattern in his life. As for myself, I must admit that to serve him did come as a wonderful opportunity. Truly speaking, I had nourished in my heart a secret desire to see him near at hand, hear his voice, talk with him, and, if possible to serve him, but never could I have imagined the circumstances under which those prayers were to be granted nor could I have dreamt how close I would come to him in the next twelve years. I have written of this period in detail in my book *Twelve Years with Sri Aurobindo*, and I shall draw on that account from time to time as we proceed.

Let me now try to explain the inner significance of the accident on November 24, 1938. We later asked Sri Aurobindo about it and he said: 'The hostile forces had tried many times to prevent things like the *darshan* but I had succeeded in warding off all their attacks. At the time the accident to my leg occurred, I was more occupied with guarding the Mother and I forgot about myself. I didn't think the hostiles would attack me. That was my mistake.' Explaining what is meant by 'hostile forces' Sri Aurobindo writes: 'These hostile forces exist and have been known to yogic experience ever since the days of the Veda and Zoroaster in Asia (and the mysteries of Egypt and the Cabbala) and in Europe also from old times. These things, of course, cannot be felt or known so long as one lives in the ordinary mind and its ideas and perceptions...but once one begins to get the inner view of things, it is different. One begins to experience that all is an action of forces, forces of Prakriti, psychological as well as physical, which play upon our nature – and these are conscious forces or are supported by a consciousness or consciousnesses behind.' Elsewhere he says: 'The lower nature is ignorant and undivine, not in itself hostile to the Light and Truth. The hostile forces are anti-divine, not merely undivine; they make use of the lower nature, pervert it, fill it with distorted movements and by that means influence man and even try to enter and possess or at least entirely control him.' These are realities of the occult world and may not be very easy to understand but as Sri Aurobindo explains: 'The reality of the Hostiles and the nature of their role and trend of their endeavour cannot be doubted by any one who has had his inner vision unsealed and made their unpleasant acquaintance.'

We must remember that world conditions at the time were particularly favourable to the workings of these malignant forces. Discerning observers had seen and warned that from the early '30s the world was drifting towards a war of unprecedented magnitude. The phenomenal rise of Mussolini and Hitler, the inability of the democracies to contain the dictators, the Spanish Civil War, the enigmatic role of Russia which went through the throes of the brutal Stalinist purges, were all indications of a gathering storm. 1938, in particular, was a year of a mounting political crisis which came to a head when Hitler invaded Czechoslovakia in September. As a result of frantic last-minute efforts by England and France, a compromise was reached with Hitler and the Munich Agreement signed on September 29, 1938. War was narrowly averted, but no one was sure how long peace would last.

There is a letter from the Mother to her son, André, written in October 1938, i.e. after the Munich Pact, which throws a revealing light on the real forces at work behind the scene. She wrote: 'Speaking of recent events, you ask me "whether it was a dangerous bluff" or whether we "narrowly escaped disaster". To assume both at the same time would be nearer to the truth. Hitler was certainly bluffing, if that is what you call shouting and making threats with the intention of intimidating those to whom one is talking and obtaining as much as one can. Tactics and diplomacy were used, but on the other hand, behind every human will there are forces at work whose origin is not human and which move consciously towards certain ends. The play of these forces is very complex and generally eludes the human consciousness; but for ease of explanation and understanding, they may be divided into two main opposing tendencies: those that work for the fulfilment of the Divine work upon earth, and those that are opposed to this fulfilment. The former have few conscious instruments at their disposal. It is true that in this matter quality compensates by far for quantity. As for the anti-divine forces they have only too many to choose from, and always they find wills which they enslave and individuals whom they turn into docile but nearly always unconscious puppets. Hitler is a choice instrument for these anti-divine forces which want violence, upheaval and war, for they know that these things retard and hamper the action of the divine forces. That is why disaster was very close even though no human government consciously wanted it. But at any cost there was to be no war and that is why war has been avoided – for the time being.'

Indeed the respite was short-lived, but it did give the democracies some much needed time to arm themselves desperately. On September 1, 1939, Germany invaded Poland and the demoniac forces represented by Hitler unleashed the Second World War which was to change the face of the world.

With the war, Sri Aurobindo's Yoga entered a new phase and the Ashram too went through many changes. These we must now consider.

Chapter XIII

The Growth of the Ashram
1939–1950

SRI AUROBINDO made good progress in his recovery from the accident. Although strictly confined to his bed, he remained completely calm and unperturbed as if nothing had happened to him, and he submitted to the doctors' directions without question or complaint. Dr. Rao used to come almost every week from Cuddalore and he often remarked that Sri Aurobindo was an ideal patient. There must have been pain and discomfort because of the unaccustomed posture but Sri Aurobindo would scarcely disturb anybody and seldom call for any assistance. We had therefore to be all the more vigilant in anticipating his needs.

The specialist, Dr. Ayer, had advised, because of the serious-ness of the case and the age of the patient, to keep the plaster on for ten weeks. Dr. Rao, on the other hand, wanted to cut short the period to six weeks and quoted his own hospital experiences in support. It pained him, he said, to see the Master being confined unnecessarily for a long wearisome period, but he also said that when he had raised the matter with the specialist, they had agreed to differ! However, none of us was willing to take any risk although Dr. Rao argued that no risk was involved and added, 'Besides, Sri Aurobindo is an extraordinary patient; we can expect him to take good care of himself.' As a result of his insistence, the Mother at last asked Sri Aurobindo to adjudicate. He replied, 'If I am an extraordinary patient I must take extraordinary precaution too. The forces are quite active. I can't trust myself not to make some awkward movement in sleep. Between ten weeks and six, let us come to a compromise and put it at eight weeks.'

Having delayed his departure as long as he could, Dr. Manilal had now left for his home town Baroda. I was reluctant to see him go as it increased my responsibilities but he gave his assurance that he would come again when the limb was released from the cast. Dr. Ayer came over from Madras at the time of removing the plaster. To our deep consternation, as soon as the limb was set free, it swelled up from the thigh downwards to almost double its size. The Mother kept an ominous silence, but Sri Aurobindo was as unconcerned as ever. However, the specialist assured us that the swelling would subside and he was satisfied that a firm union of the bone had taken place. With proper and careful treatment, massage, compress, gradual movement of the limb, the leg would return to its normal size. But the Mother was not so easily satisfied and questioned the doctor closely regarding possible complications and danger. All this time Sri Aurobindo remained unperturbed and left everything in the Mother's hands.

When Dr. Manilal returned, he helped us to tackle the problems in his usual efficient manner. As a result of gentle massage and hot and cold compress, the swelling gradually subsided, although it took some months to disappear completely. For bending the knee, the doctor prescribed an excercise called 'hanging the leg'. As soon as it was time for Dr. Manilal to come, Sri Aurobindo would say, 'Oh, Manilal is coming. I must hang my leg!' Or when he would enquire from Baroda about the progress, Sri Aurobindo would say with a smile, 'It is still hanging!' Learning to walk again proved a more difficult task. At first crutches were tried but they did not suit Sri Aurobindo. The Mother then proposed that he should walk leaning on two persons, one on either side. Purani and Satyendra were first chosen as the human supports but as their heights were different, Champaklal replaced Satyendra and this proved to be an ideal arrangement. Gradually, as Sri Aurobindo's steps gained in strength and firmness, he needed only a stick in the right hand, Champaklal continuing to support him on the left. Finally, just the stick was used. As soon as it came to be known that the Master was using a walking stick several were presented to him. Every day after the noon and night meals the Mother would come to his room and hand over a stick to him, and he would walk for half an hour in her presence.

By April, Sri Aurobindo's progress became widely known and

requests poured in for another *darshan*. Two *darshans* had been missed, and the disciples felt August 15 to be too far away. The Mother's response was sympathetic and Sri Aurobindo gave his consent. April 24, the day of the Mother's final arrival in Pondicherry, was chosen and henceforth it became the fourth *darshan* day. But the *darshan* time was changed from the morning to the afternoon and the period shortened to avoid any strain on Sri Aurobindo. It was a simple *darshan*: one by one the sadhaks stood for a brief moment before Sri Aurobindo and the Mother, received their Blessings, and departed with feelings of supernal joy.

For the first few weeks after the accident Sri Aurobindo remained mostly silent. Gradually, however, he began to take cognizance of the new conditions around him and became more communicative. In the evenings, lying on his back, he would talk with the attendants who were assembled round the bed. He spoke in a low tone and we had to draw near to hear his finely cadenced voice. Later, when he could sit up on his bed, the team would all gather round him and the conversation begin. Sometimes, talks were also held when his body was being sponged. Almost everything under the sun was discussed – serious subjects as well as comments on day-to-day events and developments. The atmosphere was relaxed and informal with Sri Aurobindo often making humorous comments and always illuminating the subjects discussed with his vast knowledge and vision. It was an unforgettable reward he granted us for our humble service. I kept a record of these talks.

At first Sri Aurobindo was served three meals daily but breakfast was soon stopped as it was too early for his appetite. However, even his first meal gradually came to be delayed till late in the afternoon. Sri Aurobindo reserved a big part of his day for what he called his personal work of concentration. After his morning ablutions, he would go through the newspapers and then the Mother would come for a while to discuss things of importance. After this, there would be a long period which he passed in complete silence. Nobody except the Mother had any idea what he was occupied with. This period was perhaps the most mysterious part of his life. Was he drawing down the Supramental Force or concentrating on a critical phase of the War or perhaps on some individual case needing some special attention? All we were told was that he had a special work to do and had to be left alone unless some very urgent business needed his attention. During this period we were strangers to him: we might have been in his room many times but we had no apparent existence. If he needed something, it was an impersonal voice calling somebody impersonal, as it were, for he would use no name, and the voice would come from afar, the tone was grave, the look elsewhere; the noise, our chatter, fell into a vacancy. Even the explosion of a bomb would have left him serene and silent. Perhaps the bomb would not have exploded in his presence! On this point I am reminded of an incident of earlier years which the Mother once recounted to the disciples. She said: 'You remember the night of the great cyclone, when there was a tremendous noise and splash of rain all about the place. I thought I would go to Sri Aurobindo's room and help him shut the windows. I just opened his door and found him sitting quietly at his desk, writing. There was such a solid peace in the room that nobody would have dreamed that a cyclone was raging outside. All the windows were wide open, not a drop of rain came in.'

It was often three or four o'clock in the afternoon by the time Sri Aurobindo was ready for his first meal. The Mother would then come, lay out the dishes on a wheeled table which had been made for him, and push it close to the bed. Sri Aurobindo relished good food and was partial to sweets, specially *rasagolla, sandesh* or *pantua*, but he had no attachment for any particular dish. The Mother used to serve the dishes to him in their proper order; otherwise, Sri Aurobindo would sometimes be so absorbed that he would lose all distinction between the different preparations. This was his principal meal of the day. At night he had a light supper, its timing being flexible, as it depended on the Mother's endless round of activities. After the meal, he practised walking and then the Mother and Sri Aurobindo would have once again their important discussions, when we were careful not to intrude in any way. Even after the Mother's departure Sri Aurobindo kept awake and only when he learnt that she had retired did our lights go out; that was at about 2 a.m.

Yet this sketch of Sri Aurobindo's daily routine cannot in the least convey an idea of the vast consciousness which was behind everything he did, and we are bound to fail if we try to read his inner consciousness from his outward activities. One day he said: 'All that I see in this room, these walls, these tables, the books, etc. and yourself, Dr. Manilal, I see as the Divine. No, it is not an imaginary vision, it is a concrete realisation.' All Sri Aurobindo's actions welled from the Divine Consciousness that he embodied: they were *yukta karma* – that is all one can say except to add that impersonality was the essence of his nature. In everything he kept his tranquil spirit, his impersonal way. He never raised his voice, did not insist on his point and when he criticised men or countries, there was no contempt in his expression. He saw the Forces of which men are unconscious instruments and the Impersonal in him looked at everything with an equal eye. All that he did, all that came from him, his ease, reserve, calm, unhurried action, even certain aspects of his humour, gave me that impression. Sri Aurobindo has said that the Supreme is both personal and impersonal at the same time. His own life is a luminous example of this truth and has given us a small insight into the working of the Divine in the world.

As soon as Sri Aurobindo had recovered sufficiently he gave his attention to a proposal which had come from the Arya Publishing House, Calcutta, to publish *The Life Divine* which had come out serially in the *Arya* long ago and had not yet appeared in book form. The Mother too was very keen on its publication but Sri Aurobindo would not consent to it without revising the text. He also wanted to write some additional chapters. This involved a good deal of work, for he made extensive revisions and wrote new chapters. It was a wonderful experience to see how he wrote. No sooner had he begun than there followed line after line as if everything was there chalked out before him. He needed no books and had no need to think. We could see what is meant by writing from a silent mind. Absorbed, perfectly poised, gazing up now and then, wiping the perspiration from his hands – for he perspired profusely as there was no fan in the room – he would go on for about two hours. The Mother would drop in with a glass of coconut water. Sometimes she had to wait for quite a while before he was aware of her presence. Then exclaiming 'Ah', he would take the glass from her hand, drink slowly, and then plunge back into his work!

The first volume of *The Life Divine* appeared in 1939 and the second volume, in two parts, in April 1940. You will remember that it was during the First World War that the *Arya* brought it out serially and it is no mere coincidence that in book form its appearance should have synchronised with the Second World War. *The Life Divine* was favourably reviewed in the *Times Literary Supplement* and Sir Francis Younghusband, an eminent Englishman with a deep interest in philosophy and mysticism, called it 'the greatest book' to come out in his time. He also wrote in a letter to Dilip Kumar Roy at the Ashram: 'This war has been a terrible catastrophe and we here in London suffered badly...but bad as it is the calamity has had one good effect; it has turned men's minds to God.... And *The Life Divine* could not have appeared at a more opportune moment.'

When war broke out in September 1939, and during the months of the so-called 'phoney war' that followed, Sri Aurobindo did not 'actively concern himself' with it, to use his own words. He followed the newspapers and since we had then no radio at the Ashram, we would get short bulletins from the town giving the latest news. Of course the war figured prominently during our talks in the evening. Apart from his deep knowledge of history, Sri Aurobindo had a masterly grasp of military strategy, although he never made a special study of the subject, and we were repeatedly struck by the prescience of his observations. In these talks he imparted to us a clear vision of the issues at stake, but never imposed his views. When we dared to differ or failed to follow him, he patiently explained to show us where we were wrong. His physical nearness made us realise, with an extraordinary lucidity, what terrible inhuman forces were trying to overcast the world. We faced an abysmal darkness from which a supreme Divine Power alone could save us.

In May 1940 the war suddenly erupted into violent action when, in a surprise move, Hitler launched a massive attack on France through Holland and Belgium. I well remember the occasion. It was evening; Sri Aurobindo was alone in his room. As soon as I entered he looked at me and said, 'Hitler has invaded Holland. Well, we shall see.' This laconic comment, with its deep overtone, still rings in my ears. Events now moved swiftly and relentlessly. In England, Churchill replaced Chamberlain as Prime Minister, a move Sri Aurobindo approved. But France, it seemed, had lost her will to fight and offered little resistance to Hitler's Panzer Divisions. The British Expeditionary Force in France was cut off and pushed back to the shores of the English Channel. The German Army irresistibly advanced towards Paris and occupied this 'open city' on June 15. Churchill's bold and magnanimous offer of a union with France was rejected by the French Government. The Mother deeply deplored this rejection and said that the offer had come as an act of Grace and for her refusal to respond to it France would have to go through immense suffering. The aged Marshal Pétain now formed a new Government in France and on June 25 signed an armistice with Hitler, accepting his harsh terms.

Meanwhile the British army in France successfully organised a mass evacuation by sea from Dunkirk and more than 300,000 British and allied troops were safely landed in England. Vast quantities of war material had to be left behind but it was a miraculous deliverance for the men who were to form the hard core of the British armies later to fight Hitler with success. As the war took this critical turn, Sri Aurobindo followed the developments with close attention. A radio was installed in a sadhak's room and an extension speaker from it was later put up for Sri Aurobindo to listen to important messages, speeches, etc.

Having won the Battle of France decisively, Hitler now turned his attention to winning the Battle of Britain. He fixed August 15, 1940, as the day on which he would complete his conquest of Western Europe and broadcast from Buckingham Palace. When Sri Aurobindo heard of this he remarked, 'That is the sign that he is the enemy of our work.' He also indicated at this time that besides August 15, September 15 too would be a day of crucial importance for Hitler. As a prelude to invasion, Hitler ordered an aerial offensive on a scale never known before. Had he won this war in the air, the fate of England would have been sealed and perhaps that of the world. But August 15 turned out to be a turning point for Britain. On that day 180 German planes were shot down in British skies, the largest toll so far taken of the dreaded Luftwaffe. Churchill himself has written in his War Memoirs: 'The 15th August was for Britain the most crucial day when she was subjected to an attack from about a hundred bombers and eight hundred planes to pin her down in the South.' A month later, on the same date, September 15, 1940, Sri Aurobindo said smiling: 'England has destroyed 175 German planes, a very big number. Now invasion will be difficult. Hitler lost his chance after the fall of France. He has really missed the bus! If after the French collapse he had invaded England, by now he would have been in Asia. Now another force has been set up against him. Still the danger has not passed.' Hitler continued his desperate bid to achieve air-mastery over Britain but by the middle of October he realised that he had failed in his objective and he indefinitely postponed the invasion. The immediate danger was indeed over: Hitler had met with his first reversal; his all-conquering march had been halted.

The outward mind finds it difficult to perceive or accept that events in the physical world can be changed by spiritual forces. But this is a superficial way of looking at things, a partial and limited outlook. Sri Aurobindo writes of a deeper vision and action: '...it is part of the experience of those who have advanced far in Yoga that besides the ordinary forces and activities of the mind and life and body in Matter, there are other forces and powers that can act and do act from behind and from above; there is also a spiritual dynamic power which can be possessed by those who are advanced in the spiritual consciousness, though all do not care to possess or, possessing, to use it, and this power is greater than any other and more effective.' He further clarifies that 'it was this force that he used...at first only in a limited field of personal work, but afterwards in a constant action upon the world forces.'

In Volume 26 of SABCL, entitled *On Himself*, there is a passage in which Sri Aurobindo has explicitly mentioned his role in the Second World War. He has referred to himself in the third person here because the passage is part of a biographical sketch submitted by a disciple but practically re-written by Sri Aurobindo himself. It reads: 'At the beginning [of the Second World War] he did not actively concern himself with it, but when it appeared as if Hitler would crush all the forces opposed to him and Nazism dominate the world, he began to intervene. He declared himself publicly on the side of the Allies, made some financial contributions in answer to the appeal for funds and encouraged those who sought his advice to enter the army or share in the war effort. Inwardly, he put his spiritual force behind the Allies from the moment of Dunkirk when everybody was expecting the immediate fall of England and the definite triumph of Hitler, and he had the satisfaction of seeing the rush of German victory almost immediately arrested and the tide of war begin to turn in the opposite direction. This he did, because he saw that behind Hitler and Nazism were dark Asuric forces and that their success would mean the enslavement of mankind to the tyranny of evil, and a set-back to the course of evolution and especially to the spiritual evolution of mankind: it would lead also to the enslavement not only of Europe but of Asia, and in it of India, an enslavement far more terrible than any this country had ever endured, and the undoing of all the work that had been done. for her liberation.'

On September 19, 1940, Sri Aurobindo and the Mother made a joint declaration in support of the Allies. It was in the form of a letter addressed to the Governor of Madras covering a token contribution to the War Fund and stated: 'We feel that not only is this a battle waged in just self-defence and in defence of the nations threatened with the world-domination of Germany and the Nazi system of life, but that it is a defence of civilization and its highest attained social, cultural and spiritual values and of the whole future of humanity. To this cause our support and sympathy will be unswerving whatever may happen; we look forward to the victory of Britain and, as the eventual result, an era of peace and union among the nations and a better and more secure world-order.' Since his arrival in Pondicherry, this was the first occasion on which Sri Aurobindo made a public pronouncement on a political issue. Moreover, the letter was placed at the disposal of the Governor for publicity in case of need.

At once there was a storm of protest in the country at the stand Sri Aurobindo had taken and some of the inmates of the Ashram, who had strong anti-British feelings and had fought for Indian freedom, were also nonplussed and greatly disturbed. How could Sri Aurobindo, who was once a mortal opponent of British rule in India, 'not merely a non-cooperator but an enemy of British Imperialism', support the cause of Britain? A disciple wrote to the Mother, 'The Congress is asking us not to contribute to the War Fund. What shall we do?' The answer given was: 'Sri Aurobindo has contributed for a Divine cause. If you help, you will help yourselves.' But the criticisms continued and some inmates, because of their hatred for the British, openly proclaimed their pro-Hitler feelings, thereby causing much embarrassment and harm to the Ashram. The Mother had to deal sternly with these disciples and Sri Aurobindo also had to write letters pointing out the grave error of the disciples and the danger of a Nazi victory. To one disciple he wrote: 'We made it plain in a letter which has been made public that we did not consider the war as a fight between nations and governments (still less between good people and bad people) but between two forces, the Divine and the Asuric. What we have to see is on which side men and nations put themselves; if they put themselves on the right side, they at once make them- selves instruments of the Divine purpose in spite of all defects, errors, wrong movements and actions which are common to human nature and all human collectivities. The victory of one side (the Allies) would keep the path open for the evolutionary forces: the victory of the other side would drag back humanity, degrade it horribly and might lead even, at the worst, to its eventual failure as a race, as others in the past evolution failed and perished. That is the whole question and all other considerations are either irrele- vant or of a minor importance. The Allies at least have stood for human values, though they may often act against their own best ideals (human beings always do that); Hitler stands for diabolical values or for human values exaggerated in the wrong way until they become diabolical (e.g. the virtues of the Herrenvolk, the master race). That does not make the English or Americans nations of spotless angels nor the Germans a wicked and sinful race, but as an indicator it has a primary importance.'

It is not difficult for us today to visualize the kind of world that would have emerged had Hitler won. The horrors he perpetrated all came out after the war – the concentration camps, the mass genocide, the slave labour and similar inhuman acts of barbarism are enough evidence to prove undoubtedly that another Dark Age would have descended on mankind, a darkness made worse by the alliance of science and technology with despotism. Yet men were so concerned then with the conflicting emotions and loyalties generated by the war and so preoccupied with surface details that few could see the real issues which were at stake.

There was a second occasion when Sri Aurobindo openly intervened in a political issue which vitally affected India's future. Japan had entered the War in December 1941 and within three months, sweeping everything before her, had reached the gates of India. Realising the extreme gravity of the situation Churchill announced in March 1942 that he would be sending Sir Stafford Cripps to India as his personal envoy to negotiate with the Congress and Muslim leaders so that a responsible Central Government could be formed to mobilise Indian resources for fighting the Japanese. He also offered to create a new Indian Union with Dominion Status and with a constitution to be framed by India's own representatives after the War. When Sir Stafford Cripps came to India to work out the details, Sri Aurobindo welcomed the mission and on March 31 sent a message to him in the following terms: 'I have heard your broadcast. As one who has been a nationalist leader and worker for India's independence, though now my activity is no longer in the political but in the spiritual field, I wish to express my appreciation of all you have done to bring about this offer. I welcome it as an opportunity given to India to determine for herself, and organise in all liberty of choice, her freedom and unity, and take an effective place among the world's free nations. I hope that it will be accepted, and right use made of it, putting aside all discords and divisions. I hope too that friendly relations between Britain and India replacing the past struggles, will be a step towards a greater world union in which, as a free nation, her spiritual force will contribute to build for mankind a better and happier life. In this light, I offer my public adhesion, in case it can be of any help in your work.' Sir Stafford Cripps replied: 'I am most touched and gratified by your kind message allowing me to inform India that you who occupy a unique position in the imagination of Indian youth, are convinced that the declaration of His Majesty's Government substantially confers that freedom for which Indian Nationalism has so long struggled.'

Cripps now entered into long discussions with the Indian political leaders but he failed to get the Congress to accept his proposals. Sri Aurobindo had seen clearly that the Cripps offer presented a great opportunity which, if taken, would lead India to both freedom *and* unity – mark that he uses both these words in his message to Cripps. He considered that a Central Government in which Hindus and Muslims worked together with a common objective, aligning India firmly against the anti-divine forces, would reduce the tension between the two communities and lead to cooperation instead of confrontation. Sri Aurobindo also saw the necessity of organising the collective strength of the country and repel the danger from Japan. He told us clearly: 'Japan's imperialism being young and based on industrial and military power and moving westward, was a greater menace to India than the British imperialism which was old, which the country had learned to deal with and which was on the way to elimination.' But the Congress leaders were impervious to these vital considerations and seemed more concerned with immediate political calculations, being probably influenced by Gandhiji's opinion that the proposals offered by the British were no more than 'post-dated cheque on a bank that was crashing'. Sri Aurobindo went to the extent of sending a personal emissary to Delhi to try and persuade the Congress leaders to accept the Cripps offer. S. Duraiswamy, a distinguished Madras lawyer and a disciple, was selected for this mission, perhaps because he was a friend of C. Rajagopalachari, one of the few senior leaders in the Congress who lent support to the Cripps proposals. However, it was all in vain: the offer was rejected by the Congress. When the rejection was announced, Sri Aurobindo said in a quiet tone, 'I knew it would fail.' We at once pounced on the words and asked him, 'Why did you then send Duraiswamy at all?' 'For a bit of *niṣkāma karma*,' was his calm reply, without any bitterness and resentment.

Many discerning observers, looking back into the past with dispassionate eyes, now consider that had the Cripps offer been accepted, the whole course of recent Indian history could well have changed. A working association of the Hindus and Muslims in government could have belied the 'Two Nations' theory, preventing Partition with its aftermath of incalculable human suffering as well as its legacy of political problems which still bedevil us. Sri Aurobindo's vision went far beyond the immediate political issues and he saw that the Cripps offer had come on the wave of a divine inspiration. The political leaders of the day, more concerned with short-term considerations, could not share this vision and so a great opportunity was lost. I should mention here that the Mother had also strongly urged that the proposals should be accepted. She said: 'My ardent request to India is that she should not reject [the Cripps offer]. She must not make the same mistake that France has made recently and gone into the abyss.' When it was announced that the offer had been rejected, she only said, 'Now calamity will befall India.'

The War brought about many changes in India, as it did practically all over the world, and it affected our life in the Ashram also. Sri Aurobindo had declared that this was 'the Mother's War' and those disciples who lived outside were encouraged to share in the war effort and, where possible, to join the fighting forces or allow their sons to do so. Two disciples each lost a son, brilliant young men who joined the Air Force and were killed in action.

And there were many disciples who lived in danger zones which were vulnerable to air attacks. The Mother exhorted them to stay at their post but her loving heart went out to their families who had to face many difficulties and she opened the doors of the Ashram to give them shelter. This is how children first came to live in the Ashram, for previously the Ashram was meant only for sadhaks who surrendered all their worldly belongings to the Mother and in return were provided with the necessities of life they required to practise yoga. The Mother took the decision to accept children in spite of the fact that the Ashram was then facing many hardships – financial difficulties, food shortages and other problems created by the War. But in her characteristic way she did everything possible to look after the needs of the children, once they were here, and it was wonderful to see the simple and spontaneous manner in which they responded to her. She also permitted a relaxation of some of the austere rules in the Ashram, for the children had not come to practise yoga, as she said, and their needs were different. In course of time, the coming of children brought about many changes in the organisation of the Ashram and the atmosphere also changed with the laughter and gaiety of the young ones.

On December 2, 1943, the Mother formally opened a school for about twenty children. She herself was one of the teachers. From this small beginning has grown the International Centre of Education with its separate School and Higher Course classes and today it constitutes one of the most important and prominent features of the Ashram. Sri Aurobindo had a deep and abiding interest in education. As a teacher, he had seen the weaknesses of our system and the poverty of its ideals. In the *Karmayogin* and later in the *Arya* he wrote a series of articles giving his views on education which were altogether different from the conventional ideas on the subject. The Mother too had a new and innovative approach to education and all this has found expression in the Centre of Education which has evolved at the Ashram. The Mother took a day-to-day interest in the growth of the school. No detail was too small for her to look into and she personally guided the teachers, who were all members of the Ashram, in introducing the new methods of teaching she wanted, as well as in planning the courses of studies for the students. The system of education now followed at the Centre, the Free Progress System, is largely her own creation and it has evoked admiration from many eminent educationists who have come to the Ashram.

As the number of children increased, the Mother felt the necessity of providing them with a system of physical education to make their growing bodies supple and strong and to inculcate a sense of discipline in them. With the help of a young disciple, Pranab Bhattacharya, who had recently joined the Ashram and had specialised in this field, a Department of Physical Education was started in May 1944. A spacious playground was constructed and a programme of exercises and drills was drawn up at first for the students and teachers, and later extended to the members of the Ashram. Gradually, the facilities were expanded and came to include a sportsground, a gymnasium, a swimming pool, tennis courts, etc. From the beginning the Mother took an active interest in the development of the Physical Education Department and helped to shape its programme. For years she spent her late afternoon and evening hours with those who took part in the physical activities. She herself played tennis regularly and those of us who played with her could see that in her younger days she must have had the makings of a champion. The sadhaks and the sadhikas too were encouraged in every way to take part in these physical activities. At first there was some resistance but soon most of us were enthusiastic participants. Overall, the atmosphere in the Ashram underwent a sea-change and physically also it became a much larger institution. In 1942 the number of inmates was around 350; it was nearly double that number by the end of the decade and a good many of the newcomers were children.

By 1945 it was clear that the Allies would emerge victorious in the War. On May 8, 1945, the war against Hitlerism came to an end and then, after the atomic explosions over Hiroshima and Nagasaki, Japan surrendered on August 14, 1945. The next day, August 15, Sri Aurobindo's seventy-third birthday, marked the first day of peace after the ravages of the Second World War. Another fortuitous coincidence? I leave you to answer.

The end of the War led to swift political developments in India. The Labour Party had come to power in Britain and they soon made it clear that they did not want to hold on to India at the cost of men and resources Britain could no longer afford. In March 1946, the British Government decided to send a Cabinet Mission to India to negotiate with Indian leaders for the eventual transfer of power to Indian hands. Sri Aurobindo was requested by the

Amrita Bazar Patrika to give his views on this important development and on March 24, 1946, the following statement was issued by him: 'Sri Aurobindo thinks it unnecessary to volunteer a personal pronouncement, though he would give his views if officially approached for them. His position is known. He has always stood for India's complete independence which he was the first to advocate publicly and without compromise as the only ideal worthy of a self-respecting nation. In 1910 he authorised the publication of his prediction that after a long period of wars, world-wide upheavals and revolutions beginning after four years, India would achieve her freedom. Lately he has said that freedom was coming soon and nothing could prevent it. He has always foreseen that eventually Britain would approach India for an amicable agreement, conceding her freedom. What he had foreseen is now coming to pass and the British Cabinet Mission is the sign. It remains for the nation's leaders to make a right and full use of the opportunity. In any case, whatever the immediate outcome, the Power that has been working out this event will not be denied, the final result, India's liberation, is sure.' You will remember that his prediction about India's freedom was made in Calcutta when he was interviewed by the correspondent of the Tamil Nationalist Weekly, *India*, and it was then published in that journal.

The British Cabinet Mission included Sir Stafford Cripps, who came to India for the second time, but in the intervening years the Muslim League position had hardened considerably and they were now adamant in their demand for a separate Muslim state. After the departure of the Cabinet Mission the negotiations were carried on by Lord Mountbatten, the last Viceroy, and eventually resulted in the freedom of India from British rule on August 15, 1947. But a bitter price had to be paid by way of a partition of the country into India and Pakistan. The story might well have been different if the Cripps offer had been accepted in 1942.

On the auspicious occasion of Independence, at the request of the All India Radio, Sri Aurobindo sent a message which was broadcast on August 14, 1947. You will find a complete text of this message as an appendix, for I am convinced that every word in it is profoundly relevant to the future of India, indeed of all mankind, and it needs to be studied in its entirety. Here I shall dwell only on the main points and add a few comments.

Sri Aurobindo begins by stating that the 'coincidence' of the date of Independence with his own birthday is not just an accident but is a mark of 'the sanction and seal' of the Divine Power that guides his steps. He goes on to say that he had hoped to see five world-movements fulfilled in his lifetime, although they had looked at first like 'impracticable dreams', and now he could see that they were on their way to achievement.

The first of these dreams was a free and united India. Sri Aurobindo tells us that today 'India is free but she has not achieved unity' and avers that unity must and will be achieved. He hopes that it will come about 'naturally, by an increasing recognition not only of peace and concord but of common action', adds that the exact form of unity 'may have a pragmatic but not a fundamental importance', and asserts that, the division must and will go. Amidst the rush of day-to-day events and the clash of conflicting forces it may be difficult to visualise today how this unity will come about, but let us remember that Sri Aurobindo's vision extends far beyond the immediate and apparently intractable problems of the day and the future will surely unfold the fulfilment of his prophecy.

The second dream was the resurgence of Asia and India's growing role and place in the council of nations. We can see that the dream has been largely fulfilled and can foresee the increasing possibilities of the future.

The third dream was 'a world-union forming the outer basis of a fairer brighter nobler life for all mankind'. Sri Aurobindo admits that there are formidable difficulties standing in the way but declares that 'unification is a necessity of Nature, an inevitable movement' and that 'human imbecility and stupid selfishness' cannot stand forever against this necessity and the Divine Will. Indeed, despite national rivalries and the tussle between the power blocs, the concept of 'One World' has taken root in the human consciousness in a way which would have been unthinkable fifty years ago, and the trend towards it is unmistakable.

The fourth dream relates to the gift by India of her spiritual knowledge to the world and here also we can see evidence of the increasing interest in Indian spirituality and yoga and of a widespread movement in this direction.

Sri Aurobindo's final dream was 'a step in evolution which would raise man to a higher and larger consciousness and begin the solution of the problems which have perplexed and vexed him since he first began to think and to dream of individual perfection and a perfect society'. This was Sri Aurobindo's sadhana for the Supramental Descent and it was for the fulfilment of this dream that he came. In his message Sri Aurobindo expresses the hope that India will have a leading role to play in these movements – the message is indeed his call to the 'new and free' India to be true to her spiritual destiny. To disregard and ignore this call would be a fatal tragedy.

The aftermath of independence was a period of grave crisis for India – I need not go into details for you all know of the horrors of the mass communal killings that followed Partition and of the tragic plight of the refugees. Truly, 'calamity' had befallen India, as the Mother had apprehended. The situation became even more critical as a result of the armed conflict with Pakistan over Kashmir. I do believe that it was Divine Grace that protected the country's newly-found freedom and gave it the strength to survive its terrible ordeals.

In December 1948, Sri Aurobindo was awarded the National Prize for Humanities at the annual convocation of the Andhra University. In his citation, Dr. C.R. Reddy, the Vice-Chancellor hailed Sri Aurobindo as 'the sole sufficing genius of the age' and said: 'He is more than a hero of a nation. He is amongst the Saviours of humanity, who belong to all ages and all nations, the Sanatanas, who leaven our existence with their eternal presence, whether we are aware of it or not.... He is a poet, dramatist, philosopher, critic, interpreter of and commentator on the Vedas, the Gita and all the transcendent lore and legend of India, and he is something higher than these, the Saint who has realised his oneness with the Universal Spirit, and fathomed the depths and brought up treasures of transcendent value and brilliance.' Dr. Reddy came to Pondicherry to offer the Prize to Sri Aurobindo in person and was granted an interview. Sri Aurobindo also sent a Message for the occasion in the course of which he expressed the view that India's national life should be founded on the principle of 'unity in diversity' which conforms to her *swabhava* and *swadharma*. Sri Aurobindo also said '...by following certain tempting directions she [India] may conceivably become a nation like many others evolving an opulent industry and commerce, a powerful organisation of social and political life, an immense military strength, practising power-politics with a high degree of success, guarding and extending zealously her gains and her interests, dominating even a large part of the world, but in this apparently magnificent progression forfeiting its Swadharma, losing its soul. Then ancient India and her spirit might disappear altogether and we would have only one more nation like the others and that would be a real gain neither to the world nor to us.... This must not and will surely not happen; but it cannot be said that the danger is not there. There are indeed other numerous and difficult problems that face this country or will very soon face it. No doubt we will win through, but we must not disguise from ourselves the fact that after these long years of subjection and its cramping and impairing effects a great inner as well as outer liberation and change, a vast inner and outer progress is needed if we are to fulfil India's true destiny.' These are words we shall do well to remember. Now that the country has achieved some outer progress, the need for a corresponding inner progress, moral and spiritual, is all the greater.

On February 21, 1949, the Mother's 71st birthday, two new journals were started. A cultural and semi-political fortnightly, *Mother India*, commenced publication from Bombay. It was edited by K.D. Sethna (Amal Kiran), a close disciple of Sri Aurobindo and a poet of distinction as well as a brilliant writer with wide intellectual interests. In writing the editorials Sethna was directly guided by Sri Aurobindo and through the columns of the journal he conveyed Sri Aurobindo's warnings regarding the expansionist designs of Stalinist Russia as well as Communist China's intentions of annexing Tibet and posing a direct threat to India, a threat which became a reality in 1962. But, as in the past, few paid heed to Sri Aurobindo's words.

The other important publication to come out on February 21, 1949 was the English-French-Hindi quarterly journal, *Bulletin of Physical Education*, brought out by the Department of Physical Education at the Ashram. The first issue contained a special message from Sri Aurobindo, written at the Mother's request, and for the subsequent issues he wrote a series of seven articles: 'The Perfection of the Body', 'The Divine Body', 'The Supermind and the Life Divine', 'Supermind and Humanity', 'Supermind in the Evolution', 'Mind of Light' and 'Supermind and Mind of Light', the last appearing in the issue of November 1950. These articles are reproduced in volume 16 of the SABCL, *The Supramental*

Manifestation. They constitute the last of Sri Aurobindo's prose writings and, as you can see from the titles, they are concerned not only with the ideal of bodily perfection but move beyond to a consideration of the nature of Supermind and the consequences of its manifestation. Indeed in these later articles Sri Aurobindo has written about the Supermind in more specific terms than in his other writings. As regards bodily perfection Sri Aurobindo's views were also briefly expressed in a letter to a disciple in December 1949 when he wrote: 'I put a value on the body first as an instrument, *dharmasādhana*, or more fully, as a centre of manifested personality in action, a basis of spiritual life and activity as of all life and activity upon the earth, but also because for me the body as well as the mind and life is a part of the Divine Whole, a form of the Spirit and therefore not to be disregarded or despised as something incurably gross and incapable of spiritual realisation or of spiritual use. Matter itself is secretly a form of the Spirit and has to reveal itself as that, can be made to wake to consciousness and evolve and realise the Spirit, the Divine within it. In my view the body as well as the mind and life has to be spiritualised or, one may say, divinised so as to be a fit instrument and receptacle for the realisation of the Divine.... That does not mean that the body has to be valued for its own separate sake or that the creation of the divine body in a future evolution of the whole being has to be contemplated as an end and not a means – that would be a serious error which would not be admissible.'

On July 9, 1950, Sri Aurobindo gave an interview to K.M. Munshi, an eminent politician and interpreter of Indian culture, who had been his student at Baroda and was now a Minister in the Central Government. Recalling the meeting Munshi wrote: 'When I visited Sri Aurobindo in 1950, after a lapse of more than forty years, I saw before me a being completely transformed, blissful, enveloped in an atmosphere of godlike calm. He spoke in a low, clear voice, which stirred the depths of my being. I talked to him of my spiritual needs. The sage replied: "...I wrote to you that I would help you and in my own way I am helping you... I will watch over your progress." Then we discussed Indian culture. I said: "The younger generation is being fed on theories and beliefs which are undermining the higher life of India." The Master replied: "You must overcome this lack of faith. Rest assured that our culture cannot be undermined. This is only a passing phase."'

I shall now turn for a while to a subject which occupies a very special place in Sri Aurobindo's life and work: his epic *Savitri*. It is a subject as vast as the ocean, indeed inexhaustible. All I can do here is to introduce you briefly to it.

It was probably at Baroda that Sri Aurobindo first thought of writing a long poem based on the well-known story of Savitri and Satyavan from the *Mahabharata*, but the earliest draft that we have goes back to August 1916. It began as 'a Tale and a Vision'. Sri Aurobindo used to work on the poem whenever he could find some time for it from his other pressing preoccupations. In its early versions the entire work did not exceed fifty typed pages; in its final form the epic contains almost 24,000 lines. There were constant revisions and retouchings, excisions and additions, and sometimes entire passages would be recast again and again until Sri Aurobindo was fully satisfied. He aimed at 'a perfect perfection', as he himself said. Again and again I was struck with awe and wonder at Sri Aurobindo's unceasing patience and his godlike labour. And slowly the massive structure of the poem emerged like one of our ancient majestic temples or like a monumental Gothic cathedral.

You may now like to know what kind of an epic *Savitri* is. It consists in all of twelve Books each containing a varying number of cantos which again are of varying length. Sri Aurobindo describes the poem as 'A Legend and a Symbol' and explains: 'The tale of Satyavan and Savitri is recited in the Mahabharata as a story of conjugal love conquering death. But this legend is, as shown by many features of the human tale, one of the many symbolic myths of the Vedic cycle. Satyavan is the soul carrying the divine truth of being within itself but descended into the grip of death and ignorance; Savitri is the Divine Word, daughter of the Sun, goddess of the supreme Truth who comes down and is born to save; Aswapati, the Lord of the Horse, her human father, is the Lord of Tapasya, the concentrated energy of spiritual endeavour that helps us to rise from the mortal to the immortal planes; Dyumatsena, Lord of the Shining Hosts, father of Satyavan, is the Divine Mind here fallen blind, losing its celestial kingdom of vision, and through that loss its kingdom of glory. Still this is not a mere allegory, the characters are not personified qualities, but incarnations or emanations of living and conscious Forces with whom we can enter into concrete touch and they take human bodies in order to help man and show him the way from his mortal state to a divine consciousness and immortal life.' She brings back Satyavan from the Kingdom of Death, thus conquering Death and the Inconscience. The Kingdom of Truth, Light and Bliss is established upon the earth....

The sheer immensity of the poem, its grandeur and creative power surpass our highest imagination. Sri Aurobindo's own vast experience in the occult and mystic domains is transcribed here in authentic mantric language, which, according to him, will be the language of the future poetry as it was that of the Vedas and the Upanishads. I can do no better than to quote to you the Mother's words:

'He has crammed the whole universe in a single book. It is a marvellous, magnificent work and of an incomparable perfection.... It is a revelation, a meditation and seeking of the Infinite and the Eternal. Each verse of *Savitri* is like a mantra which surpasses man's entire knowledge.... Everything is there: mysticism, occultism, philosophy, history of evolution, history of man, gods of the creation and of Nature.... *Savitri* is the spiritual path, the Tapasya, Sadhana.... It has an extraordinary power, it is the Truth in all its plenitude that he has brought down here on earth.'

Sri Aurobindo has encompassed all the three worlds, Heaven, Earth and the Underworlds in his wide penetrating vision. Dr. Piper of Syracuse University says about *Savitri* that it already has inaugurated the New Age of Illumination and is probably the greatest epic in the English language...the most comprehensive, integrated, beautiful and perfect cosmic poem ever composed.... It ranges symbolically from primordial cosmic void, through earth's darkness and struggles, to the highest realms of supramental spiritual existence and illumines every important concern of man, through verse of unparalleled massiveness, magnificence and metaphorical brilliance. *Savitri* is perhaps the most powerful artistic work in the world for expanding man's mind towards the Absolute.

We can say that it is the prophetic message of the divinised earth and of man's God-like possibility:

> For in the march of all-fulfilling Time
> The hour must come of the Transcendent's will...
> The frontiers of the Ignorance shall recede,

More and more souls shall enter into light,
Minds lit, inspired, the occult summoner hear
And lives blaze with a sudden inner flame
And hearts grow enamoured of divine delight
And human wills tune to the divine will...
A divine force shall flow through tissue and cell
And take the charge of breath and speech and act
And all the thoughts shall be a glow of suns
And every feeling a celestial thrill...
Thus shall the earth open to divinity
And common natures feel the wide uplift,
Illumine common acts with the Spirit's ray
And meet the deity in common things.
Nature shall live to manifest secret God,
The Spirit shall take up the human play,
This earthly life become the life divine.

Epilogue

WHEN all over the world there was a growing eagerness to know more and more about Sri Aurobindo and the interest in his work was on the increase, he suddenly withdrew from the earth-scene. Superficially, this is a terrible irony of fate. But a study of his life suggests that more than once the utterly unexpected occurred as if by a choice on his own part. One may say that such an occurrence is almost a regular feature at each decisive turn of the upward spiral of his life. We see the rising curve suddenly moving downwards when he threw away a glittering career in the ICS and retired into an unpretentious State job in Baroda. Having risen high in the Baroda Service and acted as the Principal of the Baroda College, he gave up that affluent position of security and prestige. For a time he worked from behind the scene until he appeared brilliantly upon the political horizon, and when everybody's eyes were filled with wonder and delight, his light hid itself in the shadows of the prison cell where he had one of the sovereign spiritual experiences of his life. When he came out of the prison, the nation was ready to offer him all-India leadership but he withdrew from politics altogether and went into the unknown retreat of Pondicherry. Then in 1926, after having achieved what we may call a decisive victory of his sadhana, he withdrew into complete seclusion to the surprise and disappointment of his close followers. And now on the eve of the final Victory – the descent of the Supermind in the physical – came this greatest withdrawal of all in a most unexpected manner and, as it were, almost in secrecy. But just as it is the way of the Divine to move men and forces without their knowledge, so did Sri Aurobindo prefer to act from behind the veil. All his great achievements were prepared in the secret silence of retirement, and with each emergence he brought down a greater light, a higher range of illumination and a vaster kingdom of knowledge and power.

*

On December 5, 1950, at 1.26 a.m. he left his body. Of one thing we may be sure: Sri Aurobindo did not succumb to death – for him, as for all great yogis – it was *ichha mrityu*. The Mother has said categorically: 'Our Lord has sacrificed himself totally for us.... He was not compelled to leave his body, he chose to do so for reasons so sublime that they are beyond the reach of human mentality.' Indeed the total significance of this supreme sacrifice will remain ungrasped by our limited intelligence. His body was suffused with a crimson-gold light. Power and peace and bliss filled the room. Many who came – and they came by thousands – were spell-bound, dumb and overwhelmed. Untarnished, undimmed for five days the body lay in state. On the 9th, at 5 p.m. it was interred in a vault in the Ashram courtyard under the cool shade of the 'Service Tree'.

The Mother's prayer of gratitude is inscribed in English and French on the two sides of the Samadhi:

To Thee who hast been the material envelope of our Master, to Thee our infinite gratitude. Before Thee who hast done so much for us, who hast worked, struggled, suffered, hoped, endured so much, before Thee who hast willed all, attempted all, prepared, achieved all for us, before Thee we bow down and implore that we may never forget, even for a moment, all we owe to Thee.

Appendix

The Message of Fifteenth August 1947

AUGUST 15th, 1947 is the birthday of free India. It marks for her the end of an old era, the beginning of a new age. But we can also make it by our life and acts as a free nation an important date in a new age opening for the whole world, for the political, social, cultural and spiritual future of humanity.

August 15th is my own birthday and it is naturally gratifying to me that it should have assumed this vast significance. I take this coincidence, not as a fortuitous accident, but as the sanction and seal of the Divine Force that guides my steps on the work with which I began life, the beginning of its full fruition. Indeed, on this day I can watch almost all the world-movements which I hoped to see fulfilled in my lifetime, though then they looked like impracticable dreams, arriving at fruition or on their way to achievement. In all these movements free India may well play a large part and take a leading position.

The first of these dreams was a revolutionary movement which would create a free and united India. India today is free but she has not achieved unity. At one moment it almost seemed as if in the very act of liberation she would fall back into the chaos of separate States which preceded the British conquest. But fortunately it now seems probable that this danger will be averted and a large and powerful, though not yet a complete union will be established. Also, the wisely drastic policy of the Constituent Assembly has made it probable that the problem of the depressed classes will be solved without schism or fissure. But the old communal division into Hindus and Muslims seems now to have hardened into a permanent political division of the country. It is to be hoped that this settled fact will not be accepted as settled for ever or as anything more than a temporary expedient. For if it lasts, India may be seriously weakened, even crippled: civil strife may remain always possible, possible even a new invasion and foreign conquest. India's internal development and prosperity may be impeded, her position among the nations weakened, her destiny impaired or even frustrated. This must not be; the partition must go. Let us hope that that may come about naturally, by an increasing recognition of the necessity not only of peace and concord but of common action, by the practice of common action and the creation of means for that purpose. In this way unity may finally come about under whatever form – the exact form may have a pragmatic but not a fundamental importance. But by whatever means, in whatever way, the division must go; unity must and will be achieved, for it is necessary for the greatness of India's future.

Another dream was for the resurgence and liberation of the peoples of Asia and her return to her great role in the progress of human civilisation. Asia has arisen; large parts are now quite free or are at this moment being liberated: its other still subject or partly subject parts are moving through whatever struggles towards freedom. Only a little has to be done and that will be done today or tomorrow. There India has her part to play and has begun to play it with an energy and ability which already indicate the measure of her possibilities and the place she can take in the council of the nations.

The third dream was a world-union forming the outer basis of a fairer, brighter and nobler life for all mankind. That unification of the human world is under way; there is an imperfect initiation organised but struggling against tremendous difficulties. But the momentum is there and it must inevitably increase and conquer. Here too India has begun to play a prominent part and, if she can develop that larger statesmanship which is not limited by the present facts and immediate possibilities but looks into the future and brings it nearer, her presence may make all the difference between a slow and timid and a bold and swift development. A catastrophe may intervene and interrupt or destroy what is being done, but even then the final result is sure. For unification is a necessity of Nature, an inevitable movement. Its necessity for the nations is also clear, for without it the freedom of the small nations may be at any moment in peril and the life even of the large and powerful nations insecure. The unification is therefore to the interests of all, and only human imbecility and stupid selfishness can prevent it; but these cannot stand for ever against the necessity of Nature and Divine Will. But an outward basis is not enough; there must grow up an international spirit and outlook, international forms and institutions must appear, perhaps such developments as dual or multilateral citizenship, willed interchange or voluntary fusion of cultures. Nationalism will have fulfilled itself and lost its militancy and would no longer find these things incompatible with self-preservation and the integrality of its outlook. A new spirit of oneness will take hold of the human race.

Another dream, the spiritual gift of India to the world has already begun. India's spirituality is entering Europe and America in an ever increasing measure. That movement will grow; amid the disasters of the time more and more eyes are turning towards her with hope and there is even an increasing resort not only to her teachings, but to her psychic and spiritual practice.

The final dream was a step in evolution which would raise man to a higher and larger consciousness and begin the solution of the problems which have perplexed and vexed him since he first began to think and to dream of individual perfection and a perfect society. This is still a personal hope and an idea, an ideal which has begun to take hold both in India and in the West on forward-looking minds. The difficulties in the way are more formidable than in any other field of endeavour, but difficulties were made to be overcome and if the Supreme Will is there, they will be overcome. Here too, if this evolution is to take place, since it must proceed through a growth of the spirit and the inner consciousness, the initiative can come from India and, although the scope must be universal, the central movement may be hers.

Such is the content which I put into this date of India's liberation; whether or how far this hope will be justified depends upon the new and free India.